High Performance Teams: How to Make Them Work

High Performance Teams: How to Make Them Work

Marc Hanlan

PRAEGER

Westport, Connecticut
London

Library of Congress Cataloging-in-Publication Data

Hanlan, Marc, 1952–
   High performance teams : how to make them work / Marc Hanlan.
     p. cm.
   Includes bibliographical references and index.
   ISBN 1–56720–537–2 (alk. paper)
    1. Teams in the workplace. 2. Organizational change. I. Title.
HD66.H34 2004
658.4′022—dc22   2004050965

British Library Cataloguing in Publication Data is available.

Library of Congress Catalog Card Number: 2004050965
ISBN: 1–56720–537–2

First published in 2004

Praeger Publishers, 88 Post Road West, Westport, CT 06881
An imprint of Greenwood Publishing Group, Inc.
www.praeger.com

Printed in the United States of America

The paper used in this book complies with the
Permanent Paper Standard issued by the National
Information Standards Organization (Z39.48-1984).

10 9 8 7 6 5 4 3 2 1

To my sons—Seann, Kyle, and Jesse Hanlan—
who have shown me, taught me, and changed me, more than
everyone else

Contents

List of Figures

Preface

I did not set out to write this book.

From the 1970s, I have worked with teams from many different perspectives—leader, member, consultant, and observer. I have been part of teams that soared to best-in-class and those that crashed and burned. I have guided many teams to reach beyond their imagination, and have contributed to the downfall of others. I have been part of teams that I thoroughly enjoyed and did not want to leave and have been part of teams where I could not stand coming to work each day.

Over the years, as I experienced many different perspectives of teams and their parent organizations, I found my own perspective shifting; I was changing along with the teams. As I have walked my own journey, I have tried to learn about teams and their dynamics. The more I learned about teams and worked with them, the more I discovered there are no correct answers; most textbooks and articles did not even seem to *apply*, let alone provide any answers.

But there were differences; some teams clearly functioned more effectively than others, and some of those teams had people working less to achieve more. This combination seemed to have a *multiplying* effect—not only were these "High Performance Teams" (HPTs) more effective, but most of the folks involved in the teams were actually having *fun*. As I learned and applied some of these common themes, more and more teams were able to transition to this level of all-around performance.

At the request of many teams, I have tried to document the development of these HPTs several times since 1992. Each effort confirmed that a

linear, "workbook" approach simply misses most key points of High Performance Teams—particularly the ad hoc interventions and the critically important intangible aspects. Trying an experiential approach, I then focused on helping leaders and facilitators understand the process through their own practice; although this fostered interpersonal skills, it missed the conceptual understanding.

Demystifying HPTs requires a balanced perspective: conceptual understanding of the HPT transition process; personal connection; extensive intervention skills; and a solid understanding of the business needs of the organization. If a single book, course, or workshop was able to provide these, I certainly had not discovered it.

As I worked with more and more teams, I realized that a combination of education, training, experience, and intuition would provide the most effective preparation for High Performance Teams. This would start with a prerequisite understanding of the *fundamentals* of high performance. There needed to be a reference that would provide the background, context, and processes of successful High Performance Teams, as well as specific activities that the stakeholders could perform. It would not replace the need for "real-world" experiences and interaction, but it could provide a foundation for a highly effective HPT effort.

To the limit of any written text and my own ability to share my experiences and learnings, I offer this outline of High Performance Teams. It offers a different perspective on creating and nurturing High Performing Teams, including new definitions and processes. It is my intent and hope that you will be able to build on my journey, changing and adding to it with your own discoveries.

As with my own life, this book is the result of many different people providing input, insight, and assistance. Though I wish I could single out everyone who has helped me with this book, space allows only a few. Bill Clinton, Janice Granauro, Cheryl Kuchler, Dave Orr, Bob Shuttleworth, and Eric Woodworth have each provided valuable insights throughout the preparation of this book.

Of course, without all the team members and the key players that supported and worked with them, this book would not have been possible at all. My thanks and appreciation go out to all the teams, both successful and otherwise, that have helped me to experience, learn, enjoy, and grow.

There are also many individuals who have helped me along my HPT journey. Sue Whittington provided me with important insights and concepts at a critical point in my life. Andi Sywulak showed me the light to lead the way. Art Forbes helped me to clarify many of my own thoughts and assumptions about High Performance. Michelle Fields helped me to integrate differing levels of integration. Glenn Hilditch, who has always carried the flag, has taught me about teams, spirit, faith, and myself. Dot-

tie Lyons has continually helped me to remember what is important in life and living. Most importantly, I owe more than I can say to my sons, Seann, Kyle, and Jesse Hanlan, who have shown me, taught me, and changed me, more than everyone else.

Thank you.

Introduction

Change is inevitable. Change is constant.

—*Benjamin Disraeli*

CHANGE IS A CONSTANT

From the global corporation to the sole proprietor, change is the one constant in business. As the business infrastructure rapidly changes, many companies have scrambled to try to obtain, or retain, market share and profitability. Some are able to successfully adapt to the increased rate of change—and even enjoy it—while others are being left behind.

In the scramble to keep up with changing competition and constantly changing ground rules, companies have tried many different strategies and tactics. They have tried to find a competitive edge that would allow them to stay ahead of those changes. There are at least as many strategies as there are companies attempting to change, each with its own advantages and disadvantages in supporting change.

However, as the *rate* of change accelerates, so must the change strategies accordingly change. Typically, the increased global demand for product value has also been accompanied with increased demands for worker satisfaction, environmental protection, and shareholder returns. In many areas, product cycles have shortened, regulatory oversight has increased, and employee costs have risen. Yet, customers demand more now than ever before.

For many organizations, "good" is simply not good enough. Significant change is needed to survive in changing times, and breakthrough change is needed to thrive.

Historically successful change strategies such as continuous improvement, process control, and 'command and control' are inadequate to provide the basis for major, order-of-magnitude breakthroughs. Although some companies have been able to make "quantum leaps" forward, most have continued to search for the specific strategy that would yield major competitive advantage in short periods of time.

For many companies desiring breakthrough change, a new strategy emerged in the 1980s—High Performance Teams (HPTs). In these efforts, a strategy of *total stakeholder involvement* was combined with a *complete redesign of all aspects of the work* being performed, questioning assumptions that had been barriers to improvement.

These HPTs underwent training for new ways to analyze data and their work processes, then extensively reviewed customer, shareholder, employee, and operational perspectives. Working to find new ways to add value, and to find new ways around old problems, these teams redesigned all aspects of their work to achieve breakthrough improvements in productivity, cost, value, and quality of work life.

High Performance Teams offer an effective, rapid strategy to obtain breakthrough change—in breakthrough time.

One High Performance Team:
A Case for Breakthrough Change

Throughout the 1980s, the U.S. defense industry was rapidly expanding. Domestic suppliers of complex electronic equipment dramatically increased production capacity without regard for cost containment. By 1990, however, major reductions in defense spending coupled with increased global competition resulted in a crisis at one electronic supplier. The corporate choices: reduce costs by more than half, find another (profitable) market to sell to, or close down the operations.

As sales slipped precipitously, the company tried many conventional approaches: squeezing their own suppliers for cost reductions, cutting wages and salaries, and increased layoffs. There were many attempts to redesign the product for cost reduction as well, but the long approval times required did not reduce costs quickly enough.

The company tried to penetrate new markets and made some inroads, but the specialized nature of their products did not adapt easily to these new markets. The small increase in orders was insufficient to stem the major declines in U.S. revenue.

As other production plants were being closed, the company decided to create a new facility that would incorporate state-of-the-art concepts for

workplace design. This new design would include many of the innovative ideas for global manufacturing such as computer-based workflow systems, just-in-time inventory flows, ISO-9000 equivalence, and high performance teams. Throughout the facility, teams were formed around their product. The same workers would assemble the electronics from start to finish, with full ownership for the final product. However, because cost reductions were critical, there were to be no significant capital investments for the products themselves; no retooling or dedicated automation was budgeted.

One team formed around an electronic product that had traditionally required more than 45 days to build each one; thousands of units per year were required by the Department of Defense. Using High Performance Team processes, the team reviewed all the factors influencing the product, including business, technical, and social pressures. The team worked with engineers, suppliers, customers, and key stakeholders to completely redesign the way in which the product was built.

Applying HPT principles and processes, the team quickly applied their ideas to production. The result: *Within three months, the team was producing the product in less than six days, resulting in an 85 percent reduction in cost and cycle time.*

The team's motivation dramatically increased as their costs reduced. As less and less team members were required to produce the product, the team spawned additional teams to produce other products; ex-team members became essential seeds to other production areas. Team members had dramatically increased productivity and commitment—and simply enjoyed coming to work each morning.

This is one example of dramatic, order-of-magnitude improvement in productivity. Born of the need for major improvements in profitability and effectiveness, the company made major changes in its own way of doing work. These changes included unleashing the employees' creativity and commitment, allowing them to question longtime assumptions in work practices and company policies, and following a principle-based system of revolutionary change. The company's bottom-line results made dramatic improvements.

There are thousands of successful HPTs in many different industries. Though they may have different titles, different descriptions, and diverse experiences, they have followed a common path to major change. This book describes that common path.

HIGH PERFORMANCE TEAMS (HPTs): WHAT ARE THEY?

High Performance Teams are simply those teams that

achieve a quantum leap in business results in less than a year—in all key success dimensions.[1]

Since the 1980s, companies in many different industries have implemented HPTs. These efforts have typically been driven by companies needing major improvements in profitability, productivity, customer service, and employee morale—*all at the same time.*

These successful HPTs have resulted in order-of-magnitude changes in product cycle times, quality levels, and improved cash flows. Many HPTs have the unique distinction of dramatically improving productivity and market share while increasing employee morale and motivation. A hallmark of successful HPTs is their ability to achieve breakthrough results in many different "success" dimensions—simultaneously.

HPT efforts have been able to transform their organizations from a strategy of change reaction to a competitive strategy of being a change driver. The very drive pressures that may have created initial concern are now an opportunity for market prominence and profit. Some of these efforts include the following:

- At a computer storage manufacturing division, productivity improved 60 percent and overhead reduced by more than 40 percent.
- At an electronic motor controls company, the time to produce drive electronics was reduced by 65 percent while reducing the components 30 percent, dramatically lowering the overall cost and increasing sales.
- At a Fortune 500 company, Accounts Receivable cash flows in a problem billing area were increased by $4 million, and on-time billing performance was increased to 99.7 percent.
- In a distribution organization, employee commitment was increased from a 1st percentile national ranking to 48th percentile in one year.
- A furniture company increased productivity by 74 percent in three years.

High Performance Teams are found in virtually *all* organizations, from business to government to religious organizations. For convenience in this text, however, business organizations are considered the model environment for HPTs.

Given all these successes, and many more, why are HPT efforts not a well-established change strategy?

Unfortunately, in many HPT attempts, the results have been increased costs, chaotic management, disenfranchised employees, and frustrated customers. For some companies, employees equate High Performance Teams with failed promises, and management believes these terms are synonymous with the "inmates taking over the asylum."

Until now, there seemed to be no connection between each of the failed HPT attempts—or even between successful efforts. The consideration of HPT as a strategic response to change seemed to be limited to a few unique situations. Without an effective guide to the creation and nurturing of successful HPT efforts, many organizations were inadequately prepared for the unique challenges of HPT. This text is designed to provide that guidance.

So what is required to create HPTs that achieve quantum leaps in business results and breakthrough success?

HPTs: Key Learnings

The difference between successful HPT efforts that generate breakthrough results and those efforts that degrade into chaos is evident in retrospect. Based upon a history of both successful and unsuccessful teams, common themes of success are evident.

The most successful High Performance Teams

1. Are best applied when breakthrough results are required and desired by the organization.
2. Are created and guided by those who understand the underlying dynamics taking place throughout the transition to HPT.
3. Are outwardly focused on the fundamental business criteria for success.
4. Are inwardly driven by key HPT principles.
5. Are created by a fundamental shift in culture.

Although some leaders understand each of these learnings, either intuitively or deductively, it can be very difficult to apply them in real-world practice. Further, most leaders who attempt an HPT effort are not familiar with either the principles or the underlying change dynamics that are key to a successful effort.

This text outlines the fundamental processes of change occurring during the HPT process, identifies the common gaps and barriers of traditional HPT efforts, and offers a new path for successful HPT efforts. By offering a practical, proven approach to how to make them work, this text can provide a road map to organizations needing breakthrough results in short periods of time.

ORGANIZATION OF THIS TEXT

To provide the understanding and guidance for a successful HPT effort, this text is segmented into six sections: sample case histories, the context

of HPTs, new learnings, a detailed approach to the new HPTs, the future of HPTs, and reference information. These sections include:

Section I: High Performance Teams: Background and Cases

To understand how to develop future successful HPTs, it is helpful to understand the trends of past HPT efforts. An outline of historical HPT efforts is reviewed, including their mixed record of "high performing" successes and notable failures. Common themes for success and key learnings are identified for future HPT efforts.

Section II: Why HPT? A Strategic Approach to Change

The first key to understanding HPTs is to understand the *context* of their need and application. HPTs are simply one alternative of change strategy that offers breakthrough performance improvement in a short period of time. However, HPTs are not for everyone. Understanding when they should and should not be applied, as well as HPTs' opportunities and limitations, provides the first step to the effective application of HPTs.

To better understand HPTs, it is important to understand how organizations react to the full spectrum of change pressures. In this section, a wide range of business change drivers is outlined with their corresponding change strategy. By understanding that change is a common response to business pressures for change and by understanding how the various change strategies help or hinder that response, it is possible to understand where and when HPTs are best applied.

This section reviews the change spectrum from the "status quo" organization that strives to maintain present market conditions to the "breakthrough" organization that must make fundamental changes. High Performance Teams are described and positioned within that range of strategies.

This section provides the conceptual context for creating HPTs.

Section III: How HPT? The Dynamics and Processes of HPTs

Given the experience of traditional HPT efforts, and the contexts in which they were created, this section summarizes the new learnings and opportunities that now exist for those teams and organizations.

The recent increases in organizational pressures, shortening of demand cycles, and changes in global conditions have impacted the creation of HPTs. These changes offer increased opportunities for HPTs, as well as increased difficulties in their creation. These environmental pressures are reviewed in Section III.

The most successful HPT efforts follow key "Success Principles" in their formation and development. These key principles are detailed and reviewed.

The process of *transition* to high performance is one of the most critical elements of successful HPTs. This section reviews a basic model of the multidimensional processes that underlie HPT transition. Particular focus is provided for the interventions and support necessary to create and develop effective HPTs.

Section IV: The *What* of HPT: A Template for High Performance Teams

A key HPT success principle is that there are many ways to achieve the same results. This applies to the HPT process *itself* as well as work design; there are many paths to a successful HPT effort. However, it is often helpful to build upon a pre-existing template for HPT creation and development.

Applying the new learnings to the creation of High Performance Teams, this section provides a detailed template for an HPT effort. This includes specific, real-world deliverables, activities, and processes that can create a successful HPT. Building on the HPTs' underlying processes, this section also makes extensive reference to the HPT *transition processes* and the appropriate *interventions* that can accelerate the effort.

Section V: Beyond HPTs: The Third Wave

As new HPTs build on their own successes and failures and find even greater opportunities, there are some common themes emerging. This short section outlines the potential for a third wave of quantum leaps that are possible within the team and throughout the organization.

Section VI: Bibliography, Glossary, and Index

A selected, annotated bibliography is provided for reference and further study by the reader. A glossary is provided for reference, as well as a standard index.

For those organizations needing and desiring breakthrough change and considering HPTs, this book provides a detailed guide to how to make them work.

Case Histories, Examples, and Confidentiality

This text is based upon a combination of personal interviews, consulting engagements, literature research, informal surveys, and the personal experience of the author. This input spans three decades, thousands of team members, and hundreds of teams. The author's experience in internal and external consulting, line management, and independent research comprises much of the real-world perspective included in this text.

In conventional "organizational dynamics" texts, case histories are based upon published works, publicly documented change efforts, and the willingness of stakeholders to discuss their experiences openly and honestly.

Unfortunately, much of the true history of High Performance Teams, and the real learning opportunity, lies in the *unpublished* experiences. Most HPT organizations prefer not to have their experiences published. Studying the total picture of High Performance Teams is critical to understanding the HPT process; understanding the process is critical to the successful creation of High Performance Teams.

As a means of achieving significant breakthroughs in all key business success metrics, successful HPTs are often considered a competitive advantage by their parent organization. For many HPT efforts, the increased productivity, reduced cost, and enhanced employee and customer satisfaction are significant advantages—particularly in competitive marketplaces. Most organizations do not want to reduce their competitive advantage by publishing the very processes that created that advantage.

Conversely, many organizations have attempted HPT efforts without success. In some cases, considerable time, money, and resources were spent in the attempt. For these companies, not only did the team *not* achieve its goals, it triggered significant employee resentment and chaos as a result.

For all these organizations, the desire for privacy is understandable. However, a comprehensive review of both success and failure is needed to be able to create successful HPTs in the future.

This text relies heavily on actual case histories and real-world examples. To accommodate the need for confidentiality and the need for actual HPT histories, this text does not identify any specific team or company—even those that have already been publicly documented. Uniquely identifying facts or circumstances of the teams have also been modified or excluded from this text.

In this manner, the overall perspective of High Performance Teams can be studied and considered. This is critical to learning how to make them work.

NOTE

1. For the purpose of this text, *quantum leap* means more than a 50 percent improvement, and the "key success dimensions" include customer value, operational value, shareholder value, employee value, and cultural foundation. These are described in much greater detail in chapter 4.

High Performance
Teams: Background
and Cases

1

Background: Creative Workplaces

All history becomes subjective; in other words,
there is properly no history, only biography.

—Emerson

It is beyond the scope of this text to provide a historical reference on creative workplaces in the twentieth century, or even in recent U.S. history. For those interested in case histories and the evolution of alternative work cultures, there are many excellent references available.[1]

In order to understand the present and future evolution of HPTs, however, it is helpful to understand the historical context of HPTs. Understanding previous experiments in workplace and organizational design, as well as some of the corresponding thought leadership, can be effective in understanding the nature of HPTs today and where they may evolve in the future.

THE ANTECEDENTS OF MODERN
HIGH PERFORMANCE TEAMS

As HPTs are defined as simply those groups of people "that achieve a quantum leap in performance in less than a year," HPTs have existed as long as has history. For the scope of this text, however, "history" is focused on the direct antecedents to the recent HPT efforts since the 1980s.

Throughout the twentieth century, quantum leaps in industrial output and individual productivity were possible in the conversion to "scientific

management." Through time-study reviews of production methods and detailed productivity analyses of work flows, production scheduling and control became major factors in several order-of-magnitude changes in industrial output. As a result of new thinking in manufacturing industries by pioneers such as Frederick Taylor, industrial output grew at a far greater rate than at any other time since the beginning of the Industrial Revolution. With the emergency needs of World War II, all major industrial countries had further discovered new ways to produce much more with less. Entire fields of study have evolved from this "productivity revolution," and are extensively outlined and reviewed elsewhere.

In the second half of the twentieth century, it was felt that the cognitive and technical focus of work analysis was missing a significant component: the worker. With social scientists focusing attention on many workplaces, the concept of integrating work and worker began to take shape.

In 1949, Eric Trist of the Tavistock Institute of Human Relations, London, visited a coal mine in north central England. He saw self-regulating teams working throughout the mine—the result of cooperation with the workers, managers, and union leaders. Describing the change as "responsible autonomy," Trist noted a dramatic increase in personal commitment and safety and high productivity. This was counter to the popular perception that employee motivation was inversely proportional to work output; many believed that high company output required low worker satisfaction. This coal mine case study became famous in Trist's publication in 1963 of their results and his analysis.[2] Many refer to this case study as the first post-Taylor sociotechnical team.

The interest generated by the Tavistock case study, and others, set the foundation for considerable research by social researchers into the area of work system and workplaces. Kurt Lewin's concepts of "action research" and the work of National Testing Laboratories demonstrated the impact of social psychology on real work results. Different organizations tried social and technical integration in experimental formats and in different markets. *Organizational Development* (OD) research became recognized at many industries as well as at academic institutions, codifying the study of social behaviors as applied to the workplace.

Simultaneously, systems theory became more refined throughout the 1960s and 1970s from both behavioral and analytical perspectives. Building upon new research into computer systems and mathematical models, analytical systems theory was now able to describe entire manufacturing processes and work flows. Behavioral systems theory expanded similarly, providing the basis for evaluating the whole work system from a cognitive perspective.

By the 1980s, the convergence of social systems theory, social-technical work integration, and organizational development practices created a foundation for the creation of new workplaces. This convergence seemed

to offer the potential of new productivity improvements by integrating the social and behavioral perspectives of the workforce into the technical needs of the work flow. This sociotechnical approach seemed to offer organizations a new way to achieve more with less.

At the same time, by 1981 and 1982, significant downturns in the U.S. and foreign economies were described as the worst since the Great Depression.

Whether for financial necessity or for the desire to create new work cultures, by the 1980s, many organizations were willing to try something new.

NOTES

1. Weisbord, M., *Productive Workplaces Revisited*, San Francisco, CA: Jossey-Bass, 2004, Part 1, and pgs 351–426.

2. Ibid., pgs 158–166, referencing Trist, E.L., Higgin, G.W., Murray, H., and Pollock, A.B., *Organizational Choice*, London: Tavistock, 1963; also referencing Trist, Eric, *The Relations of Social and Technical Systems in Coal Mining*, presented to the British Psychological Society, 1950.

Case Histories:
A Process Review

Example is the school of mankind,
and they will learn at no other.

—Edmund Burke

STORAGE DIVISION, COMPUTER MANUFACTURER

In the early 1980s, the field of business computers was beginning to undergo some of its greatest shifts since the entry of IBM into the field 20 years before. In 1981, the first signs of high-end market shift were being noticed. Market demand for high-volume products at low cost was beginning to be asserted.

To address this need, the company wanted to explore new ideas of sociotechnical organization and to create self-directed teams that would include a "flattened" organizational structure. With this model, the company hoped that overhead would be minimized, and cycle times would be improved.

Unlike other computer storage producers who focused on capital-intensive automation systems to improve productivity, the company wanted to invest in its people resources to produce higher-quality, lower-cost products. The plant would be team-based, with product-dedicated teams.

Each team would build a product from start to finish, taking "end to end" ownership of a particular product. This product focus would allow the team to ensure high quality and faster throughput; there would be no handoffs in any of the workflows to impede product completion.

Using several sociotechnical models, the organizational design team settled on a three-level organization model. The plant manager was the plant's CEO, responsible for the strategic decisions of the plant. A few functional managers provided leadership and guidance for major functions/product lines. The remaining operations and support employees comprised the worker level, with 65 percent working on the product and 35 percent providing technical support. There were 200 workers overall.

Over the next three years, considerable preparation and training was provided to all employees, from the plant manager to the floor workers. This training included technical aspects of their work, but the greatest focus was on the sociotechnical work system, and the unique responsibilities of each level.

In addition to conventional responsibilities of production and quality yields, the functional managers were also responsible for supporting the product teams, inverting their traditional role. Team development and integration and facilitating conflict resolution were part of the managers' role, rather than the conventional delegation to support personnel. As "boundary managers," the functional managers were also responsible for integrating key stakeholder interaction with the product teams. The functional managers were also responsible for the transition of the teams to self-directed capability; in the ideal case, the functional managers would not make any decisions per se.

The job of functional manager was much more demanding and comprehensive than a traditional management role.

Similarly, the operations teams and support teams had responsibilities that far exceeded those of conventional teams. Operating team members were expected to provide peer review, peer training, and take on more and more tasks traditionally performed by support organizations. Support team members were expected to train the operating team members and to transition major support functions to those teams.

A "pay for knowledge" compensation system was also put into place, encouraging all levels of employees to expand their working knowledge of technical and social perspectives. Computer-based training was combined with peer and expert training to assist the employees in their knowledge growth.

This focus on the social aspects of work was not limited to training and compensation. The physical plant was also designed around sociotechnical principles, providing an integrated environment for all levels of employees. Unlike a traditional factory floor, the plant's production environment included carpeting, file cabinets, and computer terminals. As the teams were product-based, all levels of employees focused on a given product line had offices and cubicles physically collocated with the product assembly and test functions.

Overall, there was considerable focus on the social aspects of work, and a great deal of attention paid to the social support systems in place, prior to production start. By 1985, after ramping up production to full operational status, the plant's performance improvements included

- 40 percent reduction in touch time (actual hands-on labor time).
- 40 percent reduction in overhead requirements.
- 50 percent reduction in scrap costs.
- doubling of production capacity and utilization.

This plant was considered highly successful; it remains one of the classic examples of High Performance Teams in the United States. However, its strong focus on employee involvement and social integration was not matched by attention to technical and external stakeholder issues.

Internally, the plant had developed an excellent system of peer integration, compensation design, and individual creativity. As the production demands increased, however, the plant was unable to maintain focus on its key performance metrics. Traditional problems of inventory turn, short production runs (where production was initiated without all necessary components), and relatively high support costs continued to be major issues. In general, the workers were more trained to work with themselves than with the traditional challenges of manufacturing.

Externally, the plant teams had not focused on stakeholder involvement; teams and management from other plants were not heavily enrolled in the new experiment. Some external teams were unaware of the sociotechnical plant; other teams had considerable resentment.

Following traditional succession planning, executive management brought in new plant management as attrition occurred. However, without the same training, orientation, and commitment of the original founding management team, these new managers tried to further improve productivity through their own traditional methods. This resulted in considerable employee resentment and had a net negative effect on productivity and commitment.

By the late 1980s, computer markets had changed dramatically, and even 50 percent increases in plant productivity were not enough to keep the company's market share. As declining markets and increased competition increased pressures for more "bottom line results," the plant was unable to continually improve its performance. In 1991, the plant was closed, and operations were merged into its traditional operations. The parent company was later sold and itself merged into other computer companies.

Although a spectacular benchmark of High Performance, the plant's history also provides an important lesson in the need for HPTs to *simultaneously* focus on technical, social, and political issues.

ELECTRONIC ASSEMBLY, AUTOMATION MANUFACTURING DIVISION

Throughout the 1980s, many large companies had tried to improve productivity through automation. With the initial successes of the automotive manufacturers in the extensive investments in robotics and the dramatic advancements in computer-based automation systems, many companies were experimenting with the use of robotics in manufacturing. Given the rising costs of human labor, health care, and other nonproduct-related costs, the prospect of being able to purchase an automated system, program it to a specific task, and let it run continuously was attractive to many manufacturing firms. The further advantage of simply "reprogramming the robot" when products changed, without significant capital investment, made the attraction even greater.

This automation manufacturer's sales had increased dramatically in the 1980s, with the surge in demand for robotics and material-handling systems. The company found it difficult to keep up with demand, and it had looked for new and flexible ways to improve its productivity and capacity.

Located near a major university, the company's electronic manufacturing division wanted to take advantage of its own robotics expertise and local academic talent. It decided to create a flexible manufacturing plant that would leverage three major productivity areas: automation, information, and people.

The organizational designers believed that *automation* would contribute more than 70 percent to productivity and flexibility. As a major provider of material-handling systems, it would be natural to design a workflow around material flows and inventory systems. This system would be dynamically reprogrammed on a weekly or monthly basis to accommodate changes in product flow and storage needs.

Information was also a key component of the designers' system; it was believed that 25 percent gains would come from an effective, distributed information system. Along with material-handling systems, the corresponding manufacturing information would also flow with the product. By having a flexible information system, the plant would be able to simply "re-program" itself for any changes in product or capacity.

People were also considered to be an important part of the integrated system. The designers intended that a 5 to 10 percent improvement would come from the organizational design. With the new design, the company wanted to empower its workforce, ensuring that it would be as flexible as the automation and information systems. This would involve significant training and orientation of all plant employees, from the plant manager to the floor workers.

Facilities were also important; the company built an entire plant around the concepts of automation, information, and people. As the physical

plant was being designed and constructed, employees were given considerable input into its layout. Significant floor space was devoted to employee support functions such as recreation areas and staffed physical fitness services.

In all implementations, flexibility was the key driver for productivity. This was not only intended to improve productivity for in-house electronics; the company hoped to leverage its investment by becoming a "production house" for external customers as well. By having flexibility built into all aspects of the organizational design, it was believed that the company would be able to produce its products, and those of many other companies, in a world-class level of productivity.

In 1984, the plant opened, ramping up its production by focusing only on its proprietary products. Within two years, the resulting output was significantly higher than other plants, demonstrating 60 percent improvements in selected product areas—particularly those requiring labor-intensive operations.

As the plant began to increase its production, it discovered that product changes and customer demands shifted constantly. Instead of automation accounting for 70+ percent of productivity improvement, the organization and social changes were contributing almost 80 percent of the overall gains. The employees' motivation and willingness to change work processes had a much shorter change cycle than the reprogramming required of the automation systems. In fact, in the first year of full operation, there were considerable production delays while flexible automation systems were reprogrammed and serviced.

Similarly, throughout the start-up period, there were delays with the information systems deployment; this resulted in occasional work stoppages as work instructions were unavailable to the employees. Overall, however, the information systems were effective at supporting the needs and decision-making of the employees.

Throughout the first two years of operation, the company discovered that its "productivity triangle" of automation, information, and people was inverted. In fact, the employees' productivity gain contributed the most improvement, followed by the information system. The automation system, originally intended to provide the greatest productivity contribution, was deemed marginally effective.

Management was very impressed with this unexpected productivity gain and provided further latitude for employees. Working teams were provided say over all major aspects of work, including selection, deselection, compensation, and working conditions.

By 1989, however, it was clear that something was wrong. Production schedules were being changed and product deliveries delayed while employees were exercising in the fitness rooms. Communication between the plant and its customers (both internal and external to the company)

had deteriorated. Customers were reporting an "arrogance" on the part of the work team members. Customer meetings and production reports were often scheduled around team members' convenience. Overall productivity was declining and management was unable to stem the decline. As one manager reported, "We asked for meetings to explain the problem, and we were told they had more important things to do."

Drastic measures were taken; the entire plant was shut down for several months, and all employees were let go, then asked to rebid for their former positions. By 1990, the plant had reopened with new management and a fraction of its former employees. Firm roles were defined, and considerable limits placed on the autonomy and flexibility of the work teams. Traditional managers filled production scheduling and production control roles, defining the specific product activity each work team would be responsible for.

Slowly, the plant's productivity and quality improved, as did its relationships to customers and suppliers. Productivity and output capacity continued to grow at a greater rate than other manufacturing plants, but never repeated their initial levels or original high performance expectations.

ASSEMBLY, DEFENSE MANUFACTURING COMPANY

As noted earlier, the defense industry was undergoing major restructuring in the late 1980s. With the dramatic reductions in U.S. and NATO defense spending after the fall of the Soviet Union, companies were losing lucrative contracts. With most defense contractors, companies had long been organized around cost-plus contracts that virtually guaranteed a profit. With decreased defense budgets, these companies were now required to compete on fixed-price contracts that required project and fiscal management. The combined factors of lowered sales and fixed-price constraints resulted in major pressures for change throughout the defense markets, both in the United States and abroad.

Though some companies were farsighted enough to plan for this scenario, most companies in the defense industry (both the contractors and their suppliers) were unprepared. When the major contracts were reduced in 1988 and 1989, many contractors had only months to compensate—or exit the market entirely.

Over the years, most defense suppliers had provided employees with lucrative benefits and high compensation, compared to their commercial counterparts. Although many defense companies and unions claimed that defense work had unique requirements justifying that level of compensation, most suppliers found that outsourcing their work to commercial firms was a rapid means of reducing cost.

In 1990, one company responded to the market drop by closing plants and outsourcing as much of its manufacturing assembly as it could. However, it soon discovered that (1) the complexity of its products exceeded its manufacturing documentation and (2) security requirements and clearances could not be easily transferred to the commercial sector. While still closing plants, it decided to build two new plants, based on global best practices, that would provide world-class productivity improvements. In other words, the overall net cost of the facilities would have to be equivalent to outsourcing and going offshore.

To prepare for this, a year was spent visiting innovative workplaces worldwide and domestically. Extensive use of consultants provided expertise, benchmarking, and guidance for the plants. Both plants would be planned similarly, yet located in separate geographic locations to correspond to key customer locations. Sociotechnical design would be used to develop product flows, work design, and physical plant layout. The financial structure of the products would also change, reflecting product duration rather than conventional "touch time"; the longer it took to produce a product, the more it would cost. Information systems would also be extensively employed, with the intent of being paperless at all process steps.

Organization was similar to the computer storage company; three levels of plant management team, technical associate, and operations associate were created, with a single level of reporting. All workers would report to the small plant management team. Employees at all levels would have to pass a rigorous series of psychological and technical tests, but preference would be given to those employees laid off at the closing plants.

Even after being hired into the new plant, the employees did not start "work." Each employee underwent six weeks of training in the plant's in-house "school." Along with training in manufacturing techniques and required certifications, the employees also learned about sociotechnical designs, team work principles, and even high-speed, high-capacity production techniques.

One team was formed to assemble and test power supplies. These power supplies were high-power, high-current devices that were very difficult to produce. During the company's previous attempt at outsourcing, two potential suppliers had defaulted on their contracts, unable to produce the supplies at the required quality and cost. Manufacturing documents were incomplete, and testing consisted of a final, operational test at the completion of the manufacturing cycle: Either it worked, or it did not.

Recognizing the challenge, the company delayed the product's transference to the new sociotechnical facility until it could identify key employees at the original manufacturing location. These de facto product experts would form the nucleus of a product team at the new facility. Though they would still have to pass the screening required of all employees, these

experts were encouraged to apply and formed the initial power supply product team.

These employees did not begin assembly work when they reported to the new plant. After their initial six-week training, they reported to meeting rooms to develop a redesign of the power supply. Over a three-week period, the team analyzed, questioned, and redesigned the manufacturing process, relying on their experience, expertise, and support from a variety of technical and organizational support personnel. Their charter was to develop a new way of manufacturing the product, using sociotechnical principles combined with high-velocity manufacturing and information flow.

Initially, the team experienced many challenges in working together, finding new alternatives and questioning traditional assumptions. It was clear at several times throughout the process that an outcome was not certain, and contingency plans would have to be made in case the team was unable to achieve its goals.

Within days, however, they began to discover fundamental flaws in the assembly process. Problems that were not detected early in the process created major delays and work stoppages at the end of the process; simple check-steps eliminated later delays. Skilling was very uneven among the team members; they discovered flexibility was not practical when individuals were only expert at one thing. A new training program was designed and put into place in a way that met the production schedule while increasing capacity.

Within a month, the team began producing the product, reducing the labor time from its traditional 512 hours to 205 hours. As the product volume was increased, deliberately timing the transfer rate from the previous plant to the new plant to account for capacity increases, the team size increased from 11 to 50 to 120 employees. As more product was transferred and work design changes implemented, the team further reduced the time to manufacture from 150 hours to 70 to 38 hours. Quality was dramatically increased within three months, with "sigma" well above 6, ensuring only three product errors in one million opportunities.

As the team size and product demand increased, so did the organizational challenges. The original team strained to train, orient, and guide new employees. As new employees came onboard, without the extensive product review of the original team, conflicts arose when new members challenged the wisdom and role of the original members. The teams quickly discovered that communication and integration between the members could no longer be accomplished the way they originally were.

The teams split, and split again, forming subteams that continually communicated. "On-the-job" training became continuous for everyone, and peer-to-peer review was completed on each step of the manufacturing process. "Integration teams" were formed with rotating membership, for

the purpose of enhancing daily communication. Organizational dynamics were shifting as the demands on the teams shifted.

There was considerable support for these teams before, during, and after the transfer of work. The leader was focused on the output metrics (production schedule, quality, and cost) as well as the transition of the team from its previous manufacturing culture to its new one. Support personnel acted as supervisors to begin with, similar to the roles they filled at the originating plant, then slowly transitioned to self-directed teams as the team members demonstrated their organizational capability. The teams were given increasing responsibility for traditional results, while the leaders were focused on the transition process. While applying these new methods of manufacturing, the plant management team leader still retained accountability for all traditional metrics. As this was a represented plant, the union leadership was an integral part of the new design and transition process. Union officers were de facto members of key teams, and shop stewards were included in each redesign. The union had understood the need for dramatic change, and worked with management to effect that change.

Within two months, the teams were producing at rates that exceeded expectation and schedule. Within four months, the teams were producing more product than the customers' accounting systems were able to document. Quality, quantity, motivation, safety, and creativity were all significantly increased.

This success was replicated throughout the plant, with team members leaving the original teams to start up new ones and forming the nucleus of new High Performance Teams. Despite the dramatic improvements in productivity, motivation, and output, however, executive management later changed, and a strong emphasis on traditional management was imposed on all plants—including the two new sociotechnical plants. The financial benefits of high performance output were seen at the customer locations, not at the sociotechnical worksites. As a result, the new plants were not able to demonstrate their considerable financial advantage, and work was ultimately transferred to plants with lower-wage employees.

MOTOR CONTROL SUPPLIER, SMALL MANUFACTURING FIRM

In many agricultural applications, the need for modern automation is often limited by the harsh realities of the farmstead environment and farmstead economics. While both large and small farms are typically benefited by the advantages of automation in all phases of their operations, the physical demand on hardware may include hot summers, cold winters, heavy rainfall and lightning strikes. When combined with the intense

competition of automation suppliers and the price sensitivity of farm owners, a successful product has to be inexpensive, sturdy, reliable, and effective.

As with the computer industry, technology in the control industry made quantum leaps in the 1980s and 1990s. New technologies opened up new opportunities in the control and automation of routine farmstead operations from the feeding of livestock to planting of seeds to milking of dairy herds.

One regional manufacturing firm, looking to leverage their own expertise in electronics and control technology, wanted to expand into the agricultural market. Their growth in conventional markets had been good, but they identified untapped potential in the market for automated control systems. If they could adapt their own products to the farmstead with minimal effort, they would be able to build on their own investments and increase their sales and profitability.

The first product area was a simple motor control circuit; a control to start, stop and reverse a drive motor in a feed system. The motor drove a simple conveyor system; it only had to move forward, stop, or move backward. While the circuitry was straightforward, it had to operate equally well in hot, cold, wet, and dry climates with all of the ambient hazards of a working farm. It would be a good test of the company's ability to expand into the new marketplace.

Initial product testing was successful; the company was able to provide controls that performed well, even in the harsh farmstead environments. The product quality was high, and projected life would be more than the competition: positive advantages on the farm. However, when the component cost was compared to the competitor's products, the cost of materials was much greater than the selling price of the competition. To attempt to sell a product that was several times more expensive than the competitive products, with no significant advantage other than total operating life, would have been a waste of money and marketing resources. The product would simply not sell.

Taking a traditional approach, the company looked at the competitive products and tried to build similar products with similar components. It hoped to gain cost advantage through proper purchasing techniques. Not only did this prove ineffective; the company soon discovered that the rest of its competition had already tried the same approach. As a result of the competitors using the same circuits, the same components, and the same suppliers, all of the markets' major products were priced at the same level, to within 1/10th of a cent. Any chance of making a profit in the market seemed remote.

At one point, the Operations Manager decided the market was untenable and declined to expand the product line. The Marketing Manager, however, wanted to pursue it.

Convinced that there was significant growth potential in the agricultural market, the Marketing Manager began to take a non-traditional approach, and formed a team that included engineering, marketing, and production expertise. Rather than focus on competitive products, the team focused on the field application of the product and the integration of the motor control with the motor.

Starting with the basics, the team looked at the fundamental switching requirements of the motor and control. Applying Boolean analysis to the switching circuit, the Engineering Manager mapped out the electrical requirements for forward operation, reverse operation, and stopping. Combining the different operational modes, the analysis showed that a simple logic circuit could be constructed with 30 percent fewer components than a conventional circuit. The team built a prototype motor control based upon the new design; it was superior to the traditional design, required less parts, and was easier to manufacture.

Upon investigation, it was discovered that the competitors had all copied each other's products, using the same circuit diagrams from the 1920s. The competitors had all assumed that the early circuits were the best, and had competed solely on price, for decades. What had initially appeared as an obstacle to entry—a highly competitive market—was now a significant opportunity for profitable growth.

The Operations Manager admitted his error and the company was able to make significant penetration into the price-sensitive market. By pricing the product well above their component cost, yet below the selling price of their competition, the company was able to significantly improve their gross profit margin. By leveraging High Performance design principles, the company was able to dramatically increase sales and profitability.

SERVICE REPAIR ORGANIZATION, ELECTRICAL UTILITY COMPANY

Throughout most of the twentieth century, electrical utilities were a fundamental part of the U.S. infrastructure, providing power to virtually all citizens in all types of terrain and weather. As a protected monopoly, private and municipal utilities operated from a cost-plus basis; all costs would be equally distributed across all ratepayers. When the costs went up, the rates went up; in theory, the rates would also be reduced when the costs were reduced.

Utilities were considered one of the safest grades of stock, sometimes rivaling government bonds in its investment grade. Individuals and pension funds often held major positions in utility stocks, depending upon the stocks' stability and annual dividend return for income.

Rates continued to rise with increased costs, increasing consumer demand for rate relief. With the advent of governmental deregulation of the 1990s, selected states began to experiment with deregulation that could potentially reduce some utilities' revenue by as much as 30 percent —without reducing the underlying costs of providing power. For utilities in those states considering deregulation, and utilities in other states concerned that it would become a national deregulation, the prospect of losing 30 percent revenue meant losing all of their profits—or worse.

One utility decided to address this challenge with High Performance Teams. It would try to change its productivity by changing the nature of the way the work is performed. If productivity could be significantly improved while increasing employee commitment and safety, it would be able to survive the potential rate cuts.

One area of high cost and customer concern was the repair of underground "faults": those disruptions in service that result from shorted or disconnected buried power cables. In order to return the customer to service, the cable fault must be located, repaired, and reconnected. Although recent technology advancements have improved some aspects of the work, it can still require a great deal of detective work, digging, and repairing. More than 500 employees, full- and part-time, were required to complete the work. To find a new way of doing the work, a High Performance Team was created.

The team was given the challenge of reducing costs by 40 percent while dramatically improving customer satisfaction, employee motivation, and safety—within six months. After a period of preparation and data gathering, a cross-functional team of 32 bargaining unit and management employees spent an intensive three weeks reviewing all aspects of the work required to repair faults. The team looked at the present culture, noting the significant levels of employee resentment and discontent, as well as the organizational handoffs that were common. Looking at the process from end-to-end, the team extensively reviewed each process step, analyzing its cost and impact on the overall process. The team further talked to managers, customers, and all major stakeholders. Working with management-imposed constraints on their ultimate design, the team struggled with and eventually developed a process that would eliminate non–value-added work, reduce redundancies, and leverage new technologies in fault locating and repair.

Throughout this analysis and design, the team members spent a great deal of time in the field, communicating their thinking and collecting input from those not on the actual design team. By the time of the team's summary report to executive management, it had incorporated ideas from across the workforce.

The team outlined a process that would achieve all its objectives *simultaneously*, and management gave its approval for a phased rollout across

the enterprise. Because the original team comprised only a small portion of the ultimate workforce involved in the process, implementation would start with a pilot test then expand geographically to incorporate more and more teams. This process was expected to be completed within six months.

Though this followed the strategy of many traditional "phased implementation" plans, it imposed unique challenges on the original team. As with the power supply team in the defense industry example, the team would have to dramatically increase its membership and volume while enrolling new members into its process. It would have to impart its own learnings and motivation to team members that had not gone through the intense work design experience that original members had. Further, to meet its aggressive financial targets, the team would have to dramatically increase its own productive output and the rate at which it was repairing faults. All this would be required, at the same time.

To do this, the team decided on a phased approach that would include a short period of training for each new team, as well as "seeding" the new teams with as many original members as practical. For the pilot phase, original team members comprised most of the pilot teams, allowing the pilot focus to be on the actual work and required integration with support organizations.

Within a month, the pilot teams had exceeded their targets, and validated their new process. Many team members were excited about the new approach and enjoyed the increased autonomy and responsibility. Several management and support groups, however, were not positive about the teams' new autonomy; many viewed it as an encroachment on their traditional areas of control. Similarly, the union, originally in favor of the teams and actively supporting them, began to view the team's independence as a threat.

With the original team's enthusiasm, the phased rollout was implemented, progressively increasing the number of teams involved in the process. Each new team member underwent three days of orientation, training, and enrollment into the HPT process, with the active support and coaching of original team members. Because the three-day period was insufficient to provide a full background and involvement, considerable on-site training and orientation were provided to each team in the field as they were doing their work. This on-site work involved process reviews, coaching, and ad hoc process redesign. This would be repeated for individual team members as required; early in the team's rollout, this included meetings several times a week. Within two months, on-site meetings were reduced to once a month.

Team members increased their communication and integration as their effective geographical territory expanded. Every week, team representatives would meet and report on their progress and raise organization-

wide issues. Some teams volunteered to cover for other teams when work-load varied, and many teams exchanged team members ad hoc.

Six months after the end of the pilot phase, the work was requiring 65 percent fewer workers; 47 full-time workers were now completing the work. Safety was dramatically improved, and customers were now offering letters of praise rather than complaint. In the original team's design, team members were scheduled to rotate in and out of the local teams; in practice, few team members wanted to leave the High Performance Team. In a nationally benchmarked survey of employee commitment and culture, the teams increased two quartiles in performance.

With rolling blackouts and bankruptcies a direct result of the "California experiment" in utility deregulation and national deregulation no longer considered priority legislation, utilities face less of a threat of arbitrary rate reduction in the mid-2000s. However, the financial consequences of Enron and other power traders has had a harsh impact on all U.S. utilities: Shareholders now demand more performance for less money. Many ratepayers are still reluctant to support rate increases when reports of accounting irregularities are commonly seen. The need for increased productivity, effective performance, and employee involvement continues. For some utilities, this will be critical for their long-term survival.

Common Themes
of Success or Missed
Opportunity

Know thyself.

—inscribed at the Oracle at Delphi

There are many examples of successful High Performance Teams and many examples of unsuccessful teams. Although the most notable successes follow the *linear work* of repetitive work flows, such as manufacturing or service industries, there are also many examples of *nonlinear* work flows, such as management teams and ad hoc committees. HPTs are found in all areas of group activities, from business to government to political groups to religious orders.

For the purpose of this text, the definition of High Performance Teams remains independent of process: Any team that achieves breakthrough results in all success dimensions is an HPT. This does not necessarily include sociotechnical teams, nor does it exclude rigid, hierarchical organizations. Any group of people, in any activity, could form as a High Performance Team.

This helps in identifying HPTs, but not in understanding them. To understand HPTs, it is necessary to thoroughly examine their underlying processes, interpersonal dynamics, and common themes. Given the very diverse nature of HPTs, it is necessary to make generalizations and simplify examples to aid in that understanding. This text reviews those processes in greater detail in Section III.

Overall, observations can be made of those teams that achieve High Performance, as well as those that are unable to. There are generalized

common themes of success that are helpful in creating HPTs. There are also, however, common themes of challenge and failure that may be of even more value when creating future HPTs.

THEMES OF SUCCESS

Success Theme: All Key Success Dimensions Are Addressed: Customer Value, Operational Value, Shareholder Value, and Employee Value

There are many teams that achieve more than 50 percent improvements in a single success dimension in less than a year. Even though legitimately published as success stories, they do not constitute High Performance Teams because they have not made those improvements in all dimensions simultaneously.

The accomplishments of these "single dimension" teams should not be diminished; they are simply out of the scope of this text. For some teams, however, this single dimension focus is unhealthy. When a team focuses solely on a single dimension, other pressures often increase significantly.

Albert Dunlap, CEO of Scott Paper, Sunbeam, and other turnaround companies, often focused companies on their shareholder value dimension to the exclusion of its employees. As he had indicated,[1]

> Employees are stakeholders but they don't deserve rights the way shareholders do, unless they've invested some money in the company they're working for. We have gone way overboard in creating rights for everybody, and companies have been pulled into that mess.

In many companies, this exclusive focus had created a highly rebellious workforce, dissatisfied customers, and poor performance. For some companies, such as Scott Paper, this was resolved by eventual liquidation of assets or the sale of the company. For other companies, such as Sunbeam, there was a significant loss of market share and shareholder value. At Sunbeam, as market share continued to decline, there were inappropriate accounting and marketing tactics, as shown by SEC investigations. Sunbeam continued to lose customers and revenue, reorganizing under Chapter 11 bankruptcy in 2001.[2]

Though *by definition*, successful High Performance Teams achieve success in all key dimensions simultaneously, it is also important to understand *why* this multidimensional approach is required. HPTs do not make design choices that deliberately sacrifice one dimension for another; they strive to find the path forward that simultaneously addresses all dimensions.

Success Theme: HPTs Are Best Applied When Breakthrough Results Are Needed and Desired by the Organization

Many successful HPT efforts occur during times of organizational stress and need for revolutionary, breakthrough results. HPTs are a very different way of approaching work. For many organizations, support and acceptance of a different work culture within themselves is very difficult. Culture clashes, employee resentment, and traditional management styles often pose significant barriers to the establishment of HPTs.

Conversely, in times of great expansion and opportunity, there is often more acceptance of differing work cultures as well. When companies start new ventures, people form new organizations, or new technologies offer new entirely new markets, there is so much room for experimentation that culture clashes are minimized and increased diversity is supported.

In both cases, the organization needs and wants breakthrough results; it is able to accommodate the different styles, approaches, and cultures of High Performance Teams.

It is important to note that this does not *preclude* successful HPTs from being formed in those organizations that do not require breakthrough results; they will simply be correspondingly more difficult to achieve.

Success Theme: HPTs Are Principle-Based

Successful High Performance Teams rely on fundamental *principles* for their guidance and cohesion, rather than on contract and agreement. Typically advanced in team development, HPT members define themselves through a set of governing principles that apply throughout their workplace, rather than through explicit "service level agreements" or procedures.

Successful HPTs do not try to predetermine situations or performance expectations. Rather, they try to communicate their *intent* through overarching principles that guide their actions. These principles typically fall into two categories; Key Business Principles and Key High Performance Principles; these are described in detail in Chapter 14.

Success Theme: HPTs Are Guided by Those Who Understand Their Underlying Processes

High Performance Teams are straightforward in focus, simple in concept, and difficult to implement. Many attempted HPT efforts end in frustration and failure due to unrealistic expectations and misunderstood dynamics.

Some executives believe that simply chartering a team to be High Performance, requiring the achievement of high goals, and telling them to do

it will achieve HPTs across their organization. Though frequently attempted, these teams rarely achieve High Performance. From the perspective of those executives chartering the teams, they are not being unrealistic; rather, *they are simply repeating a portion of what they have seen and understood from successful efforts.*

HPTs are the result of natural processes, accelerated to the point where the business needs are integrated with team members' creativity and individual desires. These processes are highly dynamic and interactive, and much of the energy of these processes is not visible to the casual observer. Many casual executives and stakeholders are not sensitive to these underlying processes.

Those HPT efforts that rely upon the guidance of effective HPT facilitators and coaches are able to effectively prepare for the teams' *transition* to High Performance. These support coaches use a combination of background experience, conceptual knowledge, and integrated intuition to help the executive, the leader, and the team members to achieve an HPT.

Success Theme: HPTs Are Created by a Shift in Culture

The most successful High Performance Teams appear to have a fundamentally different *culture* within them. Key stakeholders and visitors from other teams often remark, "It feels different on this team."

HPT team behaviors, activity priorities, and even communication are often very different than other teams. For many team members, it can be difficult to explain the differences; some refer to the enjoyment of their work; others refer to a new sense of accomplishment and satisfaction; still others may talk about a new technology they have discovered.

Though there are many definitions of culture, one of the hallmarks of High Performance Teams is, in fact, their culture and the shift they have made from their previous work styles. This is explored in more detail in chapter 23.

THEMES OF OPPORTUNITY

For those teams attempting but not achieving High Performance, "failure" is often defined as not achieving their charter goals. In learning the criteria for successful HPTs, however, it is very helpful to examine the common themes of these "failed" teams, so that they become "opportunity learnings" for future teams.

This is more than semantic. Learning from HPT efforts, particularly those that experienced challenges and barriers they could not overcome, is critical to not repeating those approaches in the future. This is particularly important because the failed efforts are typically not published.

Opportunity Theme: Runaway Empowerment

Teams who believe that empowerment is merely the chance to set their own rules and write their own checks miss the critical *responsibility* perspective. For many team members given the new opportunity to make wide-ranging recommendations, there is a belief that they can simply mandate their own rules. If not provided with appropriate limits and sense of business responsibility, these teams may be "out of control" very rapidly.

The transition to increased empowerment should be a deliberate, guided process that balances responsibility and empowerment. Leaders need to understand the transition process, knowing when to support the team and when to intervene.

Experienced facilitators and coaches can help guide the leader and the team to effective empowerment in a way that correspondingly increases accountability and autonomy.

Opportunity Theme: Disillusioned Leader and Workforce

In many HPT efforts, the teams spend considerable time and intense energy in developing new recommendations, only to discover or believe that it was all for naught. In some cases, the executives do not want to implement the teams' recommendations; in other cases, the would-be HPTs have unrealistic expectations moving forward.

The subsequent resentment can lead to disillusionment, increasing resistance to change on the part of both work teams and management. This is a common outcome of would-be HPT efforts, where the team is encouraged to develop HPT recommendations, yet no visible action is taken on them. Similarly, executives may be disillusioned when expecting breakthrough results from an HPT attempt, only to see marginal improvements in practice.

Setting firm boundaries before the work is designed—and being clear about what the team can and cannot change—is critical to a successful HPT effort. Similarly, the leaders need to continually assess their own readiness for change and their own support of the HPT process as the HPT effort begins.

A successful HPT effort is not easy; it has many challenges along the path to success. A structured process that continually checks itself against the original business needs and individual desires can be critical to HPT success.

Opportunity Theme: Chaos

In any change effort where major policies and procedures may be changed or questioned, the potential for chaos exists. Generally, the

greater the *transition* attempted, the greater the potential for confusion and chaotic activity. Although change strategies can help to alleviate this danger (see Chapter 6), the potential for major system breakdowns is great.

For unsuccessful HPT efforts that attempt major change without an effective transition period, chaos and conflict often result. This can be mitigated through a combination of effective support and contingency planning.

High Performance Team development is a strategy, as any other. Like all strategic plans, there should always be a predefined "safety exit" in event of emergency.

SUCCESSFUL HPT DEVELOPMENT DEPENDS UPON KEY LEARNINGS

Given the recent history of HPT efforts, common themes of success and opportunity, the following key learnings become critical to the creation, development, and implementation of successful HPTs:

- Understanding the environmental context of High Performance Teams
- Understanding and applying the key success principles of HPTs
- Understanding the transition process and underlying dynamics of HPTs

These key learnings are explored in detail later in this text.

To properly understand the dynamics and transition processes of HPTs, it is not enough to simply review a listing of those processes. Understanding the context of High Performance Teams is essential to understanding and applying the corresponding underlying functions. Therefore, it is helpful to first review the organizational context of the formation of HPTs, and the strategic pressures that drive the need for their creation.

NOTES

1. Dunlap, Albert J. *Mean Business: How I Save Bad Companies and Make Good Companies Great*, New York: Simon & Schuster, 1996, pg 198.

2. SEC Litigation releases 17001, May 15, 2001 and 17710, September 4, 2002.

Why HPT? A Strategic Approach to Change

Organizational Pressures for Change

Every organization is perfectly designed to achieve the results obtained.

—*W. Edwards Deming*

As with any business strategy, HPTs must minimize or eliminate the business pressures that trigger their development in the first place. It is axiomatic that successful High *Performance* Teams must in fact provide real business performance, whether that increases markets, improves profits, and/or increases employee commitment. Understanding these fundamental business pressures is critical to the successful application of HPT efforts.

In setting the context for HPTs, it is helpful to review the common responses of businesses to change pressures and to evaluate a potential HPT effort as simply one change strategy alternative among many. HPTs are not for all situations, nor are they appropriate for all organizations. When reviewed against several alternative change strategies, with corresponding advantages and disadvantages, much of the apparent mysticism of HPTs is removed and effective real-world decisions can be made.

SETTING THE HPT CONTEXT: PRESSURES AND STRATEGIES OF CHANGE

To survive, all businesses must follow the basic value imperative of success: to provide unique, perceived, value-added products and services. Further,

it is not enough to be successful in only *one* dimension. There are several dimensions of business—customer, operational, shareholder, employee, and cultural—that each business must succeed in simultaneously.

Each of these success dimensions has the potential to create *pressure for change*. For example, the customer dimension often produces a pressure on the organization for a "better, faster, cheaper" product. The employee dimension may induce pressure on the organization for more compensation and better working conditions. Each of these *change pressures* acts directly upon the organization as a whole, influencing the organization to make a corresponding shift in priorities or actions.

To view the organizational response to these change pressures, it is helpful to review the natural reaction of any organization to change pressures: Each wants to minimize change and "return things to the way they were." Each organization reacts as an individual does: It tries to minimize the impact on itself. Whether consciously or unconsciously, actively or passively, the organization spends a great deal of its energy *reacting* to the pressures impacting it.

That reaction can be disconnected and chaotic, or it can be integrated and strategic.

When the reaction to change pressure is disconnected and chaotic, the organization is often negatively impacted. In a business environment, product cycles may be increased, overhead expenses uncontrolled, and employee morale worsened. In most cases, this disconnected reaction may actually increase the external pressures on the organization that in turn becomes more disconnected and further increases the pressures. This creates a destructive cycle that may ultimately lead to dissatisfied customers, financial losses, employee stress, reductions in force, and ultimately corporate failure.

That downward spiral was evidenced at AT&T as it wrestled with regulatory agencies, court-ordered divestiture, and significantly increased competition. Throughout the late 1970s and 1980s, AT&T tried many different strategies to regain its former position as the monopolistic telecommunications service. Rather than offer a strategy for increased market share and valuation in a competitive environment, the organization maintained an external focus on regulatory adaptation and an internal priority on reorganization. This broad spectrum of activities significantly distracted executives from focusing on their core markets: the downward spiral continued.[1]

Conversely, when an organization's reaction is cohesive and integrated, the external pressures may offer the very rallying cry to action that energizes creativity, motivates employees, and impresses customers. In 1979, Chrysler Corporation was at an historical low in its stock price, had declining market position and profitability, and was in danger of bankruptcy. By the early 1980s, Chrysler's Lee Iaccoca galvanized employees

and customers by focusing attention to that very competitive threat: "If you can find a better car, buy it!"[2]

Easily stated and difficult to implement, effective change strategies are critical to an organization's success. To understand the spectrum of change strategies that are commonly employed by business organizations, it is helpful to review the fundamental business change drivers and then review typical response strategies.

THE BASIC VALUE IMPERATIVE

The basic proposition of business is that the organization provides goods and/or services to its customers in exchange for value (e.g., money). In a competitive marketplace, there is an extension to this fundamental proposition:

> To survive, any organization must offer *unique, perceived, value-added* products to its customers.

For convenience, "product" is used to refer to products, services, or a combination; it is the effective output of the business to the customer.

Unique

The organization's products or services must provide a differentiator from its competition. This differentiator can be across any criteria, including geographical, functional, cost/price, or virtual. Without a distinguishing product or service to offer the customer, the business will ultimately fail.

Perceived

Unless the customer experiences *both* uniqueness and value-added from the products, the net effect is to have neither. In some cases, organizations may try to create the perception that value and uniqueness are present when they are not; ultimately, these organizations typically fail.

Value-Added

Clearly, there must be some benefit to the customer from the organizations' products and services, else there is no incentive for the customer to select those products and services.

It is important to note that market dominance is not required for the organization to survive. However, if the company fails to provide any

unique, perceived, valued-added products to any portion of its market segments, it will ultimately fail.

COMMON BUSINESS DIMENSIONS OF SUCCESS

The pressures for change come from many sources and can be categorized in many different ways. For the context of HPT efforts, it is helpful to consider the four basic dimensions of business drivers: customer value, shareholder value, employee value, and operational value. Each value dimension has both tangible and intangible elements.

There is a fifth value dimension—cultural foundation, that is a critical success driver. It is addressed separately, as it underpins the four basic dimensions.

Customer Value-Added

A customer is defined as any individual or organization that receives the products offered and evaluates its success. This may include consumers who actually use the product, internal departments who receive services, or external regulators who evaluate the products' and companies' output.

To provide unique, perceived, customer value-added services is to provide a strong benefit directly to the customer. In this dimension, business pressures are often direct and obvious; as competition increases, customer demands increase correspondingly.

Competitive pressures are most often felt in this business dimension first as the customer often provides the first feedback to the organization that competition exists. These pressures may be felt in all areas, from quality of product to cost to functions provided.

To monitor the organization's success in this business driver dimension, conventional sales and marketing metrics are most often used. Key metrics typically include sales levels, market penetration and segmentation, customer relationship management, and more. The cycle times associated with these metrics are often very rapid. For some companies, customer value cycle times may be much shorter than the organization's ability to respond, creating the potential for rapid changes in competitive position and profitability.

Successful HPTs have a history of dramatically shortened product cycle times and significantly increased customer visibility and loyalty.

Operational Value-Added

Operational is defined as anything related to the form, fit, and/or function of the product provided to the customer. It focuses on the technical aspects and the workflows required to produce it.

In manufacturing industries, this business dimension is focused on the actual design and production of the product. In service-related industries, this dimension is typically focused on the scope, quality, and function provided.

Key success metrics include quality, cost to produce, product development cycles and costs, and form/fit/function performance. Suppliers are a key component of this value-added dimension.

Shareholder Value-Added

This business dimension includes all the desires, constraints, and concerns of the owners of the company. This will include tangible fiduciary responsibilities of the organization as well as its intangible contributions to its shareholders.

This business dimension includes the influences and pressures from the shareholders as well as other key governmental, regulatory, public relations, and other stakeholders. In most cases, this dimension is focused on direct and indirect costs and rate of return to the shareholders, but it also includes the intangible aspects of corporate good will, integrity, community standing, and industry respect.

Employee Value-Added

Clearly, the organization's traditional benefit to employees has been direct compensation. Increasingly, however, employees have required and desired more tangible and intangible return for their service to the company. These tangible benefits often include variable compensation, additional health benefits, family care, and long-term pension protection. Employee demands for intangible benefits have also increased, including improved quality of working life, increased sense of involvement and contribution, and sense of pride.

When the organization no longer provides a unique, perceived, value-added benefit to the employees, it begins to lose key employees and ultimately has to pay more and more to get less and less.

Cultural Foundation

Although not strictly a business dimension, "culture" is a critical element to business success. Defined here as an integrated sense of organizational identity, the culture provides the foundation for all other business dimensions. Without a culture that directly supports the fundamental business proposition in all key business dimensions, the organization will fail. This cultural foundation is a key to successful HPT efforts, and is reviewed extensively later in this text.

ALL VALUE DIMENSIONS, SIMULTANEOUSLY

As business cycles compress, competition increases, and stakeholder expectations rise, it is no longer "just good enough" to provide value in a single business dimension. The company that provides excellent short-term return to its shareholders yet has a disillusioned workforce will ultimately fail to achieve its financial goals. Similarly, the company that has very high employee motivation and retention yet produces poor-quality product soon discovers that its sales revenues are in significant decline.

In a high-technology, rapid-cycle, global economy, the company that does not focus on *all* dimensions simultaneously ultimately fails.

The requirement of *simultaneous* value often appears "impossible"; in fact, some authors contend that *singular* value focus is the key to success.[3] In practice, however, companies that focus on one value to the exclusion of others do not succeed. As will be seen throughout this text, High Performance Teams are one type of organizational alternative that successfully address all key dimensions simultaneously.

Thus, in order to survive long term, each business organization must provide unique, perceived value-added products in all key areas of customer value, stockholder value, employee value, and operational value. Organizational sense of identity must support and reinforce product, as well.

To be successful, every business—in fact, all organizations—must provide unique, perceived value-added in all key success dimensions all the time.

NOTES

1. Vietor, Richard, *Contrived Competition: Regulation and Deregulation in America*, Cambridge, MA: Harvard University Press, 1994, pgs 211–233.

2. Iacocca, Lee, and Novak, William, *Iacocca: An Autobiography*, New York: Bantam Books, 1988, pg 269.

3. Treacy, Michael, and Wiersma, Fred, *The Discipline of Market Leaders: Choose Your Customers, Narrow Your Focus, Dominate Your Market*, Reading, MA: Addison-Wesley, 1995, pg 19.

Change Myths

Much learning does not teach understanding.

—*Heraclitus*

As the drive for wide-scale business change increases, popular beliefs about the nature of change become widespread. These beliefs are often incomplete, yet become self-fulfilled by the leaders' and organizations' own expectations. To focus on the key change strategies, it is helpful to first recognize many of these common myths.

As is seen later in this text, many of these myths arise from an incomplete understanding of change strategies and processes. Most are also self-fulfilling; beliefs about change reinforce the beliefs about the organization itself.

COMMON MYTH #1: "JUST TELL THEM TO DO IT!"

Many leaders believe that for the organization to embrace change, the leader must simply direct the employees to perform some action (or even think a certain way). By making this mandate a requirement across the organization, the leader often believes that implementation of that change will quickly occur. "Just tell them to do it" is a form of magical thinking; in this scenario, the leader believes that simply commanding the *change* will create the result (Chapter 8).

In one change effort, the operating executive of an international wood products firm wanted to reduce costs by consolidating a widely scattered

distribution system. His intent was to reduce these many locations, each with its own staff and inventory, into a few large centers. It was felt that with careful planning by the strategic staff and expert consultants, the implementation would naturally follow. As soon as this was attempted, there was considerable resistance from all major stakeholders; the project was delayed and later reimplemented after working with the affected groups for more input, commitment, and accommodation.

The idea that change is simply the matter of "directing someone to do something" is often reinforced by the seasoned executive's long history of successfully directing projects that may have been very task-focused. In an environment of short-term, highly focused work, the command to change can appear to be very effective. In an environment where many different groups of people need to collaborate on common goals, however, it is unrealistic to expect everyone to arbitrarily change their attitudes.

A variant of this misperception is the belief that the leader can *"Grab them by their [hair]; their hearts and minds will follow!"*[1] In this method, the leader not only dictates the actions to be taken but threatens negative consequences if the dictums are not followed. This tactic is often successful in the very short-term: Compliance is usually widespread. Soon after compliance is achieved, however, there is often significant resistance, resentment, and anger on the part of the employees. This typically results in severe, negative long-term consequences for the organization.

COMMON MYTH #2: ORGANIZATIONAL CHANGE LEVERS: "JUST FIND THE LEVERS AND PUSH THEM."

A common belief is to discover the key impact areas of an organization and leverage them to make change. In this scenario, the leader identifies highly visible actions that are expected to have maximum impact on the organization. Once identified, the leader takes the action that "will energize the organization" into change. Now galvanized, the organization is then expected to make whatever changes the leader desires. In practice, this is rarely effective.

For a large electronics manufacturing firm, senior management believed there was an immediate need to significantly improve quality and reduce cost. Due to the capital-intensity of the business, it was determined that the budget was the "change lever" that was most effective; much of the middle managers' efforts throughout the year were spent in pursuit of greater budgets. It was believed that the budgets simply needed to be changed to reflect more money for quality control, and less money for ongoing production costs: This would force the production lines to improve their quality levels.

In fact, in the short run, the reduced budget *increased* the quality problems because of nonrepaired equipment and manufacturing shortcuts. In the longer term, the budgets were simply overrun in both production and quality-related areas.

This example demonstrates two major issues with the "change levers" philosophy: (1) Pushing sensitive areas only reinforces the present system; it does not change it; and (2) the obvious change levers are rarely the *real* change factors occurring within an organization.

COMMON MYTH #3: CHANGE IS CREATED BY LEADERS: TO MAKE CHANGE, CHANGE THE LEADER.

This may be the most common change strategy employed by companies feeling pressure to change—at all levels. Although it is a truism that effective leaders drive effective change, it is not true that changing the leader will automatically create a change.

For many companies, changing the leader does not make significant change. Although it often signals the *opportunity* for change, particularly in the first few months of the leader's tenure, it neither creates nor drives change by itself.

In one law enforcement organization, the leader was replaced in response to numerous complaints and problems. The new leader, though well-intentioned, did nothing to address the underlying concerns, and no significant changes occurred. In fact, resistance actually increased among the key stakeholders because expectations had been raised at the time of the leadership change; this made subsequent change much more difficult. The new leader left the organization within two years.

In many sports teams—most notably the New York Yankees in the 1970s and 1980s—changing the leader per se does not guarantee success.[2] Many times, it increases the overall stress on the organization, decreases stability, and engenders a chaotic reaction from its employees and other stakeholders.

Changing the leader is often a component of key change strategies, but it is not, by itself, an effective response.

COMMON MYTH #4: COMMUNICATION IS CHANGE: JUST COMMUNICATE, COMMUNICATE, AND COMMUNICATE

Communicating the need for change is simply one component of potential change strategies; it is not an effective strategy by itself.

Companies that strive to communicate with their stakeholders—customers, vendors, employees, shareholders, and more—often decrease potential resistance to change. In many instances, however, the company simply expands on the factors driving change and does not offer an effective path forwarding for actually dealing with those change drivers. This increases awareness at all levels, also increasing stress and apprehension. Without an apparent path forward, individual stakeholders typically *increase* their resistance to change.

As with the leader change, increased communication without a comprehensive, integrated change strategy may actually increase resistance and make it that much more difficult to guide change at a later time.

CHANGE MYTHS ARE SELF-FULFILLING

One of the powerful aspects of change myths is that people tend to see that which they expect to see. Given that change deals with so many different dimensions on so many levels, there is no single change metric that can be used to predict the effectiveness of any given change response within the organization. This often results in the leader's focusing on those events or actions that reinforce the leader's preconceptions. That focus, in turn, may make *real* change even more difficult.

In the 1930s, many people believed that their bank was insolvent, despite accounting records and government assertions to the contrary. For several banks, there was such a demand for cash withdrawals that their cash reserves were depleted—and they *became* insolvent. In 2003, some New York and Philadelphia bank branches were effectively closed when hundreds of bank customers withdrew their accounts—simply because people believed that the bank had no cash.[3] Myths often have the power to become self-fulfilling.

False change myths are more than simply misdirecting and misinforming. They often create a paradigm for all stakeholders that inherently self-limit individual and organizational change. Replacing those myths with an effective understanding of the dynamics of organizational change is critical to achieving successful, sustained change.

NOTES

1. Mathews, Chris, *Hardball: How Politics is Played Told By One Who Knows the Game,* New York: Simon & Schuster, attributed to Charles W. Colson, 1999, pg 49.

2. Appel, Martin, *Now Pitching for the Yankees: Spinning the News for Mickey, Billy and George,* New York: Total Sports Press, 2001.

3. Philadelphia Inquirer, *Rarely Seen Run on Bank,* page 1, April 24, 2003, and Philadelphia Daily News, *Hundreds Swarm Bank in Fear,* page 29, April 23, 2003.

Strategy as a Response to Change Pressures

Excess generally causes reaction, and produces a change
in the opposite direction

—*Plato*

CHANGE REACTION VERSUS CHANGE STRATEGY

As noted, all organizations react in some manner to external pressures for change. By itself, without a deliberate outcome, the organization will focus on the short-term relief of that pressure, *even when the short-term relief creates worse long-term problems.* Without learning from its own experience, the organization will continue to focus on a string of short-term problems that seem to have no relationship to each other.

In business organizations, this short-term focus is compounded by the multitude of different individuals, differing agendas, and different perceptions of the change pressures. Each individual has her/his own unique reaction to change.

As a corollary to this desire for rapid relief from change pressures, organizations will also seek the *minimum amount of effort required to alleviate* those pressures. As is seen later, this becomes a significant factor in identifying and developing appropriate strategies for change.

In most organizations, the natural response to change pressures is an amalgam of differing reactions chaotically mixed together. The challenge for the company as a whole and the leader individually is to understand, develop, and implement an effective change *strategy* that offers a cohesive

response to the pressures. Effective strategy not only addresses the short-term pressures but also eliminates their repetition.

CHANGE STRATEGY

In general, strategy can be defined as an integrated, deliberate set of actions designed to achieve a specific goal or outcome. When applied to change pressures, *change strategy* involves the development of a cohesive plan of action that minimizes or eliminates those pressures for change.

In the added context of the Basic Value Imperative and its associated "success dimension" pressures, this involves the development of a strategy that reduces or eliminates the change pressures while it increases the value-added offering in the key business dimensions.

Organizations that attempt to drive change without a specific, integrated change strategy will revert to the chaos of disparate individual reactions and responses. Similarly, an organization that attempts to drive change in a way that does not minimize or reduce the initial change pressures may, in fact, increase the negative impact on the organization.

CHANGE MANAGEMENT

As a subset of change strategy, change management (CM) is focused on the social aspects of the business dimensions. Cited by many sources[1] as the most common barrier to successful change efforts, the social resistance of key stakeholders often requires specific mitigation strategies. CM is often cited as a key success factor for organizational change.

For the purposes of this text, Change Management strategy is defined as

An integrated effort to align an organization's actions, behaviors, and processes around a single set of goals and outcomes.

In practice, this strategy is dependent upon several factors.

Level of Change Pressure

As noted previously, the organization will attempt the least amount of self-reaction required to alleviate the instantaneous pressures for change. Organizations that attempt radical change when the external change pressures are minimal most often fail in their implementation. Conversely, organizations that attempt to address major pressures with only incremental strategies typically fail.

Thus, the *optimal organizational response is that which most closely aligns with the level of change pressure.* When the strategic level of change is equivalent to the pressures driving change, the organization is able to respond most readily.

It is important to note that the change strategy is not exclusive to the level of external pressure; only that the organization will have the *least*

resistance to that level. In practice, this simply means that the change strategy may need to accommodate significantly increased resistance. Understanding the natural tendency of the organization for change is a key to development of successful change strategy.

Change Pressures Vary in Scope, Source, and Urgency

As noted in the Basic Value Imperative, the pressures for value-added products and services occur in all the dimensions all the time. With these diverse requirements, pressures for change are dynamic, variously intensifying or diminishing with the success dimension and the key stakeholder. At any one time, the change pressures on the organization may appear to be the greatest in a particular area; in reality, there are many simultaneous change pressures.

An effective change strategy needs to accommodate all these factors, recognizing that the levels of change may be varied and inconsistent. One of the hallmarks of HPTs is their ability to deal with simultaneous change pressures.

CHANGE MANAGEMENT STRATEGIES REFLECT A SPECTRUM OF RESPONSES

Given the varied pressures for change and the many diverse individuals involved in the organization, it is natural that change strategies reflect a *spectrum* of responses. There is no single panacea response appropriate to all change pressures.

Although there are as many different change strategies as there are individuals and organizations, most of the common strategies can be categorized into the degree of change that is attempted within the organization: minimal or no change, incremental change, significant change, and breakthrough change.

Each of these categories has its own typical business drivers, attributes, and strategies. Though some change strategies are more effective than others for given categories, it is important to note that no strategy is exclusive. For example, there are instances where a strategy for breakthrough change may be effective in achieving incremental change, but these are the exception. In fact, a common difficulty in HPT efforts is the *inappropriate selection of HPT as a change strategy when the organizational change conditions do not warrant it.*

Understanding when and where to apply HPTs is a critical component to HPT success. Improperly applied, HPTs typically fail; this is a common danger to the other, non-HPT change strategies, as well.

Figure 6-1 shows the relationship between these change strategies.

Attributes / Strategies / Drivers		No Change (De facto Strategy)	Incremental	Significant	Breakthrough
Attributes	*Characteristics*	• High apparent output with low/no impact • High reliance on documentary guides • Avoidance	• Policy changes • Procedural changes • Practice/task changes • <10% perf changes • No intangible change • Transitory • Very high maintenance	• Process changes • New products • New metrics • 10 to 50% perf changes • Some intangible changes • Some assmptns questioned • Moderate maintenance	• Major market changes • New corporate "identity" • Entirely new products/services • > 90% perf changes • Major focus on intangibles • Most assumptions questioned • High, then very low maintenance
	Typical	• Focus on reports • No risk / no return • Self-perpetuation focus	• Routine operations • Focus on task • Low risk/low return	• Product changes • Departmental turnarounds • Moderate productivity improvement	• Corporate turnaround • Spin-offs / divestitures • Corporate start-up
Strategies	*Approach*	• No defined approach	• Behavioral alignment • Minor behavioral change	• Attitude change • Perspective changes	• Identity change • Major individual change
	Typical	• **Status Quo** • Command and control • Chaos	• **Directive Change Mgmnt** • Leader-mandated change • Expert-mandated change • Statistical methods focus	• **Behavioral Change Mgmnt** • Aligned organization • High-involvement teams	• **Cultural Change** • High Performance Team • New organization
Drivers	*Characteristics*	• No major external drivers • Minimum competition • Guaranteed financials	• Evolutionary competition • Predictable markets	• Major competition (external or internal) • Financials threatened	• Major new markets • New "rules" • Corp survival questioned
	Typical	• Monopolistic industries • Bureaucratic orgs • Traditional government	• Well-entrenched companies • Long-term historical leaders • Very long-term product cycles	• New product areas • New services available • Market shifts needed	• Bankruptcy • New corporations/orgs • 'Intra'-preneurial orgs

Figure 6-1 The Spectrum of Change Strategies

NOTE

1. Kotter, John, et al. *Harvard Business Review on Change*, Boston: Harvard Business School Press, 1998, pgs 1–20, 139–157; also Champy, James, *State of Reengineering Report*, CSC Index, 1994, pgs 30–45.

Status Quo

Not to decide is to decide

—Harvey Cox

As defined in Chapter 6, a strategy is a deliberate response to change pressures. The maintenance of status quo is not a formal organizational strategy, but it is a common response to change. Few organizations deliberately chart a course for status quo, yet many ultimately exhibit the characteristics of a status quo organization. For this reason, status quo is considered a de facto strategy for comparison and illustrative purposes only.

In the Status Quo change scenario, maintenance of the existing organization is paramount and overrides all other change strategies. For these organizations, the principal charter is stewardship of the underlying assets and strengths rather than any fundamental change.

Status quo does not mean "no action." On the contrary, many organizations are heavily invested in maintaining their present conditions. In most status quo companies, this energy is focused on retaining current market share and rates of return.

TYPICAL KEY DRIVERS OF STATUS QUO

High levels of *perceived* success drive the deliberate selection of Status Quo as a change strategy. These are most commonly found in monopolistic industries and traditional governmental agencies. In these areas, there is a strong stakeholder belief that a significant change in any of the key

business dimensions might result in a decrease in that performance dimension.

This underlying belief that the organization has effectively reached its zenith in performance is the most common driver to a Status Quo organization.

Given all the activity of corporations in the present global economy, it would seem that few, if any, organizations would be content to maintain "business as usual." Most organizations have an explicit change strategy that typically defines its goals and general strategy for change. In practice, this stated policy often is not supported by the leaders' and stakeholders' discrete actions. When gauged by the leaders' exhibited behaviors, Status Quo is the most common of change strategy.

COMMON STRATEGIES

By definition, there is no specific strategy for change in Status Quo. However, there is often a strong focus on "keeping everything the same," ranging from a strong market and political influence to actively blocking new advances and opportunities.

In implementation, two common status quo forms appear: chaotic and command-and-control.

The Chaotic Organization

In the chaotic implementation, there is no centralized edict for maintenance of status quo; rather, the organizational culture is clearly focused on individual survival and minimal interference. The chaotic organization is typically split into numerous autonomous subgroups that independently work to maintain status quo. This split also reinforces barriers between the subgroups, further restricting change.

To the casual observer, this organization appears deeply fragmented and frustrating. The apparent conflicts between departments are typically used as reasons why changes are not practical; often, even customers become part of interdepartmental conflict. Individual employees and leaders may complain about their inability to make important changes. There may even be visible, repetitive attempts to "change the culture" and to "make fundamental change," yet each of these attempts is often forgotten by the next budget cycle.

Externally, the chaotic organization appears fractured, bureaucratic, and ineffective. In practice, however, it is very effective at its core mission: to maintain status quo.

The Command-and-Control Organization

In the command-and-control implementation, there is an overwhelming focus on hierarchy and authority. In this implementation, authority

increases toward the top of the pyramidal organizational chart, with almost total authority invested in the CEO as "commander" of the company. Lines of communication are up-down; authority passes upward toward the CEO, not laterally between departments. Each hierarchical level has complete authority over the levels below it, and reports exclusively to the level above it.

In this implementation, each stakeholder's role is clear and unambiguous. There is a strong focus on predefined practices, policies, and procedures. Any variance to established policy often results in negative consequences.

In practice, this implementation appears to have a high reliance on "paper": documents guide almost all actions of employees, customers, and external stakeholders. Any attempt to change the established policies is difficult and may require extensive review throughout the command chain.

In this implementation, bureaucracy is combined with restricted authority to result in the maintenance of status quo.

OPPORTUNITIES OF STATUS QUO CHANGE

In the short to intermediate time frame, the Status Quo organization is well positioned to provide existing services. For routine products, where there is no change required in product delivery or service quality, the organization performs as it is expected to.

In some turbulent environments, this can be a significant advantage. For example, in global areas where infrastructure is questionable, service providers are transient, and governments are unstable, having an institution that is dependable and predictable can itself be a "unique, perceived, value-added" service.

However, in the long term, the inability of the organization to change may create its own greatest challenge to long-term survival.

CHALLENGES OF STATUS QUO CHANGE

In both Status Quo implementations, there is the underlying assumption that the organization has reached its summit. In chaotic implementations, this belief may be denied verbally yet reinforced by behavior. In command-and-control implementations, this belief may be explicitly stated and followed.

In the short term, this belief is often reinforced, as any significant change in strategy tends to temporarily increase costs and decrease performance. In the medium to long term, however, these organizations often discover, too late, that their belief has been incorrect.

There are many examples of entire industries that had dramatic reversals in fortune due to their attempt to maintain status quo while new competition or market pressures were replacing them. From railroads to electric typewriters to slide rules, technology has often been a factor in undermining beliefs of corporate invulnerability. Of course, even new technologies can be undermined by the changing markets, as many "dotcoms" discovered in 2000. The wrong technology, improperly applied, can be disastrous to corporate survival as well.

In each of these cases, the organization did not fulfill the fundamental business proposition that it needed to provide *unique, perceived, value-added* products to the marketplace.

Chaotic and command-and-control organizations may seem to be at opposite ends of management style, yet both are strongly oriented to maintenance of the status quo. Given either implementation, the organization can be very effective at survival in stable markets and environments.

Incremental Change Strategy

Behavior is what a man does, not what he thinks, feels, or believes.

—*Anon.*

For many well-entrenched organizations, there is a desire for improved performance in the key business dimensions. However, this improvement is required in a way that does not jeopardize its underlying strengths and assets. For these organizations, *incremental and evolutionary change* is the preferred strategy of change.

TYPICAL KEY DRIVERS OF INCREMENTAL CHANGE

Companies that are well positioned in the market, often with a long history of high market penetration, often try to exploit that market position without endangering its existing financial returns.

Key market drivers include companies that are market dominant, yet not monopolistic. Competition may be encroaching on fringe areas without representing a serious threat to the company's market future. These often occur in markets that appreciate low-risk, low-return actions, such as semiregulated utilities and long-term capital markets.

Internal change drivers include long product development cycles that require long-term product dominance for financial return, and capital-intensive products that require significant retooling and investment for product change. These areas include transportation, energy, and infrastructure-related industries.

It is important to note that technology and regulation can change these drivers in a short period of time. In communication industries, technological drivers such as bandwidth and media have been major short-term change drivers, whereas regulatory changes and market conditions have driven many energy utilities to change their trading and investment strategies.

TYPICAL CHARACTERISTICS (ATTRIBUTES)

Companies in this environment typically display a high focus on the following areas of concern:

Policies and Procedures

A high focus on adherence to policies and procedures results in a great deal of energy spent on the maintenance of documents. Change in policy/procedure is reflected in the careful updating of the appropriate documents; typically, many groups are dedicated to updating and distribution. There are often elaborate policies and procedures required to update policies and procedures.

Task/Work Practice Focus

Changes in work practices are often focused at the operational task level, designed to optimize existing processes. Tasks are often described in considerable detail, including corresponding roles and responsibilities for all key stakeholders.

Minor Performance Improvement (Less than 10 percent)

Performance improvement is sought and achieved but is rarely more than 10 percent of discrete business metrics. This allows for constant change without increasing the risk to key resources. As with the task focus, there is often considerable detail and precision associated with the performance improvement.

Certainly, with a focus on key tasks, individual teams and efforts may experience improvements much greater than 10 percent. However, in this change scenario, the *overall* organization's improvement is minor.

Focus on Tangible, Discrete Results

A common "marker" of organizations in this strategy is their primary focus on short-term, directly measurable milestones for success. These

organizations typically focus on work-related metrics that are to be measured in real time. Longer-term metrics, as well as intangible metrics, are typically difficult for these organizations to monitor, measure, and change.

Very High Managerial Maintenance

Organizations in this scenario typically require a considerable amount of managerial review and monitoring to ensure that the processes are in control. For these organizations, regular hierarchical metric reviews and management involvement in operational tasks are common.

COMMON STRATEGIES
OF INCREMENTAL CHANGE

The most common strategy for incremental change is continuous process improvement and its corresponding work alignment. Together, these often result in a *Directive Change Management* (DCM) strategy.

Continuous Improvement

In this context, "continuous improvement" refers to the focus on *process optimization*. Continuous changes are made to the underlying processes to constantly improve the outcomes. Whether focused on production processes or human interaction, the organization is organized around process control and making the process more effective.

Pace of Work

Many DCM strategies focus on increasing the workers' *pace* as a key to improved performance and output. This focus assumes that the workforce has untapped potential for more output, without increasing the direct costs and/or number of workers, or changing the work processes.

These organizations often maintain an underlying assumption that workers inherently desire to perform the *minimum* amount of work for the *maximum* amount of pay while managers inherently desire to achieve the *minimum* amount of pay for the *maximum* amount of work. There is also an assumption that these desires are mutually exclusive.

This "pace of work" approach is typically implemented through increased supervision, strong negative and positive incentives for compliance, and continual performance monitoring.

Work Alignment

For many process-oriented organizations focused on incremental change, uncontrolled work processes and behaviors can introduce undesirable variables. As these variables are often perceived as negative influ-

ences on the core processes, the organization tries to eliminate them. This desire for "no variances" often results in a strong attempt to align work processes and work behaviors.

This work alignment is focused on the actions and behaviors throughout the organization, not on the underlying intents and motivations of the employees and stakeholders. The organization desires to achieve a smooth operation where all contributing processes, including people, are optimized and integrated. In this manner, changes are seen as predictable, controllable, and engendering little risk to the underlying assets and market strengths.

CHANGE MANAGEMENT STRATEGY: "DIRECTIVE CHANGE MANAGEMENT" (DCM)

For many organizations pursuing incremental change, the key change management strategy is DCM. In this implementation, the leader communicates the key objectives of the organization along with a corresponding set of expected actions and behaviors. As with the work processes themselves, the organization is tuned to an optimal set of supportive behaviors.

In the DCM strategy, the focus is on the organizational leader; from problem recognition to final improvement, the leader is responsible for all major change activities. This is typically implemented by strong, energetic leaders with a desire to personally drive change throughout the organization.

There are six phases of DCM.

1. *Problem identification.* The leader determines that a problem exists and sets a priority to its solution. Most often, this is a problem that endangers the core work processes. Although the initial detection of the problem may come from a variety of sources, it is the leader who determines that there is, in fact, a problem to be fixed. In this change strategy, only the leader makes the final problem determination.
2. *Problem declaration.* The leader declares the problem to exist and its reduction/elimination to be a priority of the organization. There is a clear definition of the problem with defined goals and a vision for success. This will often include a predefined set of "deliverables" that are to be completed along with the elimination of the problem. Key stakeholders understand the charter they have been given to complete; there is little ambiguity in the objectives.
3. *Communication of importance.* Key leaders, usually in consensus, communicate the significance of the problem and its importance to the organization. Through a variety of media, meetings, and incentives, management demonstrates the importance and urgency of the problem resolution. As part of the communication process, the key leaders charter a group to fix the problem.

4. *Problem resolution group.* An individual or group is chartered with the responsibility to address the problem and report back to management with a series of recommendations for change. There are several variants to this group:

    a. *Leader-mandated resolution.* In those cases where the leader may believe the answer is straightforward, not requiring analysis and review, a simple statement for change may resolve the problem. This often takes the form of a revised policy or procedure issued by the leader.

    b. *Expert-mandated resolution.* For many problems, an expert is relied upon to review the problem and recommend a solution. In this strategy, external consultants are the most common experts utilized to map the implementation plan.

    c. *Slice group-recommended resolution.* When there are many variables contributing the problem, requiring a wide variety of background, ideas, and expertise, "slice" groups are often chartered. These groups represent a slice of the organization, including external experts, and may offer a wide-ranging implementation plan to the leader.

5. *Implementation mandate.* After appropriate review by the leader, the recommended resolution—or some variant—is mandated by the leader. As with the initial organizational communication, there is unified consensus around the need for implementation and the expectation that all key stakeholders will follow the implementation.

6. *Implementation management.* As the new implementation is executed and the expectation for compliance communicated, deviations from the new policy/procedure are consequenced. Typically, there are severe negative consequences for variance.

It is important to note that this change management strategy relies on the individuals in the organization to comply with the new procedures. In the case of noncompliance, individuals may be persuaded—by simple communication or eventual discipline—to align themselves with the new work processes. In this manner, the original problem is not only addressed and reduced/eliminated, but the organization is further aligned around a common set of goals.

Directive Change Management, then, is a series of integrated actions, deliberately taken, to align the *actions* of all stakeholders. Though similar, this strategy is significantly different from the "magical thinking" of "tell them to do it," which is outlined in chapter 5.

OPPORTUNITIES OF INCREMENTAL CHANGE

As a low-risk, low-return strategy, DCM offers rapid alignment of short-term work behaviors around key work processes. This strategy requires

neither extensive understanding of change dynamics nor long-term investment. It builds on the present expertise of the leadership and allows for a wide variety of expert analysis in a short period of time.

Most DCM strategies provide rapid improvement returns, particularly when the leader has strong communication skills and effective performance incentives are put into place. Typical implementation periods range from weeks to months.

As with the Status Quo change strategy, DCM is focused on *stewardship* of the organization's assets; short-term risk is minimized.

CHALLENGES OF INCREMENTAL CHANGE

The difficulty in DCM is its focus on external behaviors and work processes more than on the internal motivations and commitment of employees and other key stakeholders. This results in an environment where *compliance* is more important than *motivation*. Although common adherence to policies and procedures is important, its over-reliance often results in stifled creativity, innovation, and competitive position.

With this high reliance on process and procedure, DCM organizations often have difficulty in dealing with individuals' performance and behaviors. Perceived as a variance to the underlying process, the DCM organization will most often attempt changes to the *process* itself, rather than working with the individual to make changes. This often results in complicated policies and procedures that attempt to account for all potential problems, rather than an effective, focused work process.

Another characteristic of DCM strategies is their transience and high-maintenance management. Because the principal incentive to comply is externally imposed, management often has to spend a great deal of time and energy reinforcing the policies and policing the organization to ensure compliance. Similarly, as management's attention is inevitably refocused on other problems, the incentive to comply is reduced and the overall impact of the original change program is minimized or even eliminated.[1]

Organizations focused on DCM often find themselves repeating programs and problem resolution over and over again, reachieving results previously thought attained. Leaders in these organizations often complain that they ". . . thought it had already been taken care of . . ." As this cycle repeats, more management energy and focus are required to obtain compliance; with each cycle, organizational resistance to change increases significantly. In many organizations, it is often the same leader who recycles the strategy, dramatically decreasing the effectiveness each time. Increased resistance, frustration, and resentment on the part of employees and other affected stakeholders requires increasing focus and disciplinary

actions on the part of the leader—until the leader is ultimately rendered ineffective at driving long-term change.

Directive Change Management is the most common form of deliberate change management strategy in organizations today.

NOTE

1. Mayo, Elton, *The Human Problems of an Industrial Civilization*, 1933, reprinted Ayer Co. Publishing, 1977.

Significant Change Strategy

Attitudes are more important than facts.

—*Karl A. Menninger*

For many companies facing pressures that drive change yet are not directly life threatening to the organization, different types of change dynamics emerge. For these companies, the challenge is to respond to those significant changes without endangering their underlying assets.

Unlike Incremental Change strategies, however, the pressures facing these companies are significant and are expected to have material impact on several basic business dimensions.

TYPICAL KEY DRIVERS OF SIGNIFICANT CHANGE

Major product competition, market changes, and short-term financial pressures may drive the organization to significant change. On a departmental level, market changes may threaten the discontinuance of product lines, closure of plants, reductions in force (RIFs), or other significant change reaction. Conversely, new technologies and market opportunities may offer the opportunity to create new plants, new product areas, and departmental start-ups. Whether positive or negative, there is significant change required by the organization to react to the business pressures.

TYPICAL CHARACTERISTICS (ATTRIBUTES)

Companies undergoing significant change typically have a strong focus on the following areas of concern.

Major Process Changes

These companies focus on whether the right processes are in place to achieve the necessary results. Unlike in the incremental scenario where the focus was on process optimization, these companies are focused on whether the correct process is even being considered. Existing processes are compared with desired results, and new alternatives are explored.

Product Changes

New product areas and new market assessments are continually reviewed for applicability to new market threats and opportunities. These companies are typically introducing new products and new product areas at a pace at least equal to their major competition.

New Metrics

Companies in this change scenario work to find new metrics that define success. These new metrics often include predictive metrics that monitor precursors of key market and product changes, as well as monitor intangibles such as employee commitment and customer relationship. Typically, the success metrics themselves are constantly changing as the organizations respond to a wider diversity of business drivers.

Moderate Performance Improvement (10 to 50 Percent)

Typically these companies focus on moderate increases in performance across the full spectrum of business dimensions. Changes in product lines and target market segments drive the need for performance improvement.

Some Assumptions Questioned

Companies undergoing significant change often begin to question some of their underlying assumptions about themselves, their products, and their marketplace. These assumptions are typically focused on customer perceptions about the company and its products.

TYPICAL CHANGE STRATEGIES: BEHAVIORAL CHANGE MANAGEMENT (BCM)

Successful companies undergoing significant change pressures typically focus on the *attitudes* of employees and key stakeholders. In this

Behavioral Change Management (BCM) strategy, the *social* considerations of the stakeholders become a critical element in successful change and transition.

In BCM strategies, there is a deliberate sequence of problem identification, organizational research, and behavioral interventions, all designed to align the organization's attitudes and desires around organizational goals. The resulting integration of technical and social perspectives into an integrated work flow can be very effective at responding to the need for significant change.

There are nine common elements of BCM strategies.

1. *Leader develops a business case for change.* The leader determines that there is a problem or concern that needs to be changed. The "business case for change" includes the fundamental change pressures and a cohesive vision for success.

2. *Deliberate process of change management strategy is developed.* The leader, with assistance and input from key stakeholders, develops a specific strategy for change management that becomes an integral part of the business case. This is typically developed with the assistance of change management consultants or others with change expertise. In this strategy, there is considerable focus on stakeholder behaviors, attitudes, and commitment to the change effort.

3. *Organizational readiness is assessed.* An assessment is made of the organization and its key stakeholders for their resistance to change and desire for improvement. This "readiness assessment" provides an overall indication of the challenges and opportunities for change, as well as an initial diagnostic tool for specific change strategies.

4. *Organization is prepared for change.* As part of the BCM strategy, the organization is kept informed and involved with the change effort. This often varies with the nature and history of the organization, from individual interviews to focus groups to "all hands' meetings," and from memos to interactive videoconferencing. The potential implementations vary with each effort but minimally involve wide communication of the business case and individuals' and departments' roles in the change effort.

5. *Data Collection.* To provide background information to the redesign of existing work, considerable data is collected. This may include historical information on the product, customers, and financial aspects of the work, as well as current information about competition, employee attitudes, and key stakeholders.

6. *Work Design / Redesign.* Given the need for change outlined in the business case and the data collected in both technical and social aspects of the work, a group of key stakeholders with a wide breadth and depth of knowledge redesign the overall work. These stakehold-

ers, most often a combination of employees and consultants, review all aspects of the current work, consider the new needs of the market and the organization, and develop new processes and products that relieve the original change pressures or take advantage of new market opportunities. A comprehensive plan for change is presented to the leader and management for review and approval.

7. *The work plan is implemented.* The work plan is implemented as appropriate throughout the organization. This may be a "total immersion" plan where the plan is implemented quickly throughout the entire organization, or a "phased implementation" plan that includes an orderly transition period.

8. *Results are monitored.* The work teams and management review the ongoing results of the implementation, including key metrics that relate directly back to the business case. In the event of variances, the work teams may alter or completely change work processes to obtain the results desired.

9. *Renewal.* At the end of the original charter period, the overall process is reviewed and compared to the original business case for change. Celebration and "lessons learned" are completed, and the overall process may be restarted.

Though there are many different applications of the BCM process, there are some special cases that provide important context for HPTs: high involvement teams, self-directed work teams, and traditional HPTs.

BCM SPECIAL CASE: HIGH INVOLVEMENT TEAMS

"High-involvement teams" (HITs) are often chartered to address a business problem, often related to employee morale. In many cases where employee intangibles and quality of work life are significant issues, many BCM companies create HITs. The common expectation is that the team will not only address the business concern but also address employee concerns, simply by virtue of their own creation.

HITs typically involve an intense review of the problem by a broad cross-section of employees and other stakeholders; in many cases, the entire team will be involved in some phase of the work review/redesign.

BCM SPECIAL CASE:
SELF-DIRECTED WORK TEAMS (SDWTs)

For many organizations facing significant change, one alternative is to create teams that are apparently self-managed and self-directed. For these teams, the traditional supervisory or managerial role is eliminated, and

the team is chartered to address the business issues as an autonomous team.

In this strategy, the social aspects of performance are considered pre-eminent to the technical aspects of work. By allowing teams to form self-governing workgroups that naturally align themselves around the work to be performed, the strategy assumes that performance will naturally optimize itself.

In many cases, high-energy teams enjoyed the increased flexibility and newfound resources to focus on the business issue; in the short term, this dramatically increased energy, motivation, and productivity. SDWTs were very popular in the late 1980s and early 1990s as short-term productivity increased significantly. In the short term, this also appeared to support a general corporate drive to reduce the total layers of management throughout the organization.

For most of these teams, however, insufficient training, transition, and support were provided for continuing success. As a result, these teams experienced conflicts with the rest of the organization and considerable frustration in dealing with real-world issues.

BCM STRATEGIES: OPPORTUNITIES

BCM-based teams, overall, are very effective at achieving their original business goals in short to moderate timeframes. These teams typically achieve significant improvement, often beyond the leaders' original expectations. Unlike conventional teams attempting to respond to business change pressures, BCM efforts typically reach their goals in more than one dimension at the same time.

BCM teams offer significant improvement over conventional change strategies in success rates of organizations facing necessary change. Overall, organizations that follow a deliberate, behavior-based strategic approach to change are more successful than those that follow strictly work-based approaches.

BCM STRATEGIES: CHALLENGES

BCM strategies are very effective at helping organizations anticipate change and accelerate the transition process. However, this very speed of change often increases the transience of the effect; many BCM teams find it difficult to maintain increased levels of innovation and productivity for sustained periods of time. This "rubber-band effect"—snapping back to previous levels—can increase frustration and resentment in the workforce long term, increasing resistance to future change.

Organizations that focus on BCM often overfocus on the social aspects of work design and inadvertently diminish the impact of other business success dimensions. In many BCM-oriented efforts, the technical and social aspects are considered in depth, yet business-related pressures and concerns remain a gap. This often results in change efforts that have very high employee buy-in and commitment, yet it is based on unrealistic business assumptions. These unbalanced efforts fail the fundamental business proposition of unique, perceived value-added product, and fail to achieve overall business success. This can further intensify the "rubber-band effect" in the workforce, customers, and other key stakeholders.

In many BCM efforts, with the increased focus on social aspects of the team, there is often a gap in the integration of the team's effort with other work and other organizations. This is particularly true in organizations that have different work cultures interfacing with the changed team. With the focus on social dimensions, BCM teams tend to focus inwardly, dealing with intrateam dynamics, and may be vulnerable to unanticipated conflicts with surrounding organizations.

Behavioral Change Management strategies often provide an effective integration of work and social change. Companies requiring significant change are very often able to create and implement effective change when comprehensive BCM strategies are employed. For those organizations requiring greater change, or those requiring permanent change, however, different strategies are needed.

Breakthrough Change Strategy

The great law of culture is:
Let each become all that he was created capable of being.
—*Thomas Carlyle*

For some organizations, change pressures are so great as to be literally a matter of "life and death." For positive opportunities, spin-offs and start-ups may face entirely new markets and organizations. In negative situations, companies may have their very survival threatened. Major changes must be made—and often must be made quickly.

TYPICAL KEY DRIVERS
FOR BREAKTHROUGH CHANGE

For new markets, new product opportunities, and application of new technologies, organizational cultures may be created to leverage major opportunities. Whether a spawned venture of existing companies or an entirely new entity, these organizations understand that their traditional structures and cultures are unable to match the new needs of the market-place. A new organization is required.

For those organizations where their very survival is threatened, break-through change is not an option. In these scenarios, the entire organization must re-evaluate its ability to meet the fundamental business proposition and make whatever changes are necessary to adapt.

In both scenarios of high growth and high cost reduction, it is simply inadequate to continue doing "business as usual"; the organization will

not survive. Even "significant" changes of processes and products are often insufficient to meet the new change pressures; the organization must fundamentally shift *itself*.

TYPICAL CHARACTERISTICS (ATTRIBUTES)

Organizations undergoing breakthrough change are typically focused on the following areas of concern.

Major Market Changes

Markets and customers that may have been taken for granted before are no longer assured; this can be positive or negative, depending on the company's previous market position. This is most often triggered by the competition of new technologies, but can also be affected by regulatory, societal, and other events. In some cases, such as pharmaceutical patent markets, the organization's own product changes can create the market shift.

Entirely New Products

Companies undergoing major upheaval typically have an intense focus on entirely new product areas and application of new technologies. In markets involving very short product development cycles, such as computer hardware and information systems, the product cycle itself may be the subject of major focus.

New Corporate Identity, Externally and Internally

As organizations reshape themselves to the new needs of the marketplace and their own survival, they often change visible signs of their identity. This may be external and overt as in the case of corporate name and logo change; or it may be more internally focused as in the case of facilities and communications changes.

Order-of-Magnitude Performance Improvement (At Least 50 Percent)

Organizations competing for their corporate lives often strive for order-of-magnitude changes in performance; they simply cannot settle for anything less. These organizations are not able to afford resources on process optimization; they need to discover entirely new processes that will achieve the desired results. Development cycles are very short, and cus-

tomer assurance and quality testing are often concurrent with the product development itself.

Consistent Focus on Intangibles

Organizations undergoing major market, product, and structural change often have significantly increased focus on the intangible aspects of each key business dimension. For new markets, these organizations will have considerable focus on customer relationships and their management. As differing workforce skills and expertise are required, employee motivation and commitment become critical issues. Trust in the organization from all stakeholders becomes critical to the organization's success, whether from suppliers believing an existing company will not be forced into bankruptcy or from new customers believing that a new company will be able to meet their needs. In times of crisis, intangibles often become much more 'mission critical' than tangible measures.

Most Assumptions Challenged

Inherent in the actions of the organization in all dimensions is an explicit challenge to conventional assumptions. Organizations in major transition often focus on the underlying assumptions. These may include fundamental questions across all of the major business dimensions. These organizations often ask questions that would be inappropriate (at best) in other change scenarios.

TYPICAL CHANGE STRATEGIES: CULTURE CHANGE

Successful organizations undergoing revolutionary change typically focus on the sense of group identity, or culture of the organization. In this culture change (CC) strategy, the *group identity* of the organization is the critical element, rather than the behaviors of DCM and the attitudes of BCM. For the purpose of understanding High Performance Teams, and other breakthrough strategies, the following definition of culture is used:

> Culture is the collective sense of group identity that makes the group unique.

Traditional definitions of culture include a "group of implicit rules, unspoken laws, and beliefs of a group of people." This "HPT culture defi-

nition" focuses on the underlying sense of *group identity* that *created* those rules, laws, and beliefs.

In the context of successful HPT efforts, it is critical to understand that culture is not the *result* of group behaviors; rather it is our fundamental sense of group identity that *drives* those behaviors. In fact, *culture is the primary way in which people define themselves as a group*. As such, culture is constantly changing and redefining itself. With every change in individual self-image and interpersonal relationship, the group's culture itself is redefined. It is this very dynamism that both fuels culture's power and makes it difficult to understand. Yet one of the keys to developing successful HPTs relies upon understanding this dynamic.

Using traditional definitions of culture, "culture change agents" typically focus on the behaviors and beliefs of an organization. This focus typically results in a change strategy that attempts to align behaviors and beliefs and to declare rules and values. Although these are valuable and effective in many change strategies, they do not shift the culture per se.

With the new definition of culture, there is a strong focus on the shift of group identity. In this focus, it is important to note that it is not possible to define a strategy that "manages" or predetermines an individual's identity. One cannot simply define another's sense of self, let alone the self-perceived identity of a constantly changing group. As will be seen, there are more effective means of influencing culture.

An important corollary of this CC concept is the heterogeneity of culture. Because culture is defined by the group's perception of its members' sense of self, the *number* of potential cultures within any given organization is (literally) exponential. For any given working group, there is an instantaneous group identity perception; for each perception, there exists a de facto culture. The interactivity of individuals and cultures within the organization yield a dynamism that is both difficult to quantify and energetic in its creativity and output. This heterogeneity becomes a significant factor in the underlying processes of High Performance Teams.

"Culture change" is fundamentally different from the "change management" strategies outlined earlier. Though there are similarities and overlaps, understanding the differences is critical to understanding the creation of successful HPTs. Where *culture change* is the dynamic shifting of the group's sense of self, *change management* is the effort to align organizational behavior around a single set of goals and outcomes. In change management strategies, the leaders deliberately develop programs and processes to achieve alignment of the organization around specific business goals. In culture change, the organization shifts its own sense of self—in a way that may or may not be aligned with predefined business goals. As will be seen, the roles of key stakeholders are fundamentally different in the two approaches.

Though culture change is different from change management, it is not exclusive of it; many organizations experience a culture shift while attempting change management. For these organizations, the resulting business changes are often more effective and long lasting. The key distinction here is the *strategic* nature of deliberate culture change versus the *incidental* culture change that may or may not occur with change management.

COMMON COMPONENTS OF CULTURE CHANGE

Effective changes in culture have common stages. Common to each of these phases is the impact on the individual; the individual's sense of self changes, which in turn changes the group's sense of self.

1. *Common Crisis, Common Drive.* This is an external event/process that drives the change. In the individual change process, it results in changed perspective and can be positive (opportunities) or negative (consequences). When it affects a group, it has the potential for catalyzing cultural change. In practice, this can range from the creation of entire companies to the prospect of lost jobs. It is usually an *environment* rather than a single event or series of events.
2. *Forging a Common Identity:* Together, through a combination of adversity and opportunity, the group experiences the same environment. The more this *common experience* occurs uniformly throughout the group, the more a common identity is forged in reaction. A greater driver, however, is the degree to which the group has a *common impact* of that common experience. Normal reaction to a common impact is to create a common sense of identity. Life-changing experiences include family, war, and other highly impactful situations that previously diverse individuals now share.
3. *Apply Common Identity to the Common Output/Product:* When that common identity, forged from a common experience and common impact, is directed toward a single outcome, it is highly reinforced. Positive consequences will further reinforce that common identity. For that identity to be reinforced, it is critical that the common identity is required to create the common output. In business, this may be the company or business unit itself, as long as it has a clearly defined and articulated charter.
4. *Apply Individual Identity to Specific Roles and Responsibilities:* Whereas a common identity is needed to bond the people together, it is also critically important that each individual's *own* needs are met; the more the individual's need is met *coincident* with the group identity,

the more the individual is reinforced within that group. To preserve individuality, however, it is also critical that the individual have individual-specific satisfaction (i.e., that everyone does not have to satisfy identical needs). In business, this is often achieved through specific role and responsibility assignment.

5. *Dynamically Reform New Identities:* The external events/processes that triggered the initial changes may have been addressed, but they often remanifest themselves in other forms. The group/team now needs to adapt itself *together* to meet those new challenges with new capabilities and capacities. The team now responds to the stimuli organically, with all members of the team adapting along with the collective gestalt. As before, individuals still are able to meet their own specific demands through the context of the overall identity. The more changes the team makes as a single entity, the more powerful the team becomes.

Change in the organization is a function of the individuals' change within the group. When these individual changes are incremental and compliant, the organization's changes are correspondingly small and evolutionary. When the individuals' changes are significant and identity-changing, the organization's changes are quantum leaps in innovation and performance.

These processes are described in more detail in Part III of this book.

CULTURE CHANGE: SPECIAL CASE: NEW COMPANIES

The effect of culture change on the organization can be seen in new departments and subsidiaries of existing companies; it is most obvious in new start-ups. When companies are formed independently of their parent organizations, the impact of group identity is clear and straightforward. It was clearly evident in the 1999 and 2000 'dot-com' companies that formed, peaked, and liquidated in very short life-cycles, but is also evident in larger start-ups, as well. In these cases, the impact of the founders' vision, egos, and personal drive comprise the essence of the new culture.

At Apple Computer, shifts in culture clearly define the company's product and services innovation. Since the 1970s, Apple's corporate culture, and its corresponding creativity and innovation, shifted significantly as the leadership focus shifted from entrepreneurial to investor-backed to established to turnaround to entrepreneurial.[1]

From Apple to General Electric to IBM to Microsoft, from start-up to industry giant, most of the high-profile success stories of the last 20 years

have been the result of significant changes in unique, perceived value-added benefits. Those changes, in turn, have been driven by significant changes in culture.

CULTURE CHANGE: SPECIAL CASE: HPTs

Highly successful HPTs have gone beyond the integration of social, technical, and business strategies; they have redefined their sense of self. This breakthrough in group identity is key to resulting breakthroughs in business performance.

In an electronics manufacturing company, there were 51 competing job classifications, requiring as many as 20 different positions to complete a single circuit-board assembly. As the HPT redesigned the work processes and the product and took start-to-finish ownership of the product, they were able to reduce the time-to-build from six weeks to three days, with a threefold improvement in quality. The team worked directly with customers and vendors to further improve the product and their effectiveness. Some team members even made calls from home to work with customers off-hours. Several months later, the team realized that they had fundamentally redefined *themselves* as owners of the product. They had shifted their own self-image—together.

In one emergency dispatch operation, conflicting agendas and priorities had severely limited the organization's ability to perform. Each key stakeholder group had become more concerned with its own processes and procedures than with the operation as a whole. As part of its redesign effort, the organization changed its leader and reaffirmed its underlying charter. Very simply, the charter was to save lives. By reaffirming the purpose and identity of the organization and clarifying how each stakeholder was a necessary part of that identity, the organization reformed itself around its charter. Within a year, the operation had achieved significantly reduced response times, dramatically improved cooperation between the stakeholders, and improved employee morale. The changed culture drove the change in performance.

Although this shift is often a natural consequence of some HPTs, the success rate of HPT efforts increases significantly when the opportunity for culture shift becomes *a deliberate part* of the HPT development effort.

However, simply changing the group identity is insufficient to catalyze major breakthroughs in business results. If this had been the case, most of the "dot bombs" of 2000 and 2001 would not have failed. Clearly, the culture change is a critical mechanism for creativity and paradigm shift, but it requires a solid grounding in the fundamental business proposition and the key business success dimension.

As will be seen, the most successful HPTs combine the tangible requirements of business needs with the intangible creativity and innovation of culture change. With the proper support, context, and business tools, breakthrough HPT results follow breakthroughs in HPT culture.

CULTURE CHANGE: THE ROLE AND IMPACT
OF THE LEADER

In change management strategies, the role of the leader is key: The change revolves around the leader. In DCM strategies, the leader determines when and where change occurs. In BCM strategies, the leader is responsible for setting the stage for change and role-modeling new behaviors. With change management strategies, the leader determines the need for change and is the one responsible for its development, implementation, and success. In these approaches, the leader manages change as a process with defined beginning, middle, and end points. With DCM and BCM, the leader is clearly able to define success metrics and evaluate the ultimate success of the change strategy.

However, the same role that requires the leader to define success and business goals also inherently limits the creativity and innovation of the organization. By predefining the end state, the leader limits potential innovation and breakthroughs. Further, the leader also inherently limits the ability of the individual to internalize and take ownership for the permanent change because it is perceived as externally imposed.

In culture change, the leader affects and influences the changes, but does not "manage" culture. It is axiomatic that the organization's culture will become whatever it will become, independent of the leader's best intentions. However, as a key member of the organization, the leader can significantly influence the cultural outcome.

Every member of the organization has impact on that organization, but the leader is prepositioned to exert more influence and impact than any other. As the leader demonstrably changes his/her own self-image and allows others to experience that changed sense of self, the leader inevitably changes the organization's identity.

It is critical to note that the leader's *impact* on the organization is a result of an internal change in sense of self; it is not merely a discrete change in behaviors and actions. Many leaders, intuitively trying to change culture, change only their outward appearance and actions. This may appear to have a cultural impact, but without the corresponding internal changes, the impact is neither permanent nor authentic. In many of these artificial culture change cases, the leaders' actions may serve to actually *reinforce* an existing cultural perception of distrust and resentment.

OPPORTUNITIES OF CULTURE CHANGE

The Power of Culture Change

There are many examples of effective culture change in business. In fact, most of the successful organizations that have made major strides in their business goals have had corresponding changes in their own sense of self: Their culture is different. For most organizations, the leader is instrumental in catalyzing that change, yet not able to simply "force" the change. Many CEOs discover that their traditional management methods of control and influence are ineffective with the overall organization; they rely on a shift in culture to create true change.

Jack Welch transformed General Electric "overnight" in two decades from an industrial, product-oriented manufacturing conglomerate to a global, interdependent organization that produces services, products, profits, and employee motivation in equal measure.[2]

Lou Gerstner has helped IBM to fundamentally redefine itself across the breadth of its entire service and customer base—potentially saving it from disastrous financial results at the same time.[3]

Other companies have been able to catalyze their investors, customers, and employees with cultures that clearly add unique, perceived, value-added products to everyone involved. From Herb Kelleher of Southwest Airlines to Robert Townsend of Avis to Sam Walton of Wal-Mart, the unique sense of corporate identity—*culture*—has resulted in major successes in all key business dimensions.

Organizational Culture as a Competitive Force

To leaders unfamiliar with the effective nurturing and support of culture change, "culture" becomes synonymous with "employee resistance" and projects become "simply impossible to implement here." The tangible impacts of the intangible forces become apparently insurmountable.

When that same cultural force is supported and appropriately allowed to grow, it becomes a significant competitive advantage—often unduplicable by other companies.

Throughout much of the 1900s, Westinghouse Electric continually tried to duplicate General Electric's products, services, and culture. Despite considerable capital investment, employee incentives, and other means, Westinghouse was unable to duplicate GE's success at innovation and profitability. Finally, by the 1980s, Westinghouse no longer attempted to duplicate GE and focused on its own products and markets: It could not compete with GE's "intangible force."

Similarly, by the 1990s, Wal-Mart had steadily increased market share with an apparently unstoppable combination of competitive pricing and

aggressive merchandising.[4] K-Mart tried to duplicate Wal-Mart's success, from store hours to sales flyers, only to lose more and more market share and profitability. Finally, in 2002, K-Mart declared Chapter 11 bankruptcy, after making major capital investments in computers, storefronts, and inventory. K-Mart was unable to duplicate Wal-Mart's sense of commitment, drive, and purpose. Wal-Mart's culture was its unstoppable competitive force.

The *Cultural Foundation* of an organization can be an effective competitive force, if appropriately positioned and valued by its key stakeholders.

CHALLENGES OF CULTURE CHANGE

Culture Change Is Often Misperceived as a Process to Be Followed

Culture change efforts are often difficult to foster and implement. Because culture refers to both tangible and intangible aspects of group dynamics and sense of identity, many organizations have difficulty trying to change the culture. In most cases, culture change is viewed as a process to be changed or a procedure to be followed, rather than as a path or journey that has already been started.

For these leaders, the attempt to arbitrarily change behavior and attitudes across the organization results in increased organizational resistance. Rather than facilitate the shift toward new goals, the organization actively resists any change.

In 1990, a U.S. medical products company had acquired a French subsidiary in the same industry. Soon after the acquisition, the executives of the parent company believed that the merger needed to be accelerated; they "facilitated" the merger by mandating that all interoffice correspondence and meetings would be in English. Not only did this demonstrate a complete disregard for the traditions and culture of the subsidiary, it also reinforced widely held beliefs that the American executives were only interested in complete control. As a result of considerable active resistance on the part of the subsidiary, the executives changed their policies and worked for more effective integration. Nonetheless, the negative impact of that original edict lasted for several years, well beyond the tenure of the original executives.

Culture Change, by Itself, Does Not Achieve Business Results

Culture change needs to be combined with genuine business goals to be effective. For some companies, culture change is initiated for the sake of change rather than to achieve specific business goals. In these instances, the organization often becomes chaotic.

In one subcontract electronic assembly company, the desires of the employees were given priority over other business objectives. With appropriate orientation, training, and understanding of the business pressures, employees were directed to become a "self-directed work team" virtually overnight. Left alone to achieve ambiguous business objectives, the employees were unprepared for the many challenges. Employee perquisites were easily available; however, capital investment had been neglected. Performance decreased dramatically, and the entire operation was closed.

Culture Clash

Another common challenge for culture change strategy is the apparent clash of differing cultures. When allowing one part of the organization to change its own identity, what happens when it competes with other, unchanged, portions of the organization? In many cases, the result is considerable conflict.

One of the pioneer sociotechnical manufacturing firms had considerable success in developing computer hardware components in the 1980s. Operating in separate facilities and with separate reporting requirements than other parts of the organization, the sociotechnical group had significantly improved productivity and dramatically improved on-time delivery. Employees were proud of their results and regularly sponsored tours through their facilities.

As the company encountered difficult economic times, it consolidated its facilities and integrated the HPTs into their conventional counterpart organizations. There was considerable conflict between the two cultures, from their differing metrics and goals to vastly different expectations and compensation of workers. Within a short period of time, the HPTs were completely subsumed by the conventional culture.

Many executives believe that merging of disparate cultures creates a new, more powerful culture. Although an advantageous/productive integration may occur in some organizations, the more common outcome is for one culture to subsume the other—often with considerable resentment and conflict on both sides. Unlike a "process" that can be mixed with other processes, culture *as identity* is not arbitrarily designed or transformed.

Some successful organizations have integrated differing cultures through a strong belief in the need for diversity and the value of the individual. In these instances, differing senses of self are nurtured rather than diminished.

As will be seen, this ability of the organization to embrace differences of culture is critical to the successful nurturing of HPTs within a non-HPT environment.

Culture Change strategies can offer breakthrough results across all major business success dimensions—typically in short periods of time. These strategies have the potential for breakthrough change, yet also depend heavily upon effective interventions and integrated support. As a key component to successful HPT creation and development, Culture Change processes are described in detail later in this text.

NOTES

1. Freiberger, Paul, and Swaine, Michael. *Fire in the Valley: The Making of the Personal Computer*, New York: McGraw-Hill, 1999; also Amelio, Gil, and Simon, William L., *On the Firing Line: My 500 Days at Apple*, New York: HarperBusiness, 1998.

2. Welch, Jack, and Byrne, John A. *Jack: Straight from the Gut*, New York: Warner Books, 2001.

3. Gerstner, Louis, Jr., *Who Says Elephants Can't Dance? Inside IBM's Historic Turnaround*, New York: HarperBusiness, 2002.

4. Walton, Sam., *Sam Walton: Made in America*, New York: Doubleday, 1992.

High Performance Teams

Take my assets—but leave me my organization, and in five years, I'll have it back.

—*Alfred P. Sloan, Jr.*

As seen, there is a broad spectrum of organizational reaction to change pressures. The actual organizational response will depend upon the impact of its previous experiences, the depth and breadth of its present change pressures, and the effective implementation of an appropriate change strategy.

High Performance Teams fit naturally into that spectrum of change strategies. As part of a Culture Change strategy, HPTs offer breakthrough thinking and breakthrough results. As with any change strategy, they have corresponding challenges and opportunities. As is seen throughout this text, successful HPT implementation is dependent upon appropriate organizational timing, placement, and support.

As one type of Culture Change strategy, there are several considerations for an HPT selection and implementation.

HPTs ARE MOST EASILY APPLIED WHEN ALIGNED WITH ORGANIZATIONAL CHANGE PRESSURES

HPTs are optimally applied when the change pressures on the organization are at a very high level. As a breakthrough strategy, HPTs are best applied when revolutionary change drivers compel the organization to

major breakthrough changes. HPTs are most easily integrated into the overall organization during times of great change, new organizational formation, or even bankruptcy.

This is not to suggest that HPTs can *only* be successful during major organizational turmoil; many companies *do* create and support successful HPTs without enterprise-wide upheaval. However, the nature of culture change within HPTs is most easily integrated when its surrounding organization is also undergoing fundamental change.

HPTs CAN BE PART OF AN INTEGRATED HETEROGENEOUS CULTURE

Since each workgroup creates it own de facto culture, most enterprise-wide organizations are comprised of diverse subcultures. In the Culture Change strategy, this diversity is leveraged to encourage creativity and energy from all organizational areas. Within this context, HPTs can be more easily integrated into a diverse culture.

In conventional change strategies, the alignment of behaviors typically includes the attempted alignment of subcultures. In both DCM and BCM strategies, cultural alignment is often equated with cultural homogeneity; a single cultural model that the organization strives to achieve. In this environment, teams that are perceived as "going against the (cultural) grain" are resisted.

When HPTs are perceived as a *different* organizational culture by their key stakeholders, there is considerably less resistance in a heterogeneous culture than a homogeneous one. This is not to infer that HPTs are impossible or impractical within a DCM-driven or BCM-driven culture; only that those organizational strategies are more resistant to HPTs than are Culture Change strategies.

HPTs ARE SIMPLY ONE TYPE OF RESPONSE STRATEGY

As seen, High Performance Teams are simply one application of the Culture Change strategy, which itself is just one of many change strategies possible for the leader and the organization. Their success or failure, as with any change strategy, is dependent upon appropriate preparation, analysis, planning, and implementation. Though HPTs offer unique opportunities for breakthrough thinking, culture shift, and breakthrough results, they are, at their core, just another strategy.

As with any strategy that requires planning and execution, it is important to understand the *transition* to High Performance that teams can achieve, and to understand the *underlying processes* that create HPTs to begin with. The next section provides an outline of those processes and models for illustration and application.

How HPT? The Dynamics and Processes of HPTs

New Learnings from HPT Efforts

With just enough learning to misquote.

—Lord Byron

Building on the many efforts, both successful and otherwise, of High Performance Teams around the United States and around the world, it remains to synthesize new learnings about the dynamics of HPT formation and the real-world constraints of their creation.

As noted in chapter 11, developing, understanding, and applying these key learnings become a critical factor in the creation and implementation of successful HPT efforts.

While reviewing the learnings, it is important to note that High Performance Teams are not exclusive to business organizations; they can be successful in *any* organization of people united for parallel goals. As throughout this text, however, most HPTs have been attempted in the business arena and so are considered in more detail here. This should not exclude nonbusiness consideration; indeed, most change pressures on business are also applicable to other organization forms (as appropriate).

THE NEW BUSINESS ENVIRONMENT

There have been many changes in business pressures over the last two decades, and HPT creation has been both positively and negatively affected by these changes. Though these environmental factors will continue to change, it is helpful to review their impact on HPT formation.

SUCCESS PRINCIPLES: BUSINESS AND HIGH PERFORMANCE TEAMS

The most successful teams are *principle-driven*; they follow general guidelines that affect all their behaviors in the workplace. Some of these principles are unique to High Performance, and some simply reflect core business beliefs; together, they comprise a set of common beliefs.

Understanding these beliefs helps to understand the perspective and culture of successful HPTs.

TRANSITION: THE UNDERLYING PROCESSES OF SUCCESSFUL HPTs

There are several dimensions of transition and development in successful High Performance Teams. From an individual perspective, being part of an HPT effort is transformational; the experience often drives introspection and self-awareness in team members and key stakeholders. Understanding the individual's growth and development through this process is key to understanding and developing successful HPT efforts. Similarly, the team's overall development is also critical; understanding the team dynamics of growth and maturation is critical to understanding HPT development.

Another dimension of change—the *depth of intervention*—is used to help guide and accelerate natural processes of transition and development. These three dimensions—individual transition, team development, and level of intervention—are interrelated, and are critical keys to HPT development. Understanding these processes, and how to support and guide an HPT effort, is one of the key learnings of successful HPTs.

The New Business Environment

The problem with the future is, it isn't what it used to be.
—*A. Paul Valery*

TRENDS: ACCELERATING AT THE RATE OF CHANGE

If change is a constant, then the *rate* of change is not. The *impact* of change continues to increase, and the *multidimensional* pressures on the organization increase commensurately. The continuing demand for employee value, customer value, shareholder value, and operational value are not only increasing; the rate of the increasing demand is increasing.

Change is axiomatic, and this acceleration of change imposes unique challenges to business in general and HPTs in particular. In the 2000s, some of these pressures are significantly different than those that faced organizations in the 1980s and 1990s when workplace alternatives were first attempted on a large scale.

These factors are helpful to consider when creating HPTs.

GLOBAL MARKETS, GLOBAL COMPETITORS

With the dramatic expansion of communications and data systems technologies, the "global village" is an increasing reality, particularly in areas of commerce. Global competition was a factor for 1980s HPTs, but it was

generally limited to potential outsourcing suppliers. For many manufacturing firms considering HPTs, the lower wage and benefits costs of foreign operations provided significant cost savings over U.S.-built products. This was a key incentive to create HPTs for their productivity performance, allowing manufacturers to keep higher-waged domestic production due to their lower total net cost to produce the product. The "business case for change" for many of these HPTs was to provide a productivity improvement equal to the cost benefit of foreign production.

As global communication and transportation costs declined dramatically, the Internet simultaneously provided an infrastructure backbone for routine data transfer. Coupled with significant reductions in global tariffs and the lowering of traditional intergovernmental restrictions, global markets and competition increased exponentially.

The impact of this globalization has both hindered and helped the formation of High Performance Teams in the United States and the European Union.

For many organizations, despite major foreign investments and mergers throughout the 1990s, global competition has continued to *increase* the *change pressures* for more productivity, lesser cost, and improved customer value. This further increases the incentives for executives to discover and create new workplace alternatives, increasing many executives' acceptance and consideration of High Performance Teams.

At the same time, in many markets, globalization also imposes new demands on HPTs; competition is often no longer significantly lower; it may be *an order of magnitude lower*. In the case of one chemical manufacturing firm in the United States, its E.U. competition was able to sell its product in Europe for less than it was paying for the raw material in the United States. For domestic steel firms, Japanese and Far Asian mills have been able to provide formed steel to U.S. customers at a fraction of the domestic firms' cost to produce. For these challenges, HPTs have to find a *new* level of "quantum leap improvement"; 50 percent improvements are no longer "good enough."

INTERCONNECTED / INTERDEPENDENT ORGANIZATIONS

Along with the globalization of commerce and economies, the increases in communication and transportation have dramatically increased the interconnectedness of business organizations. Unlike the 1980s, where vertical integration was common for both manufacturing and service industries, most companies produce only a portion of their total product. Many computer peripheral firms produce only the original design and

final test "in house"; component acquisition, subassembly, and initial product tests are done by suppliers—often by several different ones.

Although this has been very effective for cost reduction and rapid-cycle product improvement, it has also significantly decreased the potential for "end-to-end" ownership of any given workgroup. This loss of "line of sight" ownership makes it increasingly difficult for any single team to review their product as a whole.

When NASA developed the Hubble Space Telescope, it had very detailed specifications for each component and comprehensive plans for individual testing. However, there were inadequate plans for testing and integrating the overall satellite; no design team had a "line of sight" to the completed product. After all parts were assembled and launched into space, it was discovered that the telescope was incapable of detailed photographs. In this case, the lack of "line of sight" design resulted in a *literal lack of sight* in space. Only subsequent "on-station" repairs were able to finally bring the telescope to its original design parameters.

Many innovations and breakthroughs are the result of many different people being able to view the overall product and having the "CEO perspective." When limited to only a portion of the product or a "slice" of the work process, the potential for significant problems is great.

In the 2000s, however, the same infrastructure that accelerated globalization and globally interconnected manufacturing also offers the countering mechanism. Use of virtual communication technologies, Internet connectivity, and wireless technologies allow teams to form *virtual teams* and *real-time integration*. This level of virtual integration becomes a critical tool for teams continuing to look for order-of-magnitude breakthroughs.

DECREASING CYCLE TIMES; INCREASED SPEED

In the 1980s, Jack Welch of General Electric talked about "Speed, Simplicity and Self-Confidence."[1] Though GE's focus has shifted to other areas, the *need for speed* has only increased. This has included speed in all areas: speed to market, speed of production, speed of employee satisfaction, and speed of financial return for shareholders.

As business cycles change, the expectations for increased performance also change. Cycle times are decreased, and the times allowed for performance improvement are decreased.

This need for rapidly improved results has encouraged organizations to look to alternative work cultures. The ability to obtain real-world results in a short period of time is a hallmark of High Performance Teams. This has increased the visibility and consideration of HPTs in the 2000s.

For some executives, however, the demand for *rapid* improvement is translated into *immediate* return; the same change pressures that drive

breakthrough improvements also seem to encourage *immediate results*. For these executives, the time and resources required to create and develop High Performance Teams are perceived as excessive. In these cases, the organization often selects the alternatives of layoffs, outsourcing, and subsequent Directive Change Management. Because these alternative paths are typically unable to meet the need for true breakthrough improvements, the business is unsuccessful.

As a *true* response to the need for rapid, fundamental change, High Performance Teams are an effective approach. However, to be considered as a potential strategy, executives and key leaders need to have an understanding of their strategic alternatives and the key success factors of developing HPTs. This text is intended to provide that understanding.

DECREASED CYCLE TIMES VERSUS CONSTANT "EMOTIONAL CYCLE TIMES"

With ever decreasing business cycle times, there is often a subsequent pressure on key stakeholders to adapt more quickly. For new markets, customers and employees are asked to adapt, understand, and be proficient in new areas of products and services. For companies undergoing frequent changes in executive management, employees are typically asked to embrace new corporate values with each shift in management. For each compression of business cycle, individuals are expected to compress their own cycles of acceptance and commitment.

As seen in this section, *emotional cycles* are not able to follow the speed and compression of *business cycles*. This creates a significant disparity for many stakeholders and can significantly hinder the organization's overall ability to adapt to its change pressures.

For business changes involving only activity and behavioral shifts from its stakeholders, Directive Change Management can appear to be very effective at matching emotional cycles with the business cycles. Because DCM depends upon *compliance of behaviors* rather than an emotional alignment, DCM can appear to yield very rapid shifts in an organization. As seen in chapter 8, however, the longer-term negative impacts of some DCM efforts can arise later to create major barriers to change.

Appropriately applied, Behavioral Change Management can be effective in aligning personal emotional cycles with the business cycles, but this strategy also has the potential for long-term negative impact.

In the case of both DCM and BCM strategies, there is often difficulty in achieving the breakthrough improvements needed to begin with. The same pressures that shorten the business cycle are also those that often demand revolutionary change.

In the case of Culture Change and High Performance Teams, the shortening of business cycles is a common challenge to the effective formation of teams. As a strategy focused on the integration of individual and organizational needs, successful HPTs cannot be created by mandate or their development cycles arbitrarily shortened. However, as seen later in this section, their development *can* be accelerated and catalyzed to a level where they are able to achieve dramatic, order-of-magnitude improvements in a matter of weeks and months, with long-term, sustaining changes.

To be able to make High Performance Teams work, particularly with the demands of shortened cycle times and increased performance, requires a working understanding of the dynamics and processes of HPT development.

NOTE

1. Slater, Robert. *The New GE: How Jack Welch Revived an American Institution,* Homewood, IL: Business One, 1993, pg 254.

The Principles
of High Performance

Hold faithfulness and sincerity as first principles.

—Kung Fu Tze

The most successful HPTs are *principle-driven*. At their core, they are guided neither by rigid doctrine nor by contract. They are formed and driven by a series of underlying principles rather than doctrine and procedure. Though this is true of most organizations, including those having no HPTs, the most successful HPT efforts deliberately and overtly guide and evaluate themselves around key principles.

In the 1980s and 1990s, soon after the initial successes of Fortune 100 companies, many organizations attempted to create HPTs "by command." Without understanding the underlying dynamics and special needs of HPTs, other organizations tried to duplicate the original teams by simply mandating breakthrough results.

Some of these artificial HPTs achieved initial success, often due to the Hawthorne Effect,[1] and then were unable to sustain their results. Most HPT efforts attempted in this manner never achieved even initial success, and actually worsened their performance.

In reviewing successful HPTs, several common principles emerge. Some of these principles are not exclusive to HPTs, yet define a prerequisite business environment within which the HPTs can thrive. These Key Business Principles are described next.

Similarly, there are also principles that uniquely *define* the HPT process. As a principle-driven process, these Key High Performance Principles are common to the most successful HPT efforts; they are described later.

KEY BUSINESS PRINCIPLES

Survival depends upon the simultaneous achievement of a unique, perceived, value-added service/product in the areas of customer, owner, employee, and operational value.

This is the Basic Value Imperative outlined in chapter 4. Organizations that continually strive to add value in *all* these areas are the most receptive to HPT efforts.

There is no operational difference between the short term and the long term; each defines the other.

Most organizations demonstrate a strong distinction between short-term tactical considerations and long-term strategy. Key infrastructure systems, such as financial, informational, and operational, are very time-line–dependent. Organizations focused exclusively on the short-term, such as cash-flow intensive markets, may sacrifice long-term equity and shareholder value. Those focused primarily on the long-term, such as Real Estate Investment Trusts (REITs) and fixed-asset investment organizations, often compromise short-term employee and customer value.

Successful HPT efforts must accommodate both short- and long-term perspectives, and develop approaches and strategies that *simultaneously* support both needs. When HPTs are driven to focus on a single perspective, they are often unable to develop true breakthrough results.

HPTs believe that there exist a series of approaches that meet *both* long-term and short-term needs and incorporate that belief into their performance.

People are the heart and soul of the organization. The company's long-term competitive force is determined by its employees.

Although it is axiomatic that people form the nucleus of any organization, organizational *behavior* often demonstrates a contrary belief. When asked to describe the "core competency" of their organization or where their "intrinsic [asset] value" is, many leaders focus on the company's products or infrastructure. Though this focus may be correct, it is not complete.

Organizations that focus on tangible assets and tangible value tend to reinforce those assets directly. Utilities that believe their key asset is their physical infrastructure spend considerable funds to maintain and expand those facilities, yet have significantly less expenditure for training and employee development than nonutilities. Consequently, the employees

who are performing maintenance and development are decreasingly able to do so. In the short term, the utility is able to maintain effective service. Long-term, however, this ability is degraded and the utility less and less able to remain competitive.

In sales and marketing organizations, there is often a clear understanding that their employees comprise their "competitive force." Without effective employees on the "front line" to customers, these organizations lose sales quickly. In nonservice organizations, however, it is less clear. Some organizations, particularly those in monopolistic markets, may even believe that employees are *counter* to their competitive advantage. In these latter extreme cases, employees are treated as a necessary commodity to be obtained, utilized, and then discarded.

In most organizations' behavior, the value of the employee is between these extremes, where there is tacit acknowledgment of employee value. However, primary resources are often focused on nonemployee areas.

As Chrysler's Lee Iacocca said, "In the end, all business operations can be reduced to three words: people, product, and profits. People come first. Unless you've got a good team, you can't do much with the other two."[2]

HPTs thrive in organizations that value their employees and understand that the company's key resource lies within its employees' competency, creativity, and commitment.

Every organizational system is perfectly designed to achieve the results obtained.

HPT efforts are fundamentally designed to *change* the conditions and assumptions under which work is performed. Whether it is a product or process change or a change in customer relationship, HPTs strive to make breakthrough changes in their world.

The *readiness* of the rest of the organization is key to their ability to implement and institutionalize those changes.

Successful HPTs are created within organizations that are ready for change. The understanding that each system is perfectly designed for its own results recognizes that the organization *itself* is responsible for its own condition. This may seem obvious, yet most organizational behavior demonstrates a lack of responsibility—particularly in times of stress and pressure. When asked to describe their current market condition, many companies will quickly focus on governmental regulation, aggressive competition, foreign labor costs, and other external factors. Though these may be legitimate factors, the *true* underlying causes are often the organization's historic inability to deal with these issues. Once the organization accepts this responsibility, its readiness for change increases significantly. The readiness of the organization to accept change is directly proportional to the ease of implementation of HPT efforts.

Some HPTs are able to create a "bubble" of change within a larger organization that is not ready for change. Even in the best of circumstances, this is very difficult to achieve and more difficult to maintain. Their long-term success is dependent on many other factors, such as their level of interaction with the rest of their organization. Generally, the successful HPTs that can exist without the tacit support of their overall organization are the exception rather than the rule.

"If you always do what you always did, you will always get what you always got."[3]

Similarly, when faced with strong pressure for change, organizations will inherently strive to repeat their own historical successes rather than try fundamental change. This is a natural reaction to change; it is further reinforced by the tangible and intangible support systems of the organization. This pressure to "keep things as they are" is often manifested in many different ways; tangibly, it may include payroll and budgetary approval systems; intangibly, it may include leaders' own beliefs in their success and competencies.

Even when organizations agree that change is required, the change efforts are often "repackaged history." Resistance to change is considerable in any organization and often expresses itself in programs that proclaim change yet offer no real shift in behavior, actions, or effect.

This becomes a critical factor in HPT efforts, both internally and externally. Internally, HPTs will initially try to use conventional approaches to obtain breakthrough results; their new processes are strikingly similar to their historical ones. Intervention during the Work Re/Design and Implementation phases is often required to help the teams understand that they must make *real* changes to yield *real* results.

Externally, HPTs experience resistance to supporting their new changes. Most often, this resistance is expressed through the reluctance of support systems to adapt to the HPT needs. Relabeling of existing systems to purportedly support the new HPT processes is one of the most common methods of resistance.

One of the most obvious and difficult realizations for the organization in general and the HPT in particular is that a real change in results requires a real change in the way things are done.

The impossible never is.

In some of the most challenging HPT efforts, the teams were charged with order-of-magnitude productivity improvements, dramatic market improvements, and even corporate turnarounds. The consensus of most

observers (and even some of their sponsors) was that they were given an impossible task. It was felt that they could not achieve their goals.

Simply put, if a long history of smart, capable leaders had been unable to make changes previously, how could an HPT achieve it?

The first roadblock to success is the belief that it cannot be achieved.

The history of breakthroughs is the history of belief that the breakthroughs can and will occur. HPTs are no exception.

The transition of a typical team to HPT culture and performance is an intense experience of trial and discovery, frustration, and achievement. Without the strong belief that there exists a "win-win" approach somewhere, teams may fail to find just that approach. Intervention throughout the HPT transition often includes the leaders' demonstration that a breakthrough answer exists, even if its details are not yet known.

This belief is not unique to HPTs, yet without it, HPTs will most likely not achieve their breakthrough performance.

KEY HIGH PERFORMANCE PRINCIPLES

There are many ways to achieve the same results.

HPTs believe that there are many different ways to achieve the same desired goals; there is no single, correct answer that simply remains to be found. The ability to incorporate many different perspectives and follow several different paths—and still achieve the breakthrough results—is a hallmark of highly successful HPTs.

This also follows for the HPT process itself. There is no single, mandatory process that will unfailingly result in an HPT. There is no prescribed list of procedures that can be followed that will guarantee success.

There are many paths to a successful HPT effort: This text outlines some of them.

All the people who do the work actively design the work; everyone involved wants to be involved.

The HPT process is inherently a team-based process. However, "team" refers to all of the key stakeholders in the process, not just the most visible and obvious. Traditionally, a team is considered the ad hoc group that is assigned a particular task; the engineers are asked to be a team that designs the product, and workers are directed to be the "work team" that builds the product. In the HPT environment, however, "team" refers to all the people who are directly involved with the product or service, from management to bargaining unit, from sales to financial staff. When all the key people are involved in the actual design or redesign of the product, that product is significantly different than the traditional. The intangible

benefits of commitment, energy, and follow-through are significantly increased when all key employees are actively involved.

This principle is one of the most challenging to implement in practice. For most organizations creating HPTs, resources are limited and employees stressed. To allocate the time and energy during times of crisis is very difficult. Many companies believe they are unable to follow this principle completely, and compromise its implementation. A common compromise is to designate a representative team or to have different teams review different phases of the process.

These organizations often discover that an early compromise has significant long-term effects; representative teams have significant challenges in ownership and change management, whereas process-limited teams have difficulty with process integration and implementation.

Although no principle is mandatory to the HPT creation and transition process, the most successful teams have found ways to accommodate this initial investment of time and energy. By placing increased responsibility on the HPT itself to recover that investment, management can reduce its exposure of its initial investment.

Creativity results from a shift in perspective; HPT results from a shift in self and relationships. Culture is the only true change mechanism.

Creativity is often defined as a "different approach." For some creative individuals, that difference may be a permanent world-outlook, and society may view those people as artists or "highly creative." For others, creativity may be a "flash of inspiration" or moment of clarity. In all these cases, there is a fundamental shift in perspective that results in a different approach.

Creativity is an important part of the HPT transition; without a shift in perspective, the teams would merely repeat earlier approaches to the problem. A critical function of the HPT transition process, then, is to shift the perspective of each team member to a new viewpoint that incorporates different thinking and new data. The dynamics of all team members achieving a new perspective—which may or may not be unified—is key to the HPT development.

But a shift in perspective by itself is transitory. For teams that shift perspective but do not shift their team culture, individual perspectives may quickly revert to traditional thinking as soon as they face the real-world challenges of implementation. For these "ad hoc HPT" efforts, good recommendations often fail during implementation.

Culture is defined as a shift in group identity, as seen in chapter 10. When the shift in perspective is extended to a shift in intrateam relationships and a shift in self, perspective shifts become permanent.

Throughout the HPT transition process, appropriate intervention is provided to offer the opportunity for all individuals to explore their own

assumptions, their own beliefs, and their own paths forward. Because this is within the context of the HPT effort, individuals are encouraged to discover their own success through the success of the HPT effort. This dramatically increases commitment and creativity.

When this change dynamic is coupled with the interaction of all other team members, the catalytic effects are significant. Once started, each individual's own discovery is able to catalyze other members' discovery and shift. This interaction further enhances the sense of group identity that in turn increases the individual shift.

Within the proper environment, with effective intervention, the capacity for new thinking, new approaches, and new understanding is coupled with newfound levels of personal energy and employee commitment. Breakthroughs become the inevitable result.

There always exists a win-win outcome, once assumptions are eliminated. Breakthroughs are only limited by peoples' belief that they are limited.

This is an extension of the "Impossible never is" key business principle. HPTs, however, take this principle to an operational level.

When first challenged with the "impossible" goals and restrictive constraints, most HPT participants react with anger and resentment. In some HPT efforts, team members have tried to leave as soon as they learned of the goals set by management: "We can't do that! That's impossible! How can we do it when no one else has been able to?"

By the end of the transition period, the same individuals are often looking for more challenges, more "impossibilities" and more ways to make order-of-magnitude change.

Though effective intervention helps team members deal with their initial reaction, it is also their successful experiences throughout the transition that underpin their belief in this principle. From their persistence in looking for that "win-win" approach that has eluded them historically to their multiple pilots during implementation, the teams discover that the answer does exist. Those teams often offer to counsel the next generation of teams.

Clearly, the belief must exist somewhere in the HPT effort, at all times. Ideally, this should emanate from the leadership, but may also come from individuals on the team or even external stakeholders. Intervention does not create the belief, but it can reinforce the opportunity for it to evolve.

The CEO perspective is only effective when shared by everyone.

The "CEO perspective" is the "big picture" perspective that drives the organization. It includes the mission and charter of the company, but also

includes the basic strengths and weaknesses of the organization and its strategic direction.

Throughout the 1990s, there was a strong emphasis on corporate "mission statements" and "guiding principles" to help all employees understand corporate direction. The assumption was that everyone would be more effective—and more committed—to the overall corporate goals if they understood them.

At one steel manufacturer, the CEO's direct reports were asked to individually describe the purpose of the company. Much to the chagrin of the CEO, no two officers' descriptions were similar, nor did they match the CEO's perspective of the company's purpose. Each officer's perspective was determined by his/her functional role in the company; for example, the financial officer believed that the corporate purpose was to provide a minimum rate of return for its stockholders. Only the CEO held the overarching perspective of the corporate purpose; therefore, the only effective integration of its diverse functions was possible by the CEO himself. This was one of many factors that made it extremely difficult for this company to deal with foreign competition; it ultimately ceased operation.

Successful HPT efforts deliberately communicate the "CEO perspective" to everyone on the team. The "Business Case for Change" is clearly established, communicated, and believed in. These teams do not simply understand the business case; they are trained to understand the underlying causes of the business case for change. For the most successful efforts, there is direct interaction and dialog between the CEO and the team members themselves, increasing understanding and commitment. This becomes critical during the implementation phase, when HPTs are often required to change course in ways that might appear to contradict the business case yet actually address its underlying needs.

A corollary to this principle is the need to share information. For the most successful HPTs, access to corporate information is provided carte blanche, except for personnel information. In the case of sensitive or trade secret information, the team is encouraged to have a dialog with a "subject matter expert" on the subject, rather than have direct access to the information. This access to the same traditional information that management has had access to, helps the team to achieve valid and verifiable transition plans. It is also an important prerequisite for trust and commitment.

In many stressful environments, there may be significant distrust between functions, up and down ranks, and between employee groups. For HPT efforts in these environments, the participants often enter the process believing that "management already has the answer," and that "management is keeping secrets."

From the team members' perspective, access to key information demonstrates management's endorsement and support of their effort. From a

management perspective, it provides the opportunity to begin establishing accountability and responsibility for access to key information.

From a practical perspective, extensive sharing of key information is also required. With limited access to key information, teams may be unable to achieve valid approaches that meet real-world needs, and it may take significantly increased effort to establish trust.

Everyone has untapped potential to be great; everyone has potential for leadership.

HPTs are created to address key business needs and to develop new ways of doing business. As all key employees are involved in the design of the new product or service, each has an important voice in decision-making. While each team will decide how it wants to make decisions, everyone has input.

Successful HPT efforts believe that everyone's input has value; each individual's experience may provide expertise that others might not share, so all input is important. These successful teams do not limit individual input or opinion based on position or history; they believe that everyone has the potential to understand the issues and make valid choices.

Highly successful HPTs also believe that everyone has potential for leadership, whether originally placed in a leadership role or not. In fact, some of the most successful HPTs have discovered that their most effective leaders come from traditional "blue collar" ranks and not from traditional management functions.

Power and authority are dynamically shared and balanced throughout the organization as needed. Decisions are made at the point of operation by the operator.

In a traditional organization, power and authority are synonymous and tend to be "top-down" driven—that is, the highest ranking individuals have the most power and then personally dispense that power as needed down through the ranks. Although this may be effective for some traditional organizations, HPTs recognize that power and authority are distributed as required for the work function, rather than for a specific rank in the organization. For these HPTs, getting the results is more important than retaining arbitrary rank.

HPTs inherently drive for breakthrough results. As they develop their designs for the new workplace, they develop the required business processes first, then design the organization around that process. In order for the process to function, the individual performing the work needs to have the competence, training, and authority to carry out that work.

Clearly, this focus on performance over hierarchy can be confusing to some participants, and even antithetical to others. For example, in the initial stages of HPT development, the financial team member may expect to be the only individual making financial decisions for the team. Without the traditional structure of the organization and functional separation between departments, it is often difficult for individuals to adapt to the HPT's new philosophy. With appropriate coaching and intervention, however, power and authority are typically shared dynamically among team members as the overall team develops.

For the most successful HPT efforts, the transfer of power and authority to the team is a phased process; it is not done all at once. For example, during the Work Re/Design phase, the team is typically given full authority to develop new approaches and new designs, yet they are not provided the authority to implement them. After the completion of the Work Re/Design phase, and with the consent and support of the sponsoring executive, the team is then chartered to implement and execute their plans. From the beginning of the HPT effort to the fully mature stage of the effort, the transfer of power and authority is deliberately timed to ensure an optimal balance between empowerment and accountability.

Non–value-added work is ruthlessly eliminated.

Successful HPT efforts believe that "non–value-added" work—work that does not directly contribute to the final product or service—should be reduced or eliminated. The most successful HPTs work ruthlessly to eliminate any non–value-added work they discover.

From an external perspective, this may appear as a sole focus on HPT-centric issues, to the detriment of others. Internally, however, successful HPTs work hard to integrate with other groups and support non-HPT efforts. By working with other parts of the organization, working from the "CEO perspective," HPTs work hard to ensure that any non–value-added work they identify is also non value-added for other areas of the organization.

An important corollary to this principle is that any organization not providing a work output is bureaucracy. Some bureaucracy may be necessary (for example, payroll transactions are often classified as non value-added, yet are important to retaining the workforce), but its identification may raise issues of whether or not that work should be "core work" or potentially subcontracted.

People will achieve more when they understand what they are not allowed to do.

Traditionally, a process redesign team is given a series of goals and directions to follow, is allocated some resources to pursue any new design,

and is given a timetable for accomplishment. In this context, the team is inherently constrained to follow that direction, whether or not it actually achieves its goals. Even when this direction is well intentioned and deliberately vague, teams will often default to historical processes that may not provide new approaches.

In many cases, the sponsoring executive may inadvertently drive the process redesign team to a preconceived design through specific design requirements.

Early HPT efforts often provided minimum direction for the teams to develop their new designs; these were "Minimum Critical Specifications." These specifications itemized the minimum requirements that the teams had to achieve, and usually included some goals and guidelines. Some specifications were long and detailed—albeit "minimum"—whereas others were only a few sentences.

HPTs that tried to adapt to these specifications often found themselves constrained by them. Not only were the teams required to meet the aggressive goals in the specifications, they were often constrained in the type of design they could develop.

Recently, the most successful HPT efforts have used a combination of goals and constraints (also known as the "Sandbox"). The sponsoring executive outlines the performance goals for the teams that the new design/approach must achieve; these are discrete and measurable. In addition, the sponsoring executive provides a list of constraints that the team may not violate. It is up to the team to develop a recommendation that achieves the goals without violating the constraints.

Teams are inherently more creative and more effective when they develop approaches and designs that are testable against the constraints than when they try to develop a path that meets arbitrary Design Criteria.

Overall, these Key Business Principles and Key High Performance Team principles offer the most direct road map to success. The most successful HPT efforts follow all these principles; the least successful follow few of them.

NOTES

1. Mayo, Elton, 1933/1977, Ibid.
2. Iacocca, 1988, Ibid., pg 167.
3. Original author unknown, although this has been quoted many times throughout the twentieth century.

The Transition to HPT: Underlying Dynamics

Even a thought, even a possibility can shatter us and transform us.
—*Nietzsche*

The single greatest criterion for a successful HPT effort is the process of *transition* from a typical team to High Performance. Understanding and supporting this unique transition process is a critical key to developing successful High Performance teams.

In some cases, the transition process occurs naturally in the routine course of their work and interrelationships. For these teams, High Performance becomes a natural extension of their own growth. These teams may not even be aware that they have transitioned; they simply have dramatically improved results, working environment, and employee morale. Unfortunately, these teams are very rare, as most organizational environments are detrimental to "natural" HPT development.

For all other teams, the transition to HPT does not occur naturally; a deliberate external shift (or *intervention*) is required to effect the transition. When these interventions are provided in a context of strategic business change, HPT transition can be very rapid and effective, often being completed in a matter of weeks and months.

To be successful, interventions require a comprehensive understanding of the dynamics of the HPT transition process. These dynamics encompass all key stakeholders of the HPT effort, but are primarily focused on the HPT leader and team members as individuals, and the HPT team as a whole.

Within a successful HPT effort, interventions are simultaneously directed at individual stakeholders, the team as a whole, and the organizational environment. The interventions themselves may take widely varying forms. The interactivity of these interventions typically result in a unique set of interventions for each HPT effort. Because these dynamics change throughout the HPT transition and are different for each HPT effort, successful HPT efforts typically require an experienced HPT practitioner to support the transition. The successful practitioner understands the multiple dimensions of change and is able to design and apply appropriate interventions. As will be seen, however, there may be several levels of practitioners supporting different phases of the HPT transition.

To understand the transition process and the interventions that can catalyze and accelerate its development, it is helpful to review models of individual and group development within HPTs. It should always be noted that these simplistic developmental models are for illustration only; in practice, individuals and teams may change from category to category, skip entire phases, and even exhibit the characteristics of more than one phase at a time. Overall, however, using these models as a general guide is helpful in understanding the transition of traditional groups to High Performance Teams.

To understand the HPT transition process, three key models are included: individual transition, team development, and intervention depth. *Individual transition* is the normal progression of individuals as they shift their perspective; *team development* is the progression of overall team characteristics and behavior; and *intervention depth* is the level of intervention required to effect a High Performance transition. Each of these is reviewed in detail.

Individual Transition

Be not afraid of greatness; some are born great,
some achieve greatness, and some have greatness thrust upon them.
—*Shakespeare*, Twelfth Night

There are many models of personal development and growth. For the purpose of understanding HPT development, however, a simplified model of internal transition is helpful for illustration. Though applicable to all key stakeholders, the focus of this model will be on the individual team member, participating in a team trying to become a High Performance Team.

Although each phase of individual transition is listed separately, this is not a linear process. Each phase does not automatically follow another; any or all may be present at any time. However, for simplicity, these phases are presented sequentially in their natural progression.

Ten phases of individual development are presented here. (See Figure 16-1.)

OBLIVION

The individual has no awareness of the business pressures on the organization, nor any "line of sight" to the business case for change. In this phase, the individual is disconnected from the strategic pressures and from the stresses that are experienced by the leaders.

It is important to note that oblivion does not equate to obliv*ious*; the individual may have many personal stressors and behavioral drivers. In

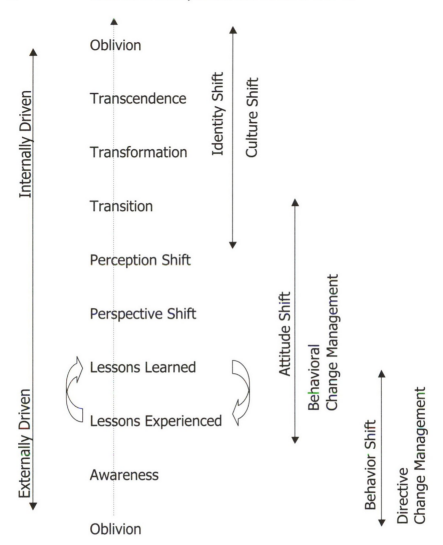

Figure 16-1 Phases of Individual Transition

most cases, however, the environmental and personal stressors are perceived as distinctly different from those identified by the organization. This is particularly true in highly polarized organizations such as those with high labor conflicts and those with executive misconduct.

Individuals in this developmental phase are often self-absorbed; if organizational issues are raised, they may be translated into exclusively personal issues. In one utility company, as management outlined the need for increased customer contact and information, individual team members

were focused on their increased workload and their ability to take breaks. There was little intersection between the organizational goals and the individuals' perceived needs.

In this phase, there is no significant pressure for change, either internally or externally.

AWARENESS

In this phase, the individual is made aware by events or circumstances that exert an impact on that individual. This action is the initial intervention for change. In the case of increased customer contact, just given the perceived workload increase is a triggering event.

During this phase, the individual is aware that something has impacted his or her environment. In conventional change efforts, this impact takes the form of initial communication of the business need for change. In this case, it is only the initial communication itself, not the resulting behavioral change demands, that provides the awareness.

This is the first contact phase; the *context* of this intervention will help determine the individual's receptivity to change throughout the change process. In most successful HPT efforts, this contact is made deliberately with all key stakeholders, providing a context that demonstrates the connection between organizational change and individual growth. Without this *contextual connection*, however, the individual may perceive the initial contact to be invasive; internal resistance will increase significantly.

Most deliberate change efforts have some initial communication or organizational preparation phase. In these efforts, there is often a discrete, structured meeting or series of communication vehicles to "prepare employees for the major changes ahead." Though this is more effective than not communicating with key stakeholders, without *contextual connection*, individuals often perceive any change announcement as an imposition on their own workday.

Successful HPT efforts deliberately design the initial contact intervention to provide a contextual connection for all key stakeholders in general and team members in particular. By communicating the need for business change in both organizational and individual contexts, and ultimately allowing the individuals to define their own individual context within the organizational framework, the transition to High Performance is significantly easier and faster.

LESSONS EXPERIENCED

In this intervention phase, the individual directly experiences the *impact* of the pressure for change. In the customer contact example, the employ-

ees may experience the need for change as soon as they have contact with irate customers. Their jobs are directly impacted by the customers' demand for time, attention, and service. Even when the individuals decline to provide those services, the customers have directly affected the individuals' workday.

In most change efforts, however, the impact of change pressure comes from management and not from outside the organization. In these traditional change programs, managers and supervisors may describe the organizational needs for change and promise negative consequences if changes do not occur. In most cases, these negative consequences are specific to the individual, such as bonus penalties, demotion, and even possible termination. Similarly, positive consequences are often promised for project success, such as promotion or bonus pay. In these cases, the connection between the organizational pressures for change and the individual impact are primarily through the manager or supervisor; the employee rarely experiences the organizational need for change on a personal basis.

This is a significant issue where distrust between management and employees already exists. In these cases, managers may become very frustrated in the employees' lack of apparent concern for the company, and employees come to believe that "management wants to take it out on employees." This quickly becomes a self-reinforcing perspective.

In successful HPT efforts, however, the individuals experience the need for change from a line of sight to the original organizational pressures. This is a critical element in building trust and providing a framework for change that integrates both organizational and individual needs.

For a defense electronics manufacturer, the team met continually with the external customers who were receiving and evaluating the product. Some team members were able to travel to the customer's location and experience the customer's perspective firsthand, further projecting the organizational impact onto the individuals' experience. By designing the opportunity for the individual to *directly experience* the organizational pressure for change, motivation, desire, and understanding for permanent, effective change increased significantly.

Clearly, this direct experience is easier to facilitate when minimal technical understanding is required, such as customer interaction. In more technical areas, such as financial and cash-flow organizational pressures, it may appear that team members are inadequately prepared. In the most successful HPT efforts, all team leaders and members are provided the orientation and training to understand the need for change.

During this phase, the individual is directly experiencing the impact of change pressures—either positively or negatively—and wants change.

LESSONS LEARNED

In this phase, the individual has experienced the pressure for change, often numerous times, and changes behavior to effect that change.

In its simplest form, this often occurs in *Directive Change Management* (see chapter 8) involving a behavioral change on the part of the employee. In this change strategy, the leader requires behavioral alignment and uses direct consequences as the means to obtain that alignment.

In many cases, that alignment occurs rapidly and superficially. At Scott Paper, Dunlap needed an alignment of employee behaviors that matched his need for increased productivity.[1] Employees were directed to increase output, minimize loitering, and improve productivity, else they would be terminated. Employees quickly realized the need to increase their individual output, often at the expense of organizational output, and became adept at individual reporting. This had the impact of appearing to increase productivity; overall, however, the negative impact on employee motivation and customer value became major contributors to the company's breakup. Later, at Sunbeam, this process became notorious as a net deflator of company value.[2]

For individuals in this phase, "learning the lessons" serves to reduce or eliminate the immediate pressures for change whether or not those learnings are beneficial to the overall organization.

In successful HPT efforts, there is a deliberate effort to integrate the organizational pressures for change with the individual's need to alleviate personal impact. This integration offers the critical learning that individual and organizational advantage are not mutually exclusive.

For many individuals, the Lessons Learned phase is attained after numerous repetitions of the Lessons Experienced phase.[3]

Change Strategy: Directive Change Management and Its Impact on Individual Transition

Transition Phases: Oblivion through Lessons Learned

As a general grouping, the phases of Oblivion through Lessons Learned represent the phases most impacted by *Directive Change Management*. In this change strategy, leaders attempt to align employees' behaviors through direct motivation (positively and negatively). Change pressures are externally induced, most often from management, and are focused on persuading the employees to act in a particular way. This strategy directly influences the employees' transition from Oblivion, through Awareness, to Lessons Experienced and Lessons Learned. However, due to significant resistance to change and corresponding resentments, it rarely motivates the employees to grow beyond those levels.

In Directive Change Management strategies, there is a significant organizational change impact on the individual, but the *context* of that impact is not defined. In these cases, particularly where there is repetitive impact without context, the individual's perspective shifts to self-centered, self-protective paradigm. Although this may be effective in the short term for the individual, it significantly increases resistance, reduces or eliminates integration into the organizational strategy, and often accelerates the very problem that triggered the need for change to begin with.

This is a major factor in the low long-term success rate of Directive Change Management strategies.

PERSPECTIVE SHIFT

As the individual experiences impact of change pressures as well as the behaviors that alleviate those pressures, his or her perspective shifts, as well. Clearly, life experiences drive most perspectives. The degree of perspective shift is often proportional to the degree of impact of the life experiences.

Informal surveys of HPT members[4] have indicated that some people believe that their perspective has shifted as a result of shift in job responsibilities. More have shifted after marriage. More than half the participants indicate that their perspectives permanently shifted after having children, and more than three quarters of those experiencing divorce strongly indicated that their long-term perspective had shifted significantly.

Within an organizational context, the individual perspective often shifts in proportion to the direct impact of change pressures. However, this shift is not necessarily a broadening of perspective; it can serve to increase the self-focus as well. For HPT efforts, the common differentiator is the context of the impact.

In the most successful HPT efforts, individuals are trained and oriented in many different areas, including customer service, budget analysis, and stakeholder concerns. Interaction with key groups is designed into the transition process, further increasing the perspective shift. Though this requires investment of time and resources early in the transition process, it significantly accelerates the transition period to High Performance. This follows the key HPT principle that *the "CEO perspective" is only effective when shared by everyone.* (See chapter 14.)

In one HPT effort involving logistics support, the individuals had maintained a strong belief of success and good performance. As part of the transition process, all team members met with and interacted with a representative group of internal customers to obtain feedback and per-

formance evaluation. The customers were candid and forceful about their experiences: The logistics group was extremely lacking in service, delivery, and quality. The customer consensus was that, given a choice, the logistics group would no longer be in service.

The team was so impacted by the interaction that they halted the HPT transition, regrouped, enrolled many additional stakeholders, and started over again. After several weeks of intense review and self-scrutiny, the team had shifted its perspective to a customer-centric viewpoint. Within six months, their customer approval rating was higher than ever before.

Perspective shift is a critical step in transition towards HPT. Without an internally shifted viewpoint, the individual is unable to truly understand differing opinions and experiences, necessary for fundamental changes in work. This is also the first phase in which only the individual can determine whether the shift has occurred. It is solely an *internal* process; it cannot be mandated by management.

PERCEPTION SHIFT

As individuals' perspectives shift, their physical *perception* shifts as well; they literally see the world differently. This is well documented from discrepancies in personal testimony of accidents to significant differences between cultures. In one classic example of perception shift, a student viewing the world through a reversing periscope actually shifted his perception to right side up; then reversed his perception again when the periscope was removed.

As individuals shift their perspective throughout the HPT transition, their actual perception of problems and solutions shifts as well. With appropriate intervention, this shift enables individuals to view nontraditional solutions to historic challenges. As Albert Einstein indicated,

> The world that we have made as a result of the level of thinking we have done thus far creates problems that we cannot solve at the same level that existed when we created them.[5]

This shift is critical to the HPTs' ability to find "breakthrough" solutions to traditional problems when other teams are unable to. Very simply, the HPTs are unable to view the problems in the same manner as before; they *cannot* view the same solutions as before.

A key HPT principle is that *creativity results from a shift in perspective* (see chapter 14). Creativity is often defined as "being different." Shifting perception provides a permanent shift in perspective; the teams become permanently "different" and highly creative.

Change Strategy: Behavioral Change Management and Its Impact on Individual Transition

Transition Phases: Lessons Experienced through Transition

As a generalized grouping, the phases of Lessons Experienced through Perception Shift are those most impacted by Behavioral Change Management. In this change strategy, management attempts to change employee attitudes, aligning employee motivation with the general business strategy of the organization. This focus is primarily externally driven, but begins to recognize internal processes within the employee. Typically, employee drive and motivation are increased, as well as some creative results. However, the impact is often transitory; as soon as the external influences are removed, employees commonly returned to their former perspectives and work methods.

In Behavioral Change Management and Culture Change strategies, the shift in individual perspective aligns with the organizational perspective. One of the differentiators between Behavioral Change Management and Culture Change is that the former attempts to force this alignment whereas the latter allows this to occur naturally and independently. This difference is significant in the development of successful HPTs.

TRANSITION

In this phase, the individual is literally changing inside. As a result of continuing lessons experienced, learned, and shifts in perspective and perception, the individual is shifting in the sense of self and identity.

Although this phase is not linear and may occur throughout the entire process, individuals in this phase realize that *something* is happening.

The key marker for this phase is that the individual *begins to believe* that change is occurring. Many team members begin to notice differences in their own behaviors and emotional responses: "I wouldn't have done that, a year ago!" Commonly, team members remark that their significant others "say I'm different."

As individuals' sense of self changes, their own identity begins to shift. As each individual's identity shifts, so must the *group sense of identity*. This is the critical precursor to *culture shift*.

Just as individuals' creativity must shift with a change in perception, so must individuals' working relationships with others shift with their change in identity. This shift in relationships between team members becomes the fundamental *team* creation of High Performance.

This Transition phase has impact on many different aspects: on the individual, on the team, and on the work. Individually, the shift in identity is profound; emotional reactions, behavior, and perception are shifted.

Between team members, relationships are different and deep; trust is dramatically increased and value is placed on commitment more than on contract. Significantly for HPT efforts, each individual's relationship to the *work itself* is also fundamentally shifted. These combine to result in a dramatic shift in how work is performed, how challenges are addressed and overcome, and how much drive, commitment, and motivation are brought forward.

"Breakthrough" results are a natural consequence of these changes.

Without appropriate intervention and alignment with organizational change pressures, however, the natural tendency of the "new" team is to create self-fulfilling, self-protective mechanisms that serve only the team. This is the primary cause of "runaway empowerment" and "entitlement" issues that doomed early HPT efforts. By ensuring that the team members include organizational issues and challenges and by including the "CEO perspective" throughout the intervention process, the team members' own transition *can include the needs of the organization*.

In Behavioral Change Management, there is a strong attempt to guide employees to the correct attitude. This includes an underlying assumption that without being shown what the proper attitudes and values are, the employees will not be able to achieve them on their own. This is often self-limiting and transitory; these efforts become programs that change as soon as the next program has management focus. When applied to HPT efforts, inappropriate interventions are sometimes used to drive the HPT toward specific conclusions, relationships, and attitudes. Most of these efforts do not achieve High Performance.

During the Transition phase, individuals often shift back and forth between old and new perspectives. Providing an emotionally safe environment for individuals to try out their new perspective without consequence often accelerates the change process.

TRANSFORMATION

In the Transformation phase, the individual has permanently changed his or her self. There has been a fundamental shift in identity; as a result, attitudes, behaviors, and relationships are fundamentally shifted.

With successful HPT efforts, this transformation has occurred with an understanding and appreciation of organizational needs and pressures. Organizational and individual needs are aligned and integrated, but *not* the same. Team members have achieved the realization that their own personal goals and needs can be met, along with the meeting (and exceeding) of organizational goals. Individuals have realized that creativity, enjoyment, and fulfillment are not antithetical to organizational constraints.

This phase is significantly reinforcing to the individual and to the team. On the individual level, achievements seem "easy" and workload seems "lighter than ever." From a team perspective, there is often a sense of euphoria and invulnerability during this phase. Continual interaction and integration with key (external) stakeholder groups can help ground the individuals' creative energy.

TRANSCENDENCE

In the Transcendence phase, the individual has fully internalized and accepted the change in self. Original issues that once were perceived as insurmountable are not even perceived as issues anymore. Individuals are focused on future opportunities and future growth for themselves and for the organization.

During this phase, considerable positive energy is directed toward new products, new markets, and new ways to express creativity.

Very simply, the individual has transcended the original change pressures that drove him or her to the transition to begin with. Though there may be recognition that the pressures exist, the individual is personally disconnected from them.

Change Strategy: Culture Change and Its Impact on Individual Transition

Transition Phases: Transition through Transcendence

The phases of Transition through Transcendence represent the phases most affected by Culture Change. By definition, the group identity is changed as the individuals' identity is shifted. The most successful change efforts are focused in these areas, providing long-term, breakthrough change. In this strategy, the drivers for change are *internal* to each individual; organizational intervention is limited to providing an accessible environment and the opportunity for self-change. In practice, this is significantly different from other change strategies.

OBLIVION

In this phase, the individual is so removed from the original change pressures that she or he becomes insensitive to it. This may create difficulties as the team members interact with key stakeholders who *are* still affected by those pressures.

At this level, entirely new change pressures are felt, and the cycle of change begins again.

NOTES

1. Dunlap, Albert, 1996, Ibid.

2. SEC Litigation releases 17001, May 15, 2001 and 17710, September 4, 2002.

3. Bridges, William, *Transitions: Making Sense of Life's Changes*, Cambridge, MA: Persus Publishing, 1980, pg. 8.

4. Hanlan, Marc, informal data collection with HPT clients, 1990-2000, dozens of focus groups and group verbal feedback.

5. Einsten, Albert, attributed by numerous sources.

Team Development

O brave new world, That has such people in't!
>—*Shakespeare,* The Tempest

High Performance Teams achieve High Performance results. Externally, these teams are seen as "super-achievers" that are able to obtain breakthrough results, often on an order of magnitude, within a year. Internally, however, HPTs are fundamentally about the members' relationships between themselves and their relationship to the work they do.

Although the underlying dynamics of creating an HPT are based on individual team members' transition, there are also phases to the overall team's development (see Figure 17-1).

Some HPTs are created from scratch; the team members have not worked together before, have not performed the work before, and may not even have been in the same organization before. Most, however, have some legacy from either the work or each other, and have a de facto team mentality prior to the HPT effort.

To help the transition to HPT, *team* interventions are necessary as well as individual interventions. In this context, a model of the team's progression to High Performance is helpful. In practice, few teams quickly progress from one extreme to the other; most commonly, teams mature slowly along the spectrum of change.

In designing HPT transitions and in developing the corresponding interventions, it is helpful to categorize the teams' initial placement on this development spectrum. In the case of ad hoc teams, individuals' pre-

| | Directive Change Mgmnt | | Behavioral Change Mgmnt | | | Culture Change |
	Calibration	Compliance	Consent	Commitment	Creativity	Culture Shift
Impact	You will be fired if you continue this behavior.	You will be the first in a layoff.	You meet expectations.	You work as hard as you can.	You find new ways to do work.	You are the best in the world.
Typical Behaviors	*Insubordinate *Policies ignored *Rebellion *Minimum performance	*Marginal performance *Passive resistance *Passive-Aggressive	*Task-focused *Gets all work done *Real-time focus *Moderate maintenance	*High energy *Work focus *Barrier elimination *Consistent approach	*Trial and error *Dead ends *Ideas challenged *Focus on design of work	*Breakthrough performance *Natural innovation *Interpersonal relationships
Interventions	*Direct consequences for actions *Immediate and consistent reaction	*Declaration *Accountability for behaviors *Authentic role modeling	*Goal accountability *Rewards *Intangible focus	*Strategic goals *Intangible goals *Individual interventions	*Goal setting *Increased responsibility for support *Shifting role of manager	*Entitlement prevention *Opportunity development *Renewal
Resources Required	*Monitoring *Preparation and planning	*Management coaching and training	*Team training *Management coaching	*Support group interaction *Key stakeholder involvement	*Benchmark info *Team and management coaching skills	*Initial support and information *Access to areas of opportunity

Figure 17-1 Phases of Team Development

conceptions and contextual connections will be major factors in the team's placement on the spectrum.

However, in times of urgent need for change, most teams are not formed ad hoc; they are re-formations of existing teams. The change pressures that trigger the need for significant change also bias a design for team re-formation rather than new team formation. In preparing for an HPT transition, preliminary assessment of a team's developmental progress helps to define an appropriate and effective intervention strategy.

WHAT IS A TEAM?

When reviewing the differing phases of team development, the basic question of team criteria is raised. When is a group of people a team? Are there practical limits to its size, composition, or purpose? How do the dynamics shift when these factors are considered? Significantly for HPT efforts attempting to change all or part of a company, can the HPT process be extended to an entire organization?

For the purpose of HPT development, *a team is defined as any group of people that have repetitive interaction for a common purpose.* In this definition, a team has no arbitrary boundaries of size or function. Rather, the *dynamics of interaction* of the team members defines the boundaries of the team. In successful HPT efforts, particularly those involving hundreds of employees, it is common for participants to consider themselves members of the overall team as well as members of subteams. For these purposes, as long as the *interactions* of the team members are similar in the overall team as they are in the subteam both groupings are considered teams.

Clearly, the nature of the teams' work may determine the size and function of the individuals' interaction and therefore the team. In some HPT efforts, however, the teams work hard to keep their interpersonal relationships the same between all members of their super- and subteams. In one electronics manufacturer, as the HPT effort increased significantly in size, the teams continually reorganized themselves to keep the subteams small, while creating interdependent "integration teams" to maintain daily interaction with all other members. In that instance, the dynamics of team development were applicable for individual workgroups in particular as well as for the overall effort.

As long as teams demonstrate the dynamics of interaction between their members, working teams may vary considerably in size, function, lifetime, and purpose. The team development phases can therefore be applied to a wide variety of environments, organizations, and enterprises.

Team Phase: Calibration

The direct method may be used for joining battle, but indirect methods will be needed in order to secure victory.

—SunTzu

In the Calibration phase, there is active resistance to authority, with continuous efforts to undermine organizational goals. The team has formed a bond that is very strong internally and very resistive externally.

Few ad hoc teams actually begin in this phase; it often requires years of negative experiences and inappropriate pressures to position a team in this category. However, once positioned in the Calibration phase, significant intervention is required to help the team move forward.

TYPICAL CALIBRATION BEHAVIORS

Rebellion

In the Calibration category, team behavior is characterized by consistent insubordination and visible behaviors of rebellion. This category is marked by outspoken individuals, verbal and written resistance to authority, and even refusal to perform assigned work. Though there may be a single, highly visible leader, most team members support the leader's active resistance and demonstrate considerable strength of belief even in private.

Typical team performance may include a single metric of satisfactory, or even outstanding, achievement with negative achievements in most other secondary performance dimensions.

In one service organization, a field team had been negatively impacted by recent corporate layoffs and downsizing. The leader of the team was strong-willed and protective of his team members. For the previous five years, the leader had consistently and verbally interpreted company directives in negative ways, and encouraged individuals' complaints and acting-out behaviors. Dysfunctional behavior within the team was disruptive and occasionally violent. The team developed a strong "siege mentality" and was characteristically unresponsive to the company's change programs. Some assigned work was simply refused.

Minimum Performance

At the same time, the "core work" performance of the team just described was good, even exemplary at times. This was interpreted by company managers as being "the reason why nothing could be done with the team." Managers attempted to change the team's behavior but were unwilling to set consequences for continuing the behaviors. Negative behaviors worsened.

EFFECTIVE CALIBRATION INTERVENTIONS

Intervention: Consequences

For teams in the Calibration category, firm management response and consistent boundaries are an appropriate intervention. For teams to progress out of this phase, effective communication with the team as a whole, and with individuals in particular, needs to occur, with well-defined consequences for specific behaviors.

In a traditional organization, managers commonly respond to active resistance by exhibiting similar behavior: "If they are going to yell at me, I'm going to yell at them—they can't get away with that!" This often serves to worsen the team's entrenchment, not better it. In the heat of the moment, management response often reflects the negative behavior of the team.

By providing firm boundaries and consistent consequences for negative behaviors and actions, managers can help the team progress forward. Effective intervention in the Calibration phase usually includes: (1) the determination of consequences, (2) communication of the unacceptability of behavior and consequences for continuing that behavior, (3) monitoring of behaviors, and (4) activation of the predetermined consequence.

In the case of the field team described earlier, management was able to determine a consequence and communicated that to the team. Very simply, if the team's behavior did not change, the team would be disbanded and individuals would be responsible for their own actions. Although

some individuals did make significant progress and discontinued their disruptive behavior, most did not believe the threat and continued. The team was disbanded, and some individuals were terminated.

Intervention: Impact of Consequence

As an example of one intervention creating another, the impact of the team's consequences can be significant. In this intervention, other stakeholders are directly affected by the original intervention. This has the effect of echoing or *multiplying* the effectiveness of the original intervention.

In the case of the example team, the impact of the team's disbanding on other teams was considerable. One of the contributing factors in the original team's refusal to change behavior was their stated disbelief that the company would follow through on its threat. The company's history of previous threats not being implemented had reinforced the team's belief that the manager was ineffectual and impotent; they continued their active resistance.

Other teams that had demonstrated a tendency toward active rebellion were closely monitoring this team's progress. Once the original team had been disbanded and the manager had reinforced the consequences, other teams quickly reduced their resistance.

Intervention: Immediacy

It is important to note that it is not the fear of retribution or the intensity of consequence that forms the intervention; it is the *consistency* and *immediacy* between the stated consequence and the subsequent implementation of consequence that creates the intervention. In many organizations, managers depend upon generalized fear to achieve their objectives, rather than a defined set of expected behaviors and consequences. With this approach, managers often increase resistance rather than reduce it.

As will be seen in other categories of team development, Calibration is unique. The interventions required do not position a team for a rapid rise to creativity and High Performance. In most cases, the emotional scarring—for both team members and managers—is considerable and may require a significant period of time to heal and move forward. However, the consequences of not intervening in a team that requires Calibration are far worse.

In the context of High Performance Team transitions, there are some instances where Calibration teams are expected to become HPTs through a structured program; the HPT transition is seen as a magic approach to the problem. This is rarely successful, and interventions required for the Calibration team are generally antithetical to High Performance development.

One of the key learnings of early HPT efforts is that *HPTs are not for everyone; not every team can directly progress to High Performance.*

RESOURCES REQUIRED TO SUPPORT INTERVENTIONS

Significant resources are required to intervene in Calibration teams. Management focus and continuous performance and behavioral monitoring are critical. In most cases, obtaining senior management approval for the predefined consequences is the most difficult resource to obtain.

Monitoring

The most common interpretation of management monitoring is to review the performance of the team and to decide the consequence. In practice, however, close monitoring of the daily behaviors of the team members is required to determine the depth and breadth of the problem. It is necessary to evaluate each individual on the team, as well as the team as a whole, to determine whether the negative pressures are coming from a single individual or whether it is team-wide. Similarly, it is important to determine whether the negative pressures are unique to the single team, or whether there are organization-wide pressures that may cause this problem to reoccur throughout the organization. Dealing with teams in this phase requires considerable management time, support resources, and close daily monitoring to determine the extent of the underlying problem.

Preparation

Obtaining prior approval for consequences is often a challenge. Because *consistency* between words and actions is a critical intervention, it is important for the operational manager to obtain prior approval for any consequences that are given to the team. In many cases—particularly in larger, multifunctional organizations—this is the most difficult and time-consuming action required. This must be completed prior to the communication with the team.

Similarly, if the consequences include the potential disbanding or reassignment of individuals within the team, the logistics of reassignment need to be completed before the consequences are implemented.

In short, all preparation for potential consequences needs to be completed *prior* to communicating with the team so that it becomes the team's behavior that immediately triggers the consequences. This connection between negative team behavior and *immediate* consequence is the essence of the effective intervention.

Team Phase: Compliance

I shall follow without hesitation;
but even if I am disobedient and do not wish to,
I shall follow no less surely.

—Cleanthes

Compliance is the phase marked by *passive* resistance and is often prevalent in initial phases of Directive Change Management and many Status Quo organizations. In this phase, the team reluctantly goes along with organizational directives while maintaining covert resistance.

Teams in this category are often considered, "too good to fire, and too poor to hire." They are the first teams considered in downsizing efforts.

TYPICAL COMPLIANCE BEHAVIORS

Compliance teams typically strive to determine exactly where management has drawn the line between consequential and nonconsequential behavior. They spend considerable energy to stay "just over the line," trying to avoid direct consequences.

Passive Resistance

Passive resistance of Compliance teams is often marked by overt agreement and covert resistance. In public meetings, no resistance may be offered to new proposals, yet active resistance may be exhibited in private.

There is often a strong dichotomy between casually observed behavior and regular, daily activity. Compliance teams most often exhibit marginal performance in all minimum performance criteria; in fact, some teams display pride in their ability to "walk the line" and to "not give the company an ounce more than they deserve."

Passive-Aggressive

Teams in the Compliance phase commonly exhibit passive-aggressive behaviors, focusing on distracting issues and mildly disruptive behaviors. Unspoken demonstrations of personal power are also common, from body language to local allocation of resources. These teams typically require very high maintenance levels from management, and are often able to continue in this phase indefinitely.

EFFECTIVE COMPLIANCE INTERVENTIONS

Setting clear expectations, boundaries, and consequences is key to helping the Compliance team move forward. Although less urgent and dramatic than the Calibration team, the Compliance team requires firm communication and consequences, as well as rapid implementation of any positive or negative consequences.

Intervention: Declaration

For most Compliance teams, apparent agreement is easily visible and actual disagreement is hidden from management. For this reason, it is important to uncover and declare the hidden resistance. This intervention process varies with the nature of the resistance, but it often includes unannounced visits with the team, casual meetings with individuals in addition to the entire team, and increased stakeholder involvement and feedback. Developing several different paths of communication and feedback with the team is essential to developing a comprehensive intervention strategy.

Similarly, Compliance teams often demonstrate resistance through body language and nonverbals, rather than written or verbal communication. When this nonverbal communication is experienced, the manager can declare it by simply stating that he or she experienced that impact. Doing this on a continuing basis, from several different stakeholders who regularly interact with the team, helps the team to identify its own behaviors and to recognize that others perceive them as well.

Intervention: Behavior Accountability

Holding the Compliance team accountable for its own behaviors, as well as its traditional results, is also key to a successful intervention. Real-

time monitoring of behaviors will also provide the team with real-time feedback.

Intervention: Authentic Role Modeling

Unlike the Calibration team, however, the Compliance team is able to accept guidance on appropriate role models of behavior and actions. Negative consequences for negative behavior can be effective, but Compliance teams are also open to beginning to look for other ways of working and behaving. For this reason, manager and key stakeholder role-modeling of desirable behaviors and attitudes is important to the team's progress. Having both consequences for actions and role-modeling for positive impact is an important intervention.

Trust is often a broken component of the relationship between management and Compliance teams. Because this is difficult to repair quickly, management behaviors become critical. The *authenticity* of behavior demonstrated by managers is critically important when working with Compliance teams. It is often more important for the manager to be authentic in communicating with the team, even when that information is not considered good news, than to demonstrate artificiality.

RESOURCES REQUIRED
TO SUPPORT INTERVENTION

As with the Calibration phase, teams in the Compliance phase require continual monitoring, feedback, and support. Traditional performance metrics should be combined with behavioral feedback to provide a continuing basis for team evaluation. Key stakeholders who have routine contact with the team should be enrolled and coached to provide similar real-time feedback to the team. All these areas can be resource-intensive.

In many organizations, managers are unprepared or unskilled to provide effective feedback, particularly when dealing with nonverbal communication. Prior to beginning a Compliance intervention, managers should be trained to develop the skills to observe and provide feedback, as well as be self-aware of their own impacts.

In many cases, the Compliance team is considered marginal and assigned to a manager noted for discipline. Although this can be effective in keeping the team away from active resistance, it can actually *increase* the team's tendency for covert resistance and reduce long-term prospects for the team. Providing the manager with effective interpersonal skills training is an important pre-intervention resource.

Team Phase: Consent

Overcome 'em with yeses, undermine 'em with grins, agree 'em to death and destruction.

—*Ralph Ellison,* Invisible Man

In the Consent phase of team development, the team begins to define itself about the work to be done. Consent teams willingly perform the tasks assigned to them and focus on operational aspects of their work. Teams typically are concerned with the tasks associated with the work rather than overall goals. Teams are often rooted in the present and concerned with real-time issues and challenges, as they come up.

TYPICAL CONSENT BEHAVIORS

Real-Time Focus

Consent teams demonstrate a strong perspective "in the moment" for their work; they are often focused on the immediate task at hand. Issues that affect future work or overall goals are generally ignored by the Consent teams, unless those issues also directly impact the immediate tasks being performed.

Focused on Task

Being task-focused, Consent teams typically complete all the work assigned to them, often on a day-by-day basis. Although these teams generally do not try to covertly sabotage their work, neither do Consent teams demonstrate an eagerness for additional work.

Dissent within the team is often ignored by team members unless it directly affects the immediate work. Similarly, problems that may affect future work are also commonly ignored by Consent teams, often with the expectation that it is "someone else's job" and will be handled—or not— accordingly. Very simply, Consent teams typically have a very short radar of issues and problems; they are focused on the work at hand, and when they are done with that work, they are done.

Given the task focus, the team's manager is often asked to provide additional work for the team to perform at the conclusion of their present task. This continuing quest for work is commonly misinterpreted as being a team that is "always hungry for work," when in fact the team is exclusively focused on the present task. As a result, Consent teams require a moderate amount of maintenance attention by management.

Consent teams are commonly found in worker and managerial levels in Status Quo and Directive Change Management organizations.

EFFECTIVE CONSENT INTERVENTIONS

Consent teams' progress is assisted by helping them to connect to aspects of their work that extend beyond the immediate work at hand, and by helping them to integrate with key stakeholder groups.

Intervention: Goal Accountability

Transitioning the team to *goal* and *project* orientation and accountability, from a task focus, can help the Consent team to appreciate medium- and long-term issues. The most effective transitions are those that are gradually introduced over a period of several months. For example, involving team members in weekly, then monthly, planning exercises can help them to appreciate many of the support issues necessary to proper work completion. Similarly, having team members attend internal or external suppliers' meetings—or even become part of a supplier team—can make for a dramatic increase in the individual's awareness horizon.

It is important to keep the team accountable for its short-term task completion, else the team may shift from an exclusively short-term focus to an exclusively long-term focus. By providing an *integration* of both task and projects necessary to complete an overarching goal, the team can be encouraged to succeed at both task and goal. This intervention may require additional training and orientation of team members to understand that integration.

Intervention: Rewards

Evaluating the team's reward system—both tangible and intangible— for its focus on integrating short- and medium-term goals can be an effec-

tive intervention. Many Consent teams' compensation systems actually reward a task focus and may discourage team members' consideration of external issues; changing the system is an effective intervention.

Intervention: Intangible Focus

As Consent teams are often focused on task issues, they commonly avoid *intangible* issues—particularly those issues that appear to create conflict. These teams actually leverage their task focus to avoid conflict on the team; this is particularly true with teams that have progressed from high-conflict phases of Calibration or Compliance. It is helpful for these teams to learn about *constructive conflict*, and appropriate ways to attend to conflicts that exist within and without the team. This often requires additional training and orientation in conflict management, as well as understanding that the team may be conflict-adverse due to traumatic effects of previous issues.

RESOURCES REQUIRED TO SUPPORT INTERVENTION

As most of the Consent interventions involve key stakeholders outside the team, as well as potential external support resources, this phase often requires considerable resources. Training and orientation support resources, as well as increased time and support by key stakeholder groups, should be planned, prepared, and allocated before the intervention is begun with the target team.

Though the Consent phase applies to any team anywhere in the organization, the most support is often required of managerial teams in the Consent phase. Because managerial teams often require more integration with external groups in their daily work, the stakeholder and training resources required to reorient the team are significantly increased. This resource requirement often impairs the Consent team's ability to progress forward.

BEHAVIOR/ACTIONS SHIFT: DIRECTIVE CHANGE MANAGEMENT

Just as the individual transition levels of Oblivion through Lessons Learned were directly impacted by Directive Change Management, so are the team phases of Compliance through Consent. Due to the strong boundary- and consequence-setting nature of Directive Change Management, that change strategy most directly impacts individuals in the early stages of transition and teams that are most resistant to change; it has the

most immediate effects and appears to offer the most immediate return. As seen by numerous case histories from academia to business, Directive Change Management often has short-term impact on productivity and apparent bottom-line results of the organization.

However, its strength is also its inherent limitation. That same short-term impact, and corresponding interventions that focus on behavior modification and consequences for variant behavior, serve to limit the individual and team focus to those specific behaviors. Consequently, teams typically do not progress beyond the levels they are required to achieve. Organizations that attempt to permanently achieve more than an incremental change are generally unable to do so with Directive Change Management strategies.

Team Phase: Commitment

> So they committed themselves to the will of God and resolved to proceed.
>
> —*William Bradford*, Of Plymouth Plantation

The teams in the Commitment phase of development are strongly attached to their work and may even sacrifice other demands on their time and energy for the sake of that work. Team members' energy is very highly focused on the team's specific jobs. Teams in this phase are typically highly praised, prized, and rewarded by the organization. For many organizations, Commitment teams are believed to be the zenith of development.

At the same time, innovation and major change appear to stymie the team in the Commitment phase; major barriers are considered insurmountable and some issues are believed to be impossible to overcome.

TYPICAL COMMITMENT BEHAVIORS

High Energy

Commitment teams are teams that have high energy—in their work, in their communication, and in their intent. Team members are constantly trying to complete the task and goal at hand, and ask for additional work. These team members ask for more work, and are often the first to volunteer for committees and ad hoc teams: They simply want to do as much as they can—for their manager, for their team, and for their organization.

Work Focus

Teams in the Commitment phase actively pursue more information about their work— ways to improve, historical benchmarking of traditional metrics, and information about the support functions necessary to do their work. They often make suggestions for process improvement and will aggressively work to reduce or eliminate barriers to getting their work done. They strive to improve their own historical benchmarks.

Barrier Elimination

Commitment teams are very effective at removing barriers to work that are straightforward and detail-oriented. In those cases where the business pressures for change can be alleviated by a great deal of work, Commitment teams excel at eliminating barriers. These barriers may include elimination of backlog, time-dependent report or grant request submission, or the coordination of many different suppliers into a cohesive plan execution. For these tangible, task-driven barriers where the deliverables are discrete and time-dependent, Commitment teams often outperform expectations.

Conversely, when business pressures are not quantifiable and involve intangibles and external factors, teams in the Commitment phase are unequipped to deal with the underlying challenges. These teams are often unable to deal with significant change pressures from customers, competitive pressures, and new requirements. Significant budget reductions, new products and new competitors, and changing customer demands are often difficult for Commitment teams to cope with.

Consistent Approach to Problems

A key marker for Commitment team members is their *intent* to find faster and better ways to do their work, though not changing their *fundamental perspective in how the work is done*. These teams often spend so much energy focused on their individual scope of work that they do not examine how their work fits into the overall organizational needs and strategic goals. Commitment teams have high energy and work hard to do their defined work to the best of their ability, but they are typically not able to generate the innovation and creativity required to make major changes in their work.

In short, Commitment teams are highly energetic, yet are limited in their overall ability to effect major change.

EFFECTIVE COMMITMENT INTERVENTIONS

Intervention: Strategic Goals

Commitment teams are often so focused on getting more work done that they have difficulty finding time to consider broader issues. They are

often so concerned with getting their work done that they lose sight of long-term issues and intangibles. Incorporating strategic goals in the team's performance metrics can help the team look at issues broader than their own traditional work.

Intervention: Intangible Goals

Similarly, developing expectations for intangible dimensions such as customer satisfaction and employee motivation can help the team to integrate their work-related energy with longer-term goals. Initially, these expectations can be expressed as specific metrics, such as customer and employee survey results, then expanded to include more comprehensive feedback and evaluation methods. Holding the team accountable and responsible for intangible results helps the team to move beyond the purely operational aspects of their work.

Intervention: Individual

Active intervention of individual transition is also important for the team's progression beyond the Commitment phase. Though the individuals' growth is key to all categories of team progression, it becomes critical in this phase. Without a change in perspective and perception on the part of the individual team members, the overall team will be unable to achieve the innovation and creativity necessary to move forward. Interventions that support individuals' own development have the most impact on the team overall.

Commonly, Commitment teams have the belief that because high energy levels and commitment to work have allowed them to progress this far, more energy and more commitment will allow them to progress further. For these teams, dramatically increased frustration and burnout occur as they discover that they cannot "brute force" creative and innovative answers. Their traditional arsenal of problem-solving techniques no longer works; they believe that their problems are just not solvable. This apparent low point is the point at which appropriate individual intervention is the most effective.

By helping individual team members shift their own perspectives, the resulting change in perception yields different approaches to traditional problems. This shift in problem solving commonly results in significant creativity and new challenges to old thinking. As will be seen in chapter 27, structured intervention for the entire team can leverage the growth of individual team members. These creative approaches are typically transient but serve to demonstrate that new thinking *is* possible and practical.

RESOURCES REQUIRED TO SUPPORT INTERVENTION

The greatest impediment to Commitment intervention often is the reluctance of the organization to change the energy level of the Commit-

ment teams. Inherently supporting the belief that further improvement and innovation are not possible from such a highly energized team, the organization often works to negate team interventions at this level. Managers may be discouraged from changing the team, while system-wide supports such as compensation systems remain geared to support high-energy, highly task-focused efforts. Developing a comprehensive intervention strategy that includes appropriate exceptions to self-limiting support systems is a key to helping the Commitment team move forward.

Team Phase: Creativity

That which is creative must create itself.

—*Keats*

Teams in the Creative phase often are trying many different things at the same time. To the casual outside observer, they may appear chaotic and disconnected from their "real" work. In fact, they are testing new ideas and trying to break down their old preconceptions about what is practical and what is not.

It should be noted that Creativity refers to the title of the team phase; it does not infer that creativity is limited to this phase. There exists differing levels of creativity in all phases of team development.

TYPICAL CREATIVITY BEHAVIORS

Trial and Error

Creativity teams are marked by a dramatic increase in their trial-and-error attempts in their daily work life and by their attempts to find unusual and nontraditional approaches to their work.

Dead Ends

Creativity teams typically have many more "dead ends" than teams in other phases, and many more "failed" trials than other teams. Creativity teams will often have significantly increased interaction with internal and external suppliers and customers, and begin to question long-held beliefs.

Ideas Challenged

Teams in the Creativity phase typically begin to exhibit a different type of intrateam conflict. Conflict in previous phases is commonly marked by a focus on interpersonal issues and power positioning. Conflict in the Creativity phase is marked by a challenge of ideas and assumptions. In this phase, team members begin to assert their own ideas and their own new perceptions about the problems and challenges facing the team.

Focus on Design of Work

Creativity teams have not lost their Commitment energy; it is simply redirected from the *execution* of work to the *design* of work. The energy that Commitment teams direct toward their jobs and volunteerism is now directed toward the exploration of new ways to perform that work. Similarly, Creativity team members are typically reviewing their own relationships with each other with the same energy with which they are reviewing the design of their work.

Shifting Relationships

During this phase, team members' relationships with each other are typically shifting from a *contract* relationship (where roles and responsibilities are specific and performance to expectations defines the success of the relationship) to a *trust* relationship (where the *intent* of each team member becomes the key relationship criterion).

Creativity teams typically have excellent performance in one or two key dimensions, and have ad hoc breakthroughs in some processes.

EFFECTIVE CREATIVITY INTERVENTIONS

Intervention: Focus on Overall Goals

Teams in the Creativity phase often experience considerable resistance from the external organization, particularly when the organization is focused on different priorities than the team. In times of urgent change, organizational focus is often on the execution and completion of work rather than on any time-consuming and unnecessary work design. This typically creates resentment and conflict in both directions: The organization may resent the apparently slower pace of the Creativity team, and the Creativity team may believe it has a unique charter.

Depending on the nature of change pressures and the charter for change provided to the team, appropriate intervention can help all key stakeholders. For the team, increasing interaction and integration with external

stakeholders can ease conflict, as well as ensure that the team stays focused on the traditional required performance metrics. The team should be providing routine reporting on its traditional progress to management and key stakeholders, demonstrating that it meets or exceeds its conventional requirements. External stakeholders can be enrolled in the team's creative process by participating as Subject Matter Experts and providing advice and suggestions at key points in the team's design work.

Internally, the Creative team can be assisted by consistent challenges to its own discoveries. Will the new approach solve the overall problem? How will the new idea be applied? What transition and change management issues will the team have to deal with in order to implement any new ideas? Helping the team to convert creative ideas into real-world solutions is a key to helping the team relate its own creative processes into business solutions. For the interventionist, it is a critical skill to be able to provide emotional support while challenging the application of new ideas.

During this phase, team members are often shared with other teams, providing a new perspective and new approach to doing work. This is often *not* the same type of work as the original team; the team member offers a new perspective of *how to approach work* rather than a new work process. The preparation and support of these team members become critical to changing the overall organization, moving forward.

Intervention: Shifting Role of Manager

Throughout the Creativity phase, the manager's role changes as well. Traditionally the manager provided tasks to be performed to the teams in the early phases of their development, expanding that to goal and project assignment for Consent and Commitment teams. During the Creativity phase, however, the manager's role changes as the team demonstrates its ability to manage its own goals and projects (it is critical that the manager's role change only *after* the team has demonstrated its ability to self-manage increasing aspects of its work). The manager's role becomes less of a work-assigning manager, and more of a coach who provides the basic strategy and resources to learn the skills. The team, however, retains the key accountability for performance and work management.

During this phase, the team and its key stakeholders are introduced to the basic concepts and dynamics of culture change. Depending on the business case for change and corresponding change strategy, this may include preparation for High Performance Teams and a roadmap for breakthrough results and relationships.

RESOURCES REQUIRED FOR INTERVENTION

As with the teams in the Commitment phase, Creativity teams most often require the support of the organization to move forward. This sup-

port is most effective when it is demonstrated through short-term resource allowance (e.g., time allowed to explore new ideas and creative approaches) and long-term integration with key stakeholders.

Providing appropriate support resources to the team, operational management, and key stakeholders is a key to helping the Creativity team move forward. This requires increasing knowledge and experience in team dynamics and real-world business requirements. When HPT transitions are considered, key HPT support resources are required to optimize this process.

Training and orientation of key stakeholders are required, and training and coaching of the team's operational management are critical. There may be a significant period of preparation prior to actual team intervention.

Resources required to support the Creative team may be significant at times; however, the bottom-line results of performance improvement typically return a very high return in a short period of time.

Team Phase:
Culture Change

By heaven methinks it were an easy leap to pluck bright honor from
the pale-fac'd moon.

—*Shakespeare,* King Henry IV

Teams in the Culture Change phase think, react, and interact very differently than other teams. They have a strong sense of team *identity* that consists of both organizational goals and individual needs. They often appear
chaotic from the outside, yet have a very defined sense of purpose and
relationship from the inside.

Culture Change teams regularly question fundamental assumptions
and do not accept the givens of traditional challenges and barriers. When
these teams are provided autonomy and accountability, they are often at
the forefront of new product development, new markets, and even new
organizations. When these teams are constrained by traditional requirements, Culture Change team members are often viewed as "problem
employees" and disruptive.

As the name implies, Culture Change team members have fundamentally shifted their own sense of self. Team members are commonly in the
Transition and Transformation stages of personal development.

HIGH PERFORMANCE TEAMS

High Performance Teams are a special type of Culture Change team that
has been formed with the integration of business needs. When individual
development is combined with the overall team's progress, both individ-

ual and team identities have significantly shifted—and *incorporated organizational goals into that shift*. This combination often results in breakthrough performance, high employee commitment and motivation, and dramatic increases in effectiveness.

TYPICAL CULTURE CHANGE BEHAVIORS

Breakthrough Performance

Properly supported, Culture Change teams consistently demonstrate breakthrough results and innovative approaches—even with "impossible" challenges. When provided with effective guidance and appropriate boundaries, these teams often provide order of magnitude improvements in all key performance dimensions. For these teams, breakthrough performance is not a single goal or short-term objective. In fact, these teams often do not view their performance as "breakthrough" at all; results become a natural consequence of the way they perform their work. Unlike traditional teams that may be intensely focused on specific goals and objectives, the Culture Change teams often focus on *how* they do their work and on their peer relationships; done properly, they know they will achieve significant improvements.

Natural Innovation

With teams in the Creative phase, innovation is a deliberate activity. Innovation and new thinking are a strong emphasis in these teams' efforts. With the Culture Change teams, however, innovation and creativity become a natural approach to the way in which they work; it is not a special effort.

In one aerospace company, several Culture Change teams had been created; they had made dramatic decreases in cost and improvements in productivity. When asked how they managed to come up with their innovations and new approaches, they said, "It just happened; it's just part of our job." When the teams' identity shifts and individuals' needs and desires are fulfilled as the teams' needs are fulfilled, innovation becomes second nature.

Interpersonal Working Relationships

Culture Change team members' relationships between themselves are often changed at a fundamental level. In one electronics manufacturing firm, work had been transferred from a closed plant, and weekly production rates had been steadily increasing throughout the year. As the team neared the end of the year, many had not used their vacation time and

were looking forward to a break. Others were concerned that, given the production demand, they would not be able to fully appreciate the end-of-year religious holidays. In a traditional environment, employee vacation schedules would have been determined by seniority and production would be shut down during specific holidays. Afterward, overtime and production pressure would traditionally be used to compensate for the downtime.

In this team, however, the dynamics were very different. When some Christian workers voiced their desire to take time off around Christmas, other Jewish workers offered to work for them as long as they would help out around Chanukah (the Christians soon learned that Chanukah is not a single day). As the holidays approached, and the team still seemed to be short of its production demand, Muslim workers offered to help out as long as they could be covered for Ramadan. This resulted in a rapid learning cycle as to the length of respective religious holidays. As it turned out, the team not only met its production demand, it exceeded it by a wide margin.

In a traditional environment, even with highly committed employees, this scenario would be highly improbable. In the case of this particular Culture Change team, however, it was a normal way of doing their daily work. The team *naturally integrates* the needs of the organization with the needs and desires of the individual team members.

Look Forward to Work

Culture Change teams are marked by an *enjoyment* of work. Although team members still have frustration and weariness about their work, they commonly look forward to coming to work. As one HPT team member said, "I don't have to set my alarm clock anymore." Another team member wanted to delay his intended retirement date so that he could continue working "to have fun." Team members experience the full range of normal emotions, but they are *energized* by the work itself and the fulfillment it provides. In a traditional team, members are often proud of their accomplishments and are fulfilled by the product or service they create. With Culture Change teams, however, most team members get energy from their working relationships.

Waiting List

Typically, many other employees want to join Culture Change teams. Though they often mistakenly attribute the team's success to tangible reasons ("they get all the good stuff"; "they get to choose their own hours"), external employees sense a fundamental difference and simply *want in*. In successful HPT efforts, the first teams are marked by a reluctance on

everyone's part to volunteer for something new. By the time these teams have reached the Culture Change phase, however, there is often a waiting list of employees wanting to join an HPT.

Evangelists

Culture Change teams typically have a strong drive to get the message out and to let other teams know about their successes. Whereas this can have a very positive effect on other teams, unconstrained it can also cause a great deal of resentment.

Low Maintenance

HPTs and other Culture Change teams typically require a moderate amount of initial attention by management. This is particularly true where their culture is dissimilar from the surrounding organization's culture. Once positioned appropriately, however, these teams are marked by their *lack* of need for managerial attention and resources. In the case of one electronics manufacturer implementing HPTs, this characteristic was embedded into the organizational design. Of approximately 1,000 workers, there were only 4 line managers and 150 technical support staff.

EFFECTIVE CULTURE CHANGE INTERVENTIONS

The most successful interventions with Culture Change teams are those that assist the team in *being* a Culture Change team. By definition, the team's identity is different than the other teams and stakeholders surrounding it; there is continuing pressure to "return to normal." Effective interventions for the Culture Change teams include both internal (team-based) and external (stakeholder-based) strategies.

Intervention: Entitlement

Internally, Culture Change teams are energized by their work and proud of their extraordinary performance. For some teams, particularly those in regular contact with traditional teams, performance pride can result in a sense of excessive entitlement: Team members want to leverage their new status for their own benefit. This may be reflected by unnecessary expenditures or special considerations for team members. At one electronics manufacturing plant, the team was tasked with designing its own workspace. Although a common task for successful teams, this team specified considerable "perqs" for itself, including gymnasium, whirlpools, personal fitness trainers, and more. Management had not pro-

vided effective guidance to the team; the amenities were built, and the team's sense of personal entitlement increased. Despite its earlier successes, the team had more focus on its personal desires than the work to be done, and performance degraded rapidly. The plant was later shut down due to poor performance.

By increasing individual and group accountability for results throughout the team's achievements, management can help the team to remember its original charter. Though team members are able to meet their own needs and enjoy the work, it is important to retain responsibility for those performance metrics—both tangible and intangible—that created the need for the team in the first place. For successful Culture Change teams, accountability is not a negative consequence; most often, it is the catalyst for celebration of good results and even failed results that led to good learnings. With appropriate intervention, Culture Change teams maintain the integration between individual, team, and organizational goals.

Intervention: Opportunity Development

As Culture Change teams improve their productivity, they often become bored with their "regular" work. The same intensity that led them to new discoveries in work processes and working relationships now serves to increase their dissatisfaction with "the easy way." By providing these teams with continuing *opportunity* challenges, individuals can channel their energy into new products, new markets, and new opportunities for growth and profitability. Typically, this is implemented by tasking individuals to be involved in new product teams or to review and analyze market opportunities. By involving team members in nontraditional roles and functions, they are able to focus their creative energies on positive opportunities. In one defense contracting team, the team was able to secure new business opportunities in areas that had been overlooked by traditional management: They obtained the order, delivered the products, and improved profitability. That is not unique for professional "new product" marketing teams, but this team was comprised of factory workers who wanted to increase sales.

Intervention: Beyond Benchmarks

In the Commitment and Creative phases, teams are often focused on benchmarks to evaluate their success; how they compare to their history or to other teams may provide motivation. With many Culture Change teams in general, and HPTs in particular, benchmarks can actually serve to limit the team's success. Typically provided a benchmark to meet or exceed, the Culture Change team may aggressively achieve the benchmarked goal and then *become complacent as soon as the goal is met*. In many

successful HPT efforts, the teams *only become as successful as their challenge goals*, despite the opportunity to further increase performance. An effective intervention is to help the team understand that they are not necessarily limited by benchmarks; they can go well beyond conventional benchmarks and create their own standards. This can be a significant issue when dealing with truly world-class teams: Their performance may be so advanced that they quickly define a "best-in-class" standard. Should this occur, the team may start to believe that they can go no further and revert to a comfort zone. Though advantageous for the organization—they have achieved "best in class"—this mentality can serve to diminish the very dynamics that helped the team to begin with. By working with the team to *define their own benchmarks* and to continually redefine those metrics, high performing Culture Change teams can continue to enjoy their work and achieve even higher levels of performance. This process of constant challenge, celebration, innovation, and creativity is critical to the health of the Culture Change team.

Intervention: Renewal

During this period of high performance, successful Culture Change teams often become bored with the same types of challenges, the same types of products and services, and the same team members. As appropriate to the overall change strategy of the organization, these teams can be tasked with their own Renewal phase: bringing new team members into their new culture, rotating existing members to other teams, and working to adapt the individual to the team and vice-versa. These dynamics become complicated as new team members bring an unshared perspective. However, the diversity in thought and perspective can help to re-energize the team in new ways. Similarly, ex-team members who are asked to rotate to non–Culture Change teams can help to energize new teams. In one manufacturing plant of 28 teams, ranging from Consent to Culture Change, this rotation resulted in a constantly changing, constantly renewing dynamic for team development.

Intervention: Management Selection and Preparation

From an external perspective, the Culture Change team can be assisted through the effective integration of their work with that of other teams. Increasing the communicating and integration responsibilities of team members, increasing the requirements of routine interaction with key stakeholders, and generally holding the Culture Change team responsible for its impact on the rest of the organization help both the team and the key stakeholders. Potential conflict between the Culture Change team and conventional teams may seem to be the most difficult area of integra-

tion, but *management acceptance and support* is typically the point of greatest conflict.

Many successful HPTs report to a succession of managers; the leaders who helped the teams transition to High Performance are often asked to repeat the success with other teams and other efforts. Consequently, the original HPTs are typically reassigned to conventional managers after their initial performance is achieved. Commonly, the new managers have inadequate training for the special circumstances of the HPT; in many cases, the new manager is tasked with leveraging the HPT into continuing levels of accountability and performance. These traditional managers then often rely on their well-used traditional techniques of consequence and motivation, with a severe impact on the HPT. In many cases, the HPT becomes confused, demoralized, and resentful.

In one manufacturing plant, Culture Change teams had been formed to lower costs and improve productivity. Despite initial successes, the plant was unable to achieve the increasing levels of productivity demanded by executive management. Traditional plant managers and production schedulers were brought in to "fix the teams," without adequate preparation or understanding of the process that had formed the teams. These managers demanded longer hours, more time on the assembly line, and higher "sweat levels" than the teams were used to. The teams were further instructed not to spend time on support activities; their motivation and spirit degraded quickly. This demotivation lowered their effective productivity, which in turn drove the managers to demand more—and so on. By the time the CEO made a plant visit, the team members wore black armbands to signify the loss of their dreams. Although productivity did ultimately improve, it never recovered to the original levels; today, the plant is effective, but only slightly above the norms for productivity and worker satisfaction.

In a similar instance, an HPT in the service industry had been transferred to a traditional supervisor with the intent of helping the supervisor learn from the team's new methods of performing work. The team's initial performance was outstanding and had already made significant improvements in productivity, cost reduction, and customer satisfaction. However, the traditional supervisor had a very clear opinion what constituted "real work" and what did not. When one team member was discovered in the office making copies of engineering documents, the supervisor's reaction was swift and unequivocal: Get back to work. This had an enormous impact on the team, resulting in considerable anger, resentment, and confusion. Only the rapid intervention of executive management and subsequent reassignment of the supervisor retained the team's overall performance.

This is not to infer that HPTs and Culture Change teams should not be supervised or challenged—just the opposite. However, the *method* of chal-

lenge and monitoring is very different from traditional teams. Culture Change teams should be held accountable for outcomes and performance; they are best given creative latitude in *how* they achieve those results. As with any team, of course, there are still practical and appropriate limits to the team's authority and autonomy; this is best specified in advance and in coordination with their responsible managers.

RESOURCES REQUIRED FOR INTERVENTION

Initial Support

In the initial stages of Culture Change teams, considerable orientation and training resources are often required as the teams expand their conventional sphere of influence and knowledge. As their investigations and issues expand beyond their traditional boundaries, these teams demonstrate a strong desire for information and training. Typical teams require orientation, training, and education to understand the new areas they review. This often requires considerable up-front resource allocation, particularly in technical areas such as finance and information systems. Support of Culture Change teams need only extend to the level required to perform the actual investigation; these teams often rely extensively on Subject Matter Experts (SMEs) for in-depth work. However, initial orientation is often required to ensure that the teams have sufficient knowledge to make appropriate decisions about their work.

Information Access

Along with significantly increased investigative scope, Culture Change teams require a great deal of information. The ability of these teams to effect change and make valid decisions is directly proportional to the depth and breadth of information they have access to. The most successful HPT efforts predetermine the level of information access that will be available; typically, this includes all information other than personnel-specific information. For many teams and organizations, this access itself is an intervention. Providing access to the appropriate information, and preparing the vehicles to transmit and store that information, can be a significant resource requirement.

Overall, Culture Change teams require unconventional resources initially, then are marked by dramatically *reduced* resource requirements as they begin to implement their ideas and culture. Typically, these teams become self-sufficient and self-managing within three to six months of initial work.

Transition to HPT: Process of Intervention

The school of hard knocks is an accelerated curriculum.

—Menander

For the most successful teams, the process of transition to High Performance is the greatest single criterion for success. Similarly, the process of *intervention* is the most significant enabler to achieving a successful transition. Appropriate intervention can accelerate a team's progress to High Performance rapidly and effectively. Conversely, inappropriate intervention may preclude the team from achieving High Performance as well as generate considerable resentment, anxiety, and chaos in the organization.

Because many different transitions are occurring at the same time— individual, team, and organizational—and because these transitions are typically interdependent, it is not practical to predefine a "cookbook" of intervention actions. At any given point during the HPT transition period, the appropriate intervention may vary dramatically depending upon the target, the environment, and the interventionist.

Though it is not practical to define all the potential intervention actions or the potential triggers for each intervention, it is helpful to review different *levels* of intervention. Throughout the HPT transition, interventions can be categorized by their primary *focus* (target) and the degree of *impact* of the invention on the target. For convenience, these types of intervention are labeled as *facilitator*, *coach*, and *catalyst* roles (Figures 24-1 and Figure 24-2). Though these are roles that the interventionist may implement, it is important to remember that these levels are actually functional levels that

Intervention Category	Role of Interventionist	Typical Intervention Levels	Primary Focus	Interventionist Key Success Factors
Facilitator	• Activity SME • Meeting facilitator • Traditional facilitator roles	• Meeting dynamics • Activity focus • Preliminary team diagnostics	• Activity participants • In the moment	• Activity knowledge and experience • Role separation between facilitator and leader
Coach	• Team development SME • Change Management SME • Traditional OD roles	• Team dynamics • Team growth through key phases • Leader coaching	• Team as a whole • Sponsoring Executive • Non-Sponsoring Executive • Team leader	• Team growth • Focus on process rather than outcome • Intervention implementation
Catalyst	• HP transition, culture change SME • Support individuals, key HPT stakeholders in design of environment that offers opportunity for fundamental, sustaining change	• Integration of team needs with rest of organization • Integration of team and individual • Relationship changes: peer, work	• Key stakeholders • Individuals in context of HPT transition • Facilitator and Coach support	• Able to synthesize unique, multilevel interventions • Business literacy • Effective boundary maintenance

Figure 24-1 Intervention Levels and Roles

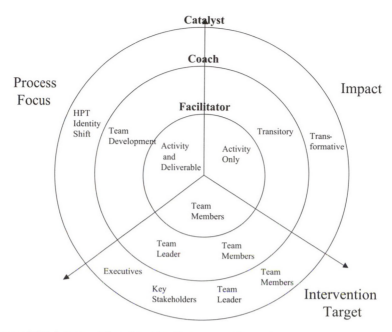

Figure 24-2 Intervention Levels: Focus and Impact

may be implemented by any individual at any time. For teams making a successful transition to High Performance, *all* these intervention levels are required.

These intervention levels are reviewed in detail in this section. As with the individual and team development models, this intervention model is simplified for illustration. In practice, there is a full spectrum of intervention strategies and implementation, appropriate to the specific HPT effort, and no level is mutually exclusive of another.

WHAT IS AN INTERVENTION?

Generally, an intervention is considered any act that "comes in or between so as to hinder or alter an action."[1] In the context of group behaviors and individual growth, this can be further expanded to

Any action or strategy designed to preclude, divert, or accelerate an otherwise natural direction or outcome.

These actions are typically designed to have a maximal impact with minimal interaction.

In working with teams, interventions often serve to preclude or divert outcomes (e.g., excessive conflict, inappropriate behaviors). In HPT

efforts, however, intervention is more often focused on the *acceleration* of natural developmental processes.

CHANGE STRATEGIES AS INTERVENTIONS

At the organizational level, change strategies are large-scale interventions designed as a response to change pressures. Directive Change Management, Behavioral Change Management, and Culture Change are the common intervention strategies that are used to reduce the organizational pressures for change.

In Status Quo (de facto) change strategies, intervention is constant yet covert. There is often considerable internal pressure to *avoid* changing direction. In many organizations, individuals work very hard to focus on tasks and issues that distract attention from the key change pressures. In Status Quo situations, intervention is clearly intended to divert a natural outcome, and is often initiated on an individual basis.

For many individuals, this intervention process is not conscious; it is often denied. Status Quo is not included as part of the spectrum of formal intervention strategies, yet many organizations exhibit its characteristic behaviors.

In Directive Change Management strategies, intervention is often very overt, with strong negative consequences for variant outcomes. The intervention is most often designed and implemented by the organizational leader, although some organizations utilize SMEs for strategy design.

For Behavioral Change Management strategies, intervention is often the result of considerable design and development prior to implementation. Typically designed by a change management SME and implemented by management, BCM works to develop a series of actions and events that result in an aligned workforce.

For Culture Change strategies, including the most successful HPT efforts, however, intervention is fundamentally different. HPT intervention can be defined as

> the design and implementation of an environment that offers an accelerated opportunity for teams and individuals to change their identity in a way that integrates individual and organizational interests. This identity shift changes the team members' relationship to the work they do and the relationship between themselves.

Although HPT interventions have a great deal in common with conventional change management interventions, the differences are critical to a successful HPT effort. In the other strategies, a predetermined outcome is defined and interventions are typically developed to evoke a particular response (usually from the workforce). With HPT efforts, however, there is no specific, predefined result, other than achievement of specific business goals. The *culture*, behaviors, and actions are allowed to develop

independently within appropriate boundaries. This is critical to the development of new individual and team identities.

WHO IS THE INTERVENTIONIST?

In its simplest form, the interventionist is anyone who initiates an intervention. To be an effective HPT interventionist, however, requires an in-depth understanding of the dynamics occurring throughout the transition process. The effective interventionist is able to initiate a deliberate set of actions that help the HPT effort stay on its path toward High Performance and accelerate the time required to achieve High Performance. These intervention actions continuously occur throughout the overall HPT effort, and may be targeted to a specific individual or the effort as a whole.

In rare cases, effective HPT intervention is performed by the team leader or from within the team; this is the case with naturally occurring HPTs. For most successful HPT efforts, however, effective intervention requires support people who understand the transition process, have extensive experience in guiding successful teams, and who are able to maintain appropriate emotional and psychological boundaries.

From a practical perspective, it is often difficult to identify and retain expert HPT interventionists, particularly for sustained or organization-wide HPT efforts. For small HPT efforts, the interventionist function is typically performed by a single person acting as a consultant to the team. In larger efforts, interventions may be performed by many different people, in different roles, throughout the effort. Most successful efforts use a combination of internal and external consultants, in varying interventionist roles, to create a virtual support team.

As noted, the intervention levels of facilitator, coach, and catalyst are labeled as *roles*, rather than individuals. Because the requisite skillsets and expertise vary considerably between these levels, many HPT efforts segment the interventionist responsibilities. For example, the facilitator role may be filled by internal support staff, whereas the catalyst role may be filled by external consultants. This can be effective in staffing an overall HPT effort. However, it then becomes critically important to provide continuous *integration* and *coordination* between the different support individuals, else the interventions may become mutually exclusive and disruptive. For these HPT efforts, there is often significant preparation, training, orientation, and integration of the support staff required, before the onset of the actual HPT transition process.

The following chapters detail the roles of facilitator, coach, and catalyst.

NOTE

1. *American Heritage Dictionary*, Boston: Houghton Mifflin, 2000.

Intervention Level: Facilitator

And all the way, to guide their chime, With falling oars they kept the time.

—*Andrew Marvell*, Bermudas

The facilitator provides the routine activity interventions required to help the team stay focused on its appropriate activities. Unfacilitated teams often prefer to solve major issues and address the most significant opportunities, ignoring the practical day-to-day requirements of their work. The task-based focus of the facilitator not only helps the team to achieve its required deliverables; it also helps the team mature.

FACILITATOR INTERVENTION ROLE

For the most successful teams, the facilitator is present at all team meetings and activities. The facilitator is the SME for the specific activity and can offer advice and counsel to the team and its members throughout the activity.

As a "meeting facilitator," the facilitator is also present to provide traditional facilitator support, such as agenda, timekeeping, and record-keeping as appropriate. Typically, there is one facilitator for each team, sub-team, and ad hoc team. This role is most frequently filled by trained team members or organizational support staff.

TYPICAL FACILITATOR INTERVENTIONS

Meeting Dynamics

The facilitator assists the leader and team members in traditional meeting support. Conventionally, the facilitator performs traditional support functions, such as meeting preparation, agenda development, timekeeping, and record-keeping. In most HPT transitions, this support function is quickly transferred from the support person to team members. By transferring the *responsibility* for minor support needs as early as possible and increasing the team's responsibilities throughout the transition, the team's accountability is commensurate with its empowerment.

Activity Focus

As the activity SME, the facilitator provides expertise on the preparation, execution, and follow-up on each activity. With the diverse background of most HPT team members, there is often a considerable learning curve with most transition activities; the facilitator acts as an educator and SME for the specific activity. When this learning curve is combined with the many different activities that are integrated together in HPT Work Re/Designs, this is a significant responsibility for the facilitator.

The facilitator also provides feedback to the team regarding its pace and direction, given the timing needs of the activity. The effective facilitator does not force a given outcome; rather, the team is reminded of its activity deliverables, and the facilitator offers choices to the team for moving forward.

Preliminary Deliberation Analysis

The facilitator assists the team with its initial attempts at decision-making and organizational skills. From the initial meeting of the team members, the team as a whole begins to form itself around its decision-making process. The facilitator provides preliminary guidance and feedback to the team, particularly in its early stages where it is still practicing decision-making. This practice becomes very important in the later stages of Work Re/Design, as the team is typically called upon to make many decisions in short periods of time.

Preliminary Team Diagnosis

As the team's first line of support, the facilitator provides initial diagnosis and feedback of potentially critical issues for the team. The facilitator is trained to be observant for *diagnostic behaviors*: those "trigger" behaviors or events that may reflect a significant issue to the team or its members.

Depending upon the trigger, the facilitator may provide real-time feedback to the team, or simply refer the issue to a coach or catalyst for follow-up.

This becomes a critical skillset in identifying potential areas of conflict and pressure, particularly in highly stressful change efforts where individuals' jobs, careers, and futures are at stake.

FACILITATOR'S PRIMARY INTERVENTION FOCUS

Activity Participants

The primary focus of the facilitator is the team itself. Whether the team is the actual HPT operational team, a subteam, or an ad hoc group formed for a specific activity, the facilitator is focused on the people and task(s) at hand. This small-scale focus for the facilitator allows for attention to the activity, and how the team members will complete the activity.

"Real Time"

The facilitator is focused in the moment, staying in touch with the activity participants in a way that monitors and provides real-time feedback. Whether the feedback is related to activity variance, behavioral issues, or team-formation considerations, immediacy is a key to the feedback's effectiveness. When the facilitator is operating in real-time, the team is more able to relate to the point being made, and interventions are much more effective.

Similarly, the facilitator role-models attention to real-time detail for the team. For many teams faced with "impossible challenges" and breakthrough goals, maintaining a real-time task focus is important to the team's ultimate success.

FACILITATOR: KEY SUCCESS FACTORS

Activity Knowledge and Experience

Clearly, a complete understanding of the immediate activity is critical to the facilitator's success. The facilitator needs to be able to educate the team members in the specific activity and be able to monitor its progress to provide feedback and support to the team. In HPT transitions, it is also critical that the facilitator understand the *context* of the activity and how the activity's outputs are integrated into future activities and deliverables. For example, in the Work Re/Design examples shown later in this text (see chapter 35), the Process Mapping facilitator must understand not only the activity of Process Mapping, but also how the information will be

used, to help the team determine the appropriate level of detail required in the Process Mapping activity.

Role Separation

Given the facilitator's role as activity SME and responsibility for providing orientation and feedback to the team on the activity's progress, it is often easy to confuse the role of the facilitator and the leader. This is particularly cogent when the facilitator attends more team activities than the leader. Given the facilitator's activity knowledge and intervention responsibilities, boundaries between leader, team member, and facilitator are often confused.

The leader remains the person most accountable for results (this is transferred to the team as a whole as the HPT transition progresses) and the person who initially evaluates the team's efforts. Because this can appear similar to the facilitator's activity monitoring and guidance, key stakeholders may demonstrate role confusion.

In some HPT transition efforts, particularly those that involve many different teams under intense time pressure, leaders' meeting attendance is often limited. As a natural reaction, teams look toward the expert to substitute for the role of the leader. This dynamic can further confuse the boundary between leader and facilitator.

To be successful, the team members must take on the responsibility of the tasks at hand and be accountable to the team leader for their successful completion. The facilitator, acting as the activity SME, should be acting as the "activity consultant" to both team members and the team leader, but not take on the leader's roles and responsibilities.

In practice, this can be very difficult. By providing feedback mechanisms, such as daily review of dynamics and performance, peer-to-peer feedback, and regular check-ins with the team, all activity stakeholders can keep appropriate boundaries.

Intervention Level: Coach

Never doubt that a small group of people can change the world.
Indeed, it is the only thing that ever has.

—Margaret Mead

The coach provides the process expertise for team and leadership development, as well as interventions to assist in the general progress of the team. The coach provides the expertise in team development and change management; this role is often filled by Organizational Development internal or external consultants. Interventions provided at the coach level often include team exercises, executive coaching, and change management strategy development.

COACH INTERVENTION ROLE

Team Development SME

The coach understands the natural progression of the team from formation to maturation and attrition and is able to provide education and feedback to the team regarding this progression. The coach is able to educate the team and its key stakeholders about typical barriers and challenges and provide consulting to the team throughout this period. The coach works with the HPT effort leader to design and implement team development strategies throughout the transition.

Change Management SME

As an SME in change management strategies, the coach provides orientation and consulting services to the team and its key stakeholders on change management, communication, and integration issues. Knowledge of business processes, organizational development, and organizational behavior are key components of the coach's expertise.

Applying this background knowledge, the coach helps the team to design, develop, and implement its own strategies for working with the overall organization. For successful HPTs developing a change management plan integrated into their overall transition plan, the coach provides the support and guidance necessary for an effective plan.

Process Consultant

The coach provides key *process consultation* to the HPT team and its leader. By observing team behaviors and decisions and providing feedback on the process and impact, the coach can help the team to make deliberate decisions about its own development. By coaching the leader and providing individual feedback, the coach can significantly reduce the time and energy required for HPT transition.

TYPICAL COACH INTERVENTIONS

Team Dynamics

The coach assists the leader and team members in the design and execution of workshops and exercises designed to accelerate the team's normal development. Whereas the facilitator provides work-related activity support, the coach provides development-related support. This support is typically a combination of preplanned workshops and exercises, as well as ad hoc, real-time interventions.

For many HPT transitions, the coach also works with the leader and key stakeholders to design integration sessions with suppliers and customers. Before and during the session, the coach provides active support to all participants, providing process consulting throughout. Afterward, the coach works with key team members to help them assimilate and integrate the outcomes of the session.

Working with the team leader and team members to design a team development strategy, the coach supports the team's developmental progress. Throughout the team's routine work, the coach actively intervenes at key points to provide observation, feedback, and questions to the team in ways that aid the acceleration of team maturation.

Deliberation Analysis: The Process of Decision-Making

A major factor in HPT's eventual development of a unique identity is decision making. The process of making decisions is the most common expression of team identity throughout the HPT transition; as such, the integration and maturation of those involved in that process are critical.

As a team dynamics SME, the coach is able to provide education of basic decision-making alternatives, as well as provide real-time feedback and counsel to the leader and the team members. These alternatives offer the team a real-world set of options that can be used for varying needs and situations. The team's "tool box" for problem solving is enhanced by understanding and implementing different options.

At the same time, however, the team is actually practicing different models of its own identity. By "trying on" different decision models, the team is able to experience different sets of its own identity assumptions. The conflict that often accompanies those models becomes a transitioning experience in its own right.

The coach provides both the educational underpinning for decision making and offers feedback to the team as it practices different decision-making models.

Leader Coaching

The coach provides considerable support to the Sponsoring Executive, Non-Sponsoring Executive, and team leader throughout the HPT effort. Typically, this support is provided in individual counseling and coaching sessions, and are outlined next.

COACH'S PRIMARY INTERVENTION FOCUS

Team Leader Coaching

The coach works closely with team leaders to provide orientation and consultation about team development and the leaders' impact on that development. Aligned with strategic development planning, the coach educates the leaders about the team development process and its major components.

Working with the leaders on a routine basis and the team members on an ad hoc basis, the coach provides real-time feedback about key interactions and behaviors. For the leader, the coach provides appropriately timed feedback about the leader's impact on the team. For the team members, the coach provides real-time and general feedback about their peer-to-peer interactions. Though this feedback is most often in the context of team development, the coach also provides individual transition feedback as appropriate.

The role of the leader is one of the most critical aspects for successful HPT efforts. Many unsuccessful efforts include a leader who is uninvolved, uneducated about the HPT process, and disconnected from the team's development. Along with the catalyst, the coach provides a critical support role for the leader's functions and role throughout the HPT transition process.

HPT Sponsoring Executive

As a change management SME, the coach provides early planning and strategic support to the Sponsoring Executive. This becomes critical to the development of effective organizational goals and integration of the HPT effort into the organization itself. Establishing key performance expectations and integrating those into the overall strategic direction of the organization are critical to the HPT effort's success. The coach provides this planning and education support to the executive in particular and key stakeholders in general.

As with the team leader, the coach also provides counsel and feedback about the impact of the executive's actions and behaviors on the team. This may involve two-way consultation; not only does the executive impact the team, but HPTs often profoundly affect the executive. The coach can help both the team and the executive set an appropriate context for this impact.

Nonsponsoring Executive (NSE)

The NSE is often a senior manager in the organization, not directly associated with the HPT effort. As a key stakeholder, however, the NSE often has regular interaction with the HPT effort and with team members in particular. Because the HPTs follow a very different process than traditional teams, it can be very helpful to provide coaching and preparation to the NSE prior to extensive involvement. The coach provides this support.

Similarly, a team undergoing HPT transition is often unprepared for the NSE, particularly in "closed-shop" environments where there is little traditional interaction between organizational functions and levels. In conjunction with the team leader, the coach provides preparation and feedback for the team's interaction with the NSE to help set the appropriate context.

COACH: KEY SUCCESS FACTORS

Team Development Knowledge and Experience

As the team development SME, the coach must have experience and expertise in the natural progression of teams. Though this includes a solid

grounding in theoretical frameworks, it is imperative that the coach also has a working knowledge of effective individual and group interventions that help the team progress.

As part of this intervention design and implementation expertise, the coach also requires an expertise and comfort level in supporting the conflict that results. Supporting the team and involved stakeholders through the conflict is critical to the learnings and maturation that can occur.

A Focus on Process Rather Than Outcome

As with most effective process consulting, it is critical that the coach remain focused on the behavioral processes going on within the team, rather than on the outcomes per se. The coach needs to establish and maintain an effective boundary that does not encroach on the leader's accountability for outcomes and deliverables. This is a difficult challenge for many process consultants, even in traditional change efforts.

In the HPT transition process, it is more so: more challenging and more critical. The individuals' and team's development in an HPT effort are rapid and at times very intense. As part of the deliberate acceleration of normal processes, HPT transitions often have compressed maturation cycles and intense points of conflict. The coach must have a level of interaction and involvement that both monitors that progress and maintains a high level of trust. Simultaneously, the coach must not be perceived as a stakeholder in the process; to be perceived as such fundamentally shifts the process itself.

The effective coach maintains an appropriate balance between *participant connection* and *nonstakeholder consultant*. The actual level of connection and involvement will vary constantly, depending on the events, the team, the dynamics, and the coach. The experienced coach is aware of these factors and works to keep all in appropriate balance.

Intervention Implementation

As a key player in strategy and team development, the coach is often called upon to implement HPT interventions at key points in the HPT transition cycle. The ability to understand the intervention, support its implementation, and provide feedback on its effectiveness is an important skill set for the coach.

This is straightforward when working with predefined intervention exercises where all participants are expecting an experience that will offer new insights or perspectives. In these interventions, the coach has a preconceived role of interventionist that is implicitly accepted by all participants. For these workshops and exercises, the coach must be able to provide observations and feedback to all key stakeholders in a way that helps

them to shift their own perspective. This is often an expected part of the coach's role; it is often direct and straightforward.

However, many interventions occur ad hoc when it is not expected by the participants. Many key intervention points are "invisible" to the team, yet need to be recognized, supported, and acted upon by the coach. At these times, the coach needs to be effective in the intervening actions, even though the participants may not perceive a value in that intervention. In fact, for most HPT intervention activity in the early stages of transition, the teams perceive the intervention as a distraction at best and manipulation at worst. Some teams are so focused on their tasks at hand, they may not even perceive the initial intervention at all. These ad hoc intervention points are critical to an HPT's development, yet the coach typically encounters significant resistance to them.

The ability of the coach to gain trust, provide education, and be able to implement effective interventions—all at the same time—is critical to the success of the coach and of the team in transition.

Intervention Level: Catalyst

cat-a-lyst: a substance that modifies and increases the rate of a reaction without being consumed in the process
—*American Heritage Dictionary*

For many successful high performance team efforts, the catalyst function has been intuitive, provided by the leader or by experienced consultants on the basis of personal values and individual, sometimes idiosyncratic, experience. Many leaders and team members of successful HPTs refer to "doing what is right" and "being true to their beliefs." Subsequent attempts by other teams to replicate the original team's successes, however, often end in frustration and chaotic organization.

In the catalyst level, the interventions are deliberate, designed, and implemented in such a way that both individuals and the team as a whole are enabled and encouraged to make choices about their work, their relationships, and themselves. Typically, catalyst interventions are designed to work on several different levels at the same time (that is, individual transitions and team progress for multiple stakeholders, simultaneously).

By its nature, the catalyst level of intervention tends to be invisible to most key stakeholders, including the team leader and sponsoring executive. For most successful high performance team efforts, however, the catalyst interventions are mission critical to a successful transition to high performance.

CATALYST INTERVENTION ROLE

HPT Transition SME

The catalyst is the key SME for culture change and the overall HPT transition. Well grounded in both conceptual understanding and practical experience with the special circumstances of HPT transitions, the catalyst provides the support expertise for the transition itself.

The catalyst provides education and context for all phases of the HPT transition, from initial identification and preparation through implementation and renewal. Able to understand the individual transition, team development, and the multiple levels of intervention required for accelerated transition, the catalyst has a complete end-to-end knowledge of the transition process.

It is important to note that this process expertise is not limited to theoretical or conceptual models of HPT transition. The most successful HPT efforts are supported by catalysts who have a comprehensive understanding of the HPT transition, including academic, practical, experiential, and intuitive perspectives. The most successful catalysts are those who are able to build on their theoretical foundations with real-world HPT experiences (and vice-versa). As noted earlier in the Individual Transition and Team Development sections, HPT transition processes are highly nonlinear; each engagement is different. The most effective catalysts are those who are able to synthesize new transition designs for each engagement; this often requires a multidimensional approach and understanding.

Environmental Designer: Change Opportunity

The catalyst supports the sponsoring executive and the HPT team leader in the design, development, and implementation of an effective *environment* for change. In this sense, "environment" is the overall situation in which the team will undergo transition. Although this includes the traditional sense of physical environment (room, logistics, etc.), it also includes the team's interaction with stakeholders, access to information, orientation, and so on. The catalyst helps the leaders to design an overall environment that offers new ideas and new thinking to the team. The catalyst is able to help the leaders convert the environment into an intervention by itself.

As a culture change SME, the catalyst understands the need to allow teams to grow independently of a prescribed outcome, yet appropriately integrated with organizational needs and desires. Rather than attempt to predetermine the outcome, the catalyst designs environments and activities that help the team to make choices about its future and its identity. Although that criterion may appear trivial, it has a crit-

ical impact on the team's overall development. The catalyst understands the intervention requirements and provides support and guidance to the leaders accordingly.

As a business process SME, the catalyst understands the effective integration of organizational constraints and pressures and includes those factors in the environmental design. As the team makes design choices about its own future, it needs to recognize and integrate the needs of the organization that created it in the first place. The catalyst is able to support the team's integration of its own desires with those of the organization, in a way that does not prescribe an outcome or diminish the team's identity.

TYPICAL CATALYST INTERVENTIONS

By the very nature of the end-to-end process expertise of the catalyst, there is no formal set of interventions that catalysts perform. The catalyst designs and implements specific interventions both ad hoc and strategically planned in a way that helps the team make its transition. As a catalyst that is not directly part of the intervention, however, the actual implementation may involve many different stakeholders supported by the catalyst. For simplicity of illustration, "implementation" here is considered the support required to execute the intervention, not necessarily the person actually performing the intervention.

Integration of Team Needs and Desires
with Organizational Environment

The catalyst designs and implements interventions for the team, as does the coach. With the catalyst, however, the interventions are designed to help the team understand that it can integrate its own needs and desires with the actions and pressures of the organization that surrounds it. These interventions are *not* designed to force the team to integrate with the organization per se. Rather, they are designed to help the team *achieve a level of understanding of the opportunities and challenges* if they do decide to align with their organizational environment. The catalyst's intervention is designed to offer a *choice* to the team and its members about their alignment with the external culture.

This intervention can superficially appear identical to the coach's role of team development and may also appear superficially to support a strategy of behavioral change management. In fact, the differentiator is the issue of *intent* and *independence* of the team to form its own identity. Simple in concept, this is often difficult in practice as it often appears to run counter to the team's organizational charter. For many Sponsoring Executives attempting their initial HPT effort, the option of team choice is syn-

onymous with "giving the inmates the keys to the asylum"; it can be very difficult.

For this reason, successful intervention with the HPT leader and team members is often contingent upon successful preparation and intervention with the Sponsoring Executive. It is also the reason why the change pressures of the organization are often directly proportional to the readiness for HPT. Without the strong pressure for breakthrough change, executives and key stakeholders are often unwilling to grant teams the option of determining their own future. In practice, of course, *all* teams determine their own future; this realization is part of the paradigm shift for all stakeholders.

Some teams choose not to integrate with their surrounding organization; most of these teams fail to achieve their objectives and often result in significant conflict and chaos. It is critical, however, that the teams be offered a *true* choice in their own course, and that they *perceive* that choice. Without the element of choice, true identity shift is very difficult. The catalyst understands the difference and designs interventions accordingly— including the accountability and responsibility of team members who choose not to align with their organizational environment.

For the most successful HPT efforts, making a deliberate choice about their identity and the level of alignment with their surrounding organization drives a *unique interdependence* that characterizes High Performance Teams. For most teams, however, this process is invisible; teams are not aware of the conscious identity shifts and design decisions they make— particularly in the early phases of their transition. The catalyst designs and implements appropriate interventions to support this dynamic.

Integration of Team and Individual Desires, Needs, and Identity

The catalyst provides interventions for the team as a whole as well as individuals *at the same time*. Although the models of individual transition and team development have been presented separately in this text for simplicity of illustration, both the individual and the team progress in symbiosis with the other. The individual's beliefs and expressions of self clearly impact the team, and the team's progress and dynamics profoundly affect the individual. Neither can be separate from the other.

Consequently, effective intervention design requires an understanding of this symbiotic interdependence. The catalyst understands and operates within this framework, designing interventions that are able to affect *both* dynamics simultaneously. The most effective interventions are those that operate on *multiple intervention levels simultaneously*. The catalyst designs interventions that have simultaneous impact and interdependent outcomes.

For example, the catalyst may design an intervention for team development that includes role-playing on the part of different individuals. The overall team may have new experiences and learnings that help them progress, but individuals also experience an impact *unique to themselves*. The outcome dynamics of the overall team and the individual team members then interact as both entities are affected. This interaction, in turn, often creates its own intervention that further impacts the team and its members. The most effective interventions literally take on a life of their own as these impacts reverberate throughout the team.

This continuing intervention effect and its interaction with other interventions are one reason why the most effective interventions are intuitive and experiential. It is very difficult to quantitatively define the interactive effects in multiple nonlinear systems.

The most effective interventions are not linear; they are not able to be prescribed.

Identity Shift

As seen in the Individual Transition and Team Development models, a shift in identity is a common factor in developing breakthrough thinking and High Performance Teams. By definition, the catalyst is unable to directly change any individual or group sense of self. However, the catalyst is able to design and implement interventions that accelerate the process of self-knowledge, -expression, and -change.

The catalyst constantly monitors the *diagnostics* and *expression of identity* from individuals and from the team as a whole. As a natural consequence of interaction, all entities display evidence of their own identity; the effective catalyst is sensitive to this evidence and dynamically evaluates the corresponding shift in identity.

Through the design and implementation of effective interventions, the individuals and the team are more able to make the shift and become more aware of the shift in themselves. This dual dynamic is a natural outcome of the catalyst's interventions.

As the identity shift progresses in the team overall and in each individual, the drive and desire for change also progresses from the intervention to the team or individual. This is also a deliberate outcome of the catalyst's interventions.

Relationship with Peers, Relationship with Work

As the team shifts its group identity and individuals shift in their own self-awareness of self-identity, the relationship between peers and stakeholders must correspondingly change. The shift in peer-to-peer relationships is clearly visible in High Performance Teams. When viewed in con-

trast to typical teams, this shift is clearly visible, even to casual observers.

The catalyst in a successful HPT transition may provide interventions around peer interaction, but more frequently views peer interaction as an *outcome* of an identity-related intervention. The catalyst ensures that peer relationships shift as a result of identity shifts that are precipitated by identity-related interventions.

More significantly, the individuals'/team's relationship to their work is fundamentally shifted. As a result of identity shift, culture change and organizational integration, the individuals' *relationship to their work* is changed. Team members fundamentally view their work differently than other team members.

The effective catalyst helps to support and accelerate this shift *as an outcome of other interventions*. By focusing on interventions that support the shift in identity and culture, and the integration of the organizational needs and pressures, the catalyst is able to include the individuals' relationship to their work as a key outcome.

This relationship shift is essential for the creation of High Performance Teams.

As noted, there are many different interventions and many different levels of intervention that help to create and accelerate the transition to High Performance. Each of these interventions is further complicated by its interaction and interdependence with other interventions. The catalyst understands and operates within this context to design, develop, and implement those interventions.

CATALYST'S PRIMARY INTERVENTION FOCUS

The catalyst provides the most impactful interventions in the HPT transition; actual design and implementation of those interventions vary with each team and each individual within each team. Just as it is impractical to define the catalyst's typical interventions, it is also impractical to define primary intervention foci. For illustration, however, it is helpful to highlight some areas of focus.

Key Stakeholders

By the nature and scope of the catalyst's interventions, the catalyst's focus may include any individual or entity that interacts or affects the potential HPT. This shifts as the HPT transition progresses, but typically includes all key stakeholders at some point during the transition. It is important for the catalyst to have an underlying relationship with each key stakeholder in order to implement effective interventions.

Most catalyst interventions require some degree of trust between the catalyst and the stakeholder "target" group. In cases of organizational distrust and/or instances where the catalyst has not established trust with the stakeholder group, there may be considerable effort required *before* the actual intervention is practical. This trust building typically varies with the stakeholder group, yet may range from a simple introductory phase to a series of interventions designed to build trust and build an environment within which the actual intervention can be implemented.

Since the catalyst's overall objective is the effective transition of the core team to High Performance, the catalyst's focus will accordingly shift to those key stakeholders who most directly affect the team's progress during that phase of development. Accordingly, the catalyst will most typically focus on sponsoring executives during the initial phases, team individuals and team leaders through the Work Re/Design phases, and the team and external stakeholders during the implementation phases.

Individuals in Context of HPT Transition

The individuals comprising the local HPT effort are the key target of the catalyst's intervention. Typically, the HPT effort is team based; the success of the HPT transition is measured by the business successes and performance results of the teams. The catalyst's interventions are therefore most visible and most expected to be focused on the target teams.

Early in the team's transition, the catalyst's interventions are often anticipated and supported. The team *expects* the catalyst "to do something," and traditional interventions are anticipated, such as workshops, exercises, and the like. In inadequately prepared HPT efforts, there may even be resentment toward the catalyst when there is no visible intervention; the team expects the catalyst to transform the team into High Performance as the result of a few sessions.

In reality, the catalyst focuses on the individuals that comprise the team, both from an individual transition and overall team development perspective. As noted, the catalyst designs and implements interventions that support and accelerate the transition process on many different levels simultaneously.

Facilitator and Coach Support

In small HPT transitions, where the roles of facilitator, coach, and catalyst are fulfilled by a single person, the knowledge, experience, and expertise of the catalyst are extended to the other intervention roles. In this case, the roles are often blended together in a simultaneous intervention process. Rather than distinct actions and interventions, the "simultaneous interventionist" typically operates at the deeper levels of interven-

tion—that is, most interventions are performed at the catalyst role even while in the *apparent* role of facilitator and/or coach.

For most HPT efforts, however, the roles are differentiated by support personnel, and facilitator, coach, and catalyst roles are fulfilled by separate people. For these engagements, it is important to provide integration of interventions between the roles and ensure that the context of all interventions is aligned.

The catalyst is typically responsible for this intervention alignment, often providing both consulting and orientation to the facilitator and coach. As the HPT SME, the catalyst is responsible for ensuring that the interventions implemented by the facilitator and coach are effective and integrated with the overall HPT transition. In practice, this typically involves orientation, co-design of all interventions, and observation/feedback to the other roles by the catalyst.

This level of integration and alignment is critical to the acceleration of the HPT transition, particularly given the interdependence and interaction of interventions on the team, the team members, and key stakeholders. The catalyst supports not only the team but other interventionists as well.

CATALYST: KEY SUCCESS FACTORS

Able to Synthesize Unique Multilevel Interventions

As noted, the catalyst must be able to design and implement interventions on many simultaneous levels. The interactivity of the multiple levels further requires the catalyst to be able to synthesize interventions that complement each other. The ability of the catalyst to design, support, and implement multiple interventions is a critical skillset.

For many persons fulfilling the catalyst role, this process of synthesis is very nonlinear and intuitive—and may even be unconscious. When asked how they "thought to do that, right now," many successful catalysts reply, "It just felt right." Ergo, their own design process is not necessarily a deductive one. Many catalysts are only able to synthesize effective simultaneous, multilevel interventions when they operate on their intuitive level.

Whatever the internal process, the effective catalyst is able to design situations and activities that yield the opportunity for individuals and teams to shift their sense of self.

Single, Integrated Intervention Design

The most effective catalysts view *all* interventions as a single, integrated intervention that is designed to dynamically shift with the needs, desires, and identities of the team and its members. When properly implemented,

the "single" intervention process appears seamless; each interventionist is interdependent with the other(s). Some catalysts have referred to this synchronicity as a "choreographed" intervention process.

Dynamic Intervention Design

One of the fundamental keys to HPT transition is the underlying ability of the individuals and teams to define their own identity; making a *voluntary* shift in identity and culture is critical to transition success. Thus, interventions that are predesigned and preconfigured to achieve a specific outcome may be helpful as *templates* to actual intervention design and implementation, but they cannot *by themselves* provide the autonomy required by the team.

To be an effective intervention or series of interventions, the interventionist must have the ability to dynamically shift the intervention to best match the needs and progress of the individuals and team. The ability to "design on the fly" is critical to the intervention success of the catalyst. In practice, when interventions are instantaneously redesigned, it is critical to coordinate and integrate the resulting redesign with other interventionists. The most effective HPT efforts have a well-integrated team of interventionists who have established the working and trusting relationships between themselves to allow this dynamism to thrive.

Strong Organizational and Business Perspective

In theory, the interventionist need have no understanding or expertise in the client universe; indeed, as seen in the coach role, success depends upon the interventionist's focus on process over content. In practice, however, the effectiveness and applicability of intervention design depend heavily upon the catalyst's ability to understand the underlying business and organizational pressures that created the need for the HPT to begin with.

The catalyst needs to fully understand the *business need for change* and the subsequent *pressures for change* that are present in the organizational environment. These change pressures constitute the "crisis points" around which individual and group identities tend to form. Similarly, the organizational environment predefines the expectation of work that is required of the team. This environment, then, forms the *context* within which the team is expected to perform and the initial *relationship to work* that each member is expected to have. Having a firm understanding of this environment and its corresponding political, social, and economic pressures for change is critical to the development of successful interventions.

Interventions that do not take these factors into account are often ineffective; worse, they may drive outcomes that are perceived as dangerous by the organization and result in severe consequences for the team and its

members. This organizational naiveté can be disastrous in the catalyst's design of interventions.

The most effective catalysts are those who understand the real-world business needs and processes, integrate the political realities of the organization, and *still* help the team to develop its own identity and breakthrough thinking.

Effective Boundary Maintenance

Given this requirement for both facilitator and coach, it may seem redundant to list this for the catalyst; in fact, it is more critical for the catalyst than the other levels.

With the many different levels and interactivity of HPT interventions and the dynamic redesign of interventions throughout the transition process, maintaining effective emotional and psychological boundaries becomes "mission critical" for the catalyst. This is particularly true for those catalysts who create intuitive designs; without this grounding in self-identity, the catalyst may easily integrate her or his own desires and issues into those of the HPTs. As the principal HPT process designer, this is most critical for the catalyst.

Intervention: Putting the Pieces Together

> Synergy means behavior of whole systems unpredicted by the behavior of their parts.
>
> —*R. Buckminster Fuller*

As seen, the change processes of Individual Transition and Team Development are interdependent; each impacts the other. The progress of any individual, though different from that of the team, has considerable impact on the team. Similarly, the lack of individual progress may have a corresponding blocking impact on overall team development. Without external influence or intervention, it is common for individuals and teams to remain frozen in their respective developmental phases.

For most work teams, there is often a corresponding relationship between the stages of individual and team development. In a team comprised of individuals early in their Individual Transition, a corresponding early stage of Team Development is often found. Although not precluded, it can be very difficult for a Calibration or Compliance team to transition directly to a Culture Change stage of development.

As shown, for teams and individuals early in their transition process, a Directive Change Management strategy is most commonly employed to move the organization forward. In this context, the DCM strategy is an organizational intervention, with interventions generally limited to a focus on specific activities and actions. When applying the DCM strategy to teams and individuals, an organizational intervention level of facilitator intervention is typically utilized.

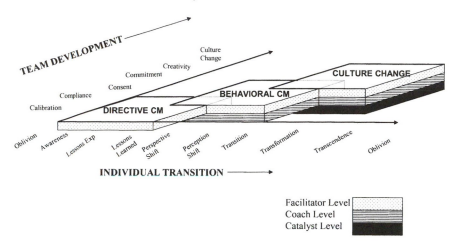

Figure 28-1 Integration: Transition, Development, and Intervention

Similarly, for those individuals and teams in their intermediate development stages, a Behavioral Change Management strategy is typically most effective. This strategy utilizes the organizational intervention levels of facilitator and coach.

Finally, for those teams and individuals in their mature development stages, a Culture Change strategy is effective, building upon all intervention levels: facilitator, coach, and catalyst.

Figure 28-1 shows the relationship between the developmental transition dimensions and the level(s) of intervention employed.

For any given team at any given point on their development, there may be a wide range of interventions and change strategies required to accelerate their transition to High Performance.

IV

The *What* of HPT:
A Template for High
Performance Teams

Transition Template

Man, unlike any other thing organic or inorganic in the universe,
grows beyond his work, walks up the stairs of his concepts, emerges
ahead of his accomplishments.

> —*John Steinbeck,* The Grapes of Wrath

TURNING CONCEPT INTO REALITY

Based on the history of successful and unsuccessful HPT efforts, it
remains to integrate all the diverse success factors into a consolidated,
comprehensive High Performance Team. Due to the highly interactive
and dynamic nature of the key success factors, each HPT effort is different; each requires a different set of interventions and support. *There is no
"cookbook" recipe that will provide a predetermined outcome.*

At the same time, reinventing an entirely new process from scratch for
each new HPT effort is unnecessary. In practice, it is possible to outline a
basic *template* of activities that are common to successful teams, and mod-
ify it as appropriate, for each individual HPT transition effort. This template can provide leaders, teams, interventionists, and other key stakeholders a starting plan for discussion and design.

This section provides that template.

A TEMPLATE FOR TRANSITION

Caveat: A Template Is Only a Template

This transition template is intended to offer a framework for only *one type*
of HPT transition. Just as HPTs discover many different approaches to

achieve their "impossible" goals, so are there many different ways to guide the transition of teams toward High Performance. *No two HPT efforts are the same*; to be effective, they *cannot* be. If this template is followed precisely, without adaptation to the particular pressures, circumstances, and needs of the High Performance Team, the HPT effort will most likely fail.

Activities to Create a Business Plan

The template is based around a series of *activities* that are performed with specific stakeholders, supported by an interventionist. These activities are briefly outlined, with corresponding deliverables listed as appropriate. These deliverables are often required later in the transition template; the process builds upon itself as the team progresses through the activities.

As a template, the duration and detail of each activity will vary considerably between HPT efforts. The process is intended to be flexible in accordance with the needs of the specific team. For some teams, a specific activity may require days of effort with considerable detail. For other teams, the same referenced activity may be only a 10-minute discussion.

Overall, the transition activities are built around the creation of an effective *business plan for action* that the team recommends to management for approval. Upon approval, the team is then responsible for the successful execution of that business plan.

This process, by itself, does *not* create or even suggest High Performance; in fact, many non-HPTs have used this process flow in their own business plan development. It does, however, help ensure that practical, measurable results are a natural outcome of the team's transition.

One of the key learnings for successful HPTs is that they are outwardly focused on the fundamental business criteria for success. By following a business plan process that addresses all business fundamentals, the HPT is clearly focused on business success.

Subject Matter Experts (SMEs)

For many activities, an SME is indicated. In these cases, it is recommended that someone with unique expertise in that area provide direct support to the team. For example, when working with social surveys and diagnostics, a social SME should be available to provide orientation and guidance on the appropriate use of social diagnostics and their interpretation. When financial areas are concerned, a financial SME should directly assist the team. As the team deals with involved technical and operational issues, there are often many different SMEs supporting the team. This will vary with the nature of the team's work and the complexity of their charter.

Mission-Critical Questions

For each major section of activity, there are key *"Go / No Go"* questions. Because the process is self-building and subsequent activities are dependent upon successful completion of the earlier activities, each of these should be answerable in the affirmative before proceeding to the next section. *If the questions cannot be answered in the affirmative, the transition process should be discontinued and rechartering of the effort considered.*

These "Go/No Go" questions offer an opportunity for intervention with the leader and the team. For some, simply asking these mission-critical questions is sufficient to catalyze individual self-awareness and prompt regular assessments of the team's development. For others, a negative answer to the questions offers the opportunity to deal with fundamental barriers and issues. The *least* effective use of these questions is to simply accept simple affirmative responses and to move on.

HPT Transition Is Dependent upon Intervention

As noted, effective transition to High Performance is dependent upon appropriate intervention. Whereas some of these interventions are activity dependent (i.e., they can be expected at given points in the template), most of the critical interventions are ad hoc. These ad hoc interventions are dependent upon the dynamics and interactions of individuals and the team, and may occur at any time throughout the transition; they are independent of any specific activity.

The actual interventions—and consequently, the success and pace of transition to High Performance—will vary considerably, depending upon the individuals, the team, and key stakeholders. Most of these interventions are ad hoc; many are "offline." *Only the activity-based interventions are listed in this template.*

TEMPLATE ACTIVITIES

Beginning with the original selection of HPT as a strategy, through Work Re/Design, to implemented results, there are seven major sections of work activity (referenced by applicable chapter).

1. *Strategy and Purpose (Chapter 30).* The executive defines and clarifies the initial change pressures on the organization.
2. *Readiness Assessment (31).* Expanding the case for change, increasing the organizational awareness of the change pressures, there is also an evaluation of the readiness for change for all key stakeholders.
3. *Leaders' Preparation (32).* Increases the leaders' awareness of the HPT transition process, and provides for planning, resource allocation, and other real-world preparation work.

4. *Data Collection (33)*. Gathers key data that will be used extensively in the Work Re/Design phase, including benchmarking and assessment instruments.
5. *Team Preparation (34)*. Establishes the team selection and preparation, as well as the final logistics preparations required for the Work Re/Design phase. Includes extensive contingency planning.
6. *Work Re/Design (35)*. The most intense and visible phase of the HPT transition, this phase develops the recommendations for change. It is often mistaken as the only critical phase of transition.
7. *Implementation (36)*. The actual work performance phase for the team. This includes templates for "full immersion" and "phased implementation" plans.

For planning convenience template calendars of activity are included (Figure 30-1, 35-1, 36-1, and 36-2).

Template: Strategy and Purpose

Only connect the prose and passion, and both will be exalted.

—E.M. Forster

The first set of activities identifies and clarifies the business change pressures that have caused the organization to consider High Performance in the first place. This section supports the *Common Crisis, Common Drive* culture change phase listed in chapter 10. It also defines and applies the Basic Value Imperative for the organization.

BUSINESS CASE: THE NEED FOR CHANGE

The reason for HPTs is to change the way things are done, to change the way people behave and their attitudes, and to change the tangible and intangible business results. If there is no driving need for those business results to change, there should be no HPT effort.

Typically, the need for stability and predictability overshadows any desire for change. To support a case for change, the executive needs to be very clear on the direction of the company and the values that will help motivate all stakeholders to go in that direction.

Activity: The need for change. Explore and define the leader's commitment to change and level of desire for that change. Questions: As the executive, do you really want your business results to change? Do you want them to change significantly? Are you willing to spend time, energy, and resources to change them?

Preparation

Sunday	Monday	Tuesday	Wednesday	Thursday	Friday	Saturday
CHAPTER — 30	1	2	31 — 3	4	31 — 5	6
EXECUTIVE DATA COLLECTION TEAM TEAM PREPARATION	CASE FOR CHANGE VISION DEFINITION		READINESS ASSESSMENT		INITIAL EXECUTIVE PREPARATION	
7	32, 33 — 8	32, 33 — 9	32, 33 — 10	11	32, 33 — 12	13
	DATA COLLECTION START TEAM LEADERS IDENTIFIED	BENCHMARKING START TECHNICAL HISTORY DATA COLLECTION START	EMPLOYEE & CULTURAL DATA COLLECTION START TEAM LEADERS NOTIFIED		BENCHMARKING COMPLETED TEAM LEADER PREPARATION	
14	33, 34 — 15	33 — 16	17	18	33 — 19	20
	VENDOR DATA COLLECTION START TEAM MEMBERS SELECTED	CUSTOMER DATA COLLECTION START			VENDOR DATA COLLECTION END TECHNICAL HISTORY COLLECTION END DATA REVIEW	
21	34 — 22	34 — 23	33, 34 — 24	25	33 — 26	27
	GOALS DEFINED SANDBOX DEFINED TEAM MEMBERS NOTIFIED	CUSTOMER PANEL IDENTIFIED & INVITED	CUSTOMER DATA COLLECTION END EMPLOYEE DATA COLLECTION END		FINAL DATA REPORT-OUT	
28	34 — 29	30	34 — 31	32	34 — 33	34
ORGANI	ZATIONAL COMMUNICATION TEAM MEMBER PREPARATION	WORK	RE/DESIGN PREPARATION FACILITIES PREPARATION	FI	NAL WORK RE/DESIGN PREPARATION	

Figure 30-1 Template Calendar: Preparation

Deliverable: Statement of desire for change

Typical intervention level: Catalyst

BUSINESS CHANGE DRIVERS

There are many drivers to change the business, many of which are obvious. Unfortunately, many drivers that undermine companies are initially invisible to the leaders. By detailing these drivers, teams are able to address them; however, the process of accepting them may be difficult.

Activity: Change pressures. Itemize the pressures that the company is presently undergoing; these are both tangible and intangible pressures that either (1) prevent the company from effectively accomplishing its

charter or (2) drive the company to go in directions with which it is not comfortable. Itemize the nature, frequency, and impact of these pressures on individuals, roles, and the company overall. These may range from political pressure in general to work and time pressures specifically.

Deliverable: Itemized list of pressures, including impact and frequency to each corresponding stakeholder.

Typical intervention level: Coach

Activity: Change constraints. What are the boundaries that preclude or restrain the company from change? There may be many levels of constraints, ranging from inconsequential to "showstoppers," from employees to federal regulations and laws. Itemize the specific, practical constraints that may prevent/preclude specific actions or recommendations, including boundaries set by the executive.

Deliverable: Itemized listing of constraints on the change effort, including scope and scale of constraint.

Typical intervention level: Coach

Activity: Change stakeholder. Who are the key stakeholders in the effort? Who most influences the final outcome? This list should be specific, by name if possible, and indicate typical role, change process role, influence and impact, and frequency of contact.

Facilitated deliverable: Itemized stakeholder map

Typical intervention level: Coach

SUCCESS METRICS

These metrics define the potential for success. Note that these are not necessarily the goals of the change effort, merely the dimensions/metrics that would define how success will be *measured* on a routine basis.

Activity: Customer value metrics. These metrics may include traditional dimensions as revenue and market share, but may also include key metrics as customer relationship, customer satisfaction, and perceived customer value.

Deliverable: Listing of key customer value metrics for success.

Typical intervention level: Facilitator, SME

SHAREHOLDER VALUE SUCCESS METRICS

These metrics typically include cost and returns on investment, but may also encompass intangible shareholder value metrics, such as goodwill, community respect, and fiduciary integrity.

The combination of shareholder value and operational (performance) value is often considered a measure of productivity (e.g., cost per unit); for some efforts, a productivity metric is used in addition to the overall shareholder value metric.

Deliverable: Listing of key shareholder value metrics for success

Typical intervention level: Facilitator, SME

Activity: Operational value success metrics. These metrics are related to the form/fit/function of the product or service. They may include quality, production levels, process cycle times, performance criteria, velocity, up/downtime, or other dimensions. Typically, this is directly related to the customer's acceptance criteria.

Deliverable: Listing of key operational metrics for success

Typical intervention level: Facilitator, SME

Activity: Employee value success metrics. These metrics may include culture and individual commitment, employee motivation and individual skillsets. These may range from traditional Human Resource metrics (e.g., demonstrable core competencies) to sociotechnical dimensions (normative stakeholder behaviors, value-based organization, etc.).

Deliverable: Listing of key social metrics for success

Typical intervention level: Facilitator, SME

Activity: Vision for changed organization. The *vision* for the new organization/product/service is a description of how things look, feel, and are perceived in the future lives of the stakeholders. What is the first impression the customer/employee/shareholder will have of the company? What will have been *fundamentally* changed about your company? What gets everyone up in the morning and want to work for or do business with you? What incites *passion*?

For some change efforts, the *behavior* of the executives is different than their stated beliefs. This is an important diagnostic; the catalyst should consider this a key indicator of potential underlying conflict. Where present, this dichotomy may be perceived by others as insincerity and hypocrisy; individual intervention and coaching are appropriate for their potential impact.

For diagnostic purposes, executive *behaviors* should be the key dimension, not just their expressed beliefs or commitment.

Deliverable: Description of the future

Typical intervention level: Catalyst

Deliverable: Description and displayed behaviors of how key stakeholders express their passion for the company in the future

Typical intervention level: Catalyst

KEY "GO / NO GO" PROGRESS TEST, STRATEGY AND PURPOSE

The sponsoring executive and all originating stakeholders should affirmatively answer the following:

- Is there a clear and expressed passion for significant change on the part of leadership?
- Is the Basic Value Imperative met?
- Once the goals and objectives are met, will the identified change pressures be eliminated or significantly reduced?

Template: Readiness Assessment

I think the necessity of being ready increases. Look to it.
—Abraham Lincoln,
Letter to Governor Curtin, 1861

Readiness Assessment is the second set of activities, designed to continue the Culture Change process of *Common Crisis, Common Drive* by identifying differing cultural groups and assessing the impact of change on each. All key stakeholders are included in the assessment.

As part of the stakeholder readiness assessment, an initial assessment is also made of key stakeholders' positions and progress along the HPT transition dimensions of team development and individual transition. These assessments will aid the interventionist in supporting the team as a whole and key stakeholders in particular.

Readiness Assessment is more than a simple, arbitrary test to determine whether the organization is ready for change. Because there are many dimensions to change and impacts of that change can range from trivial to life-changing, it is important to understand that response to change occurs across the entire spectrum. From the individual level to the overall organization, the ease of implementation will be proportional to the flexibility, resiliency, and motivation of the organization to change. There are no "right" or "wrong" answers to readiness, and no single test can ensure success or predict failure. However, it is possible to use information from several instruments to determine whether the readiness of the organization matches business change pressures and the executive's passion for change.

It is important to note that the assessment mechanisms *themselves* often represent an intervention; for some key stakeholders, the data gathering involved in the assessment process may be the first communication regarding the change. How the assessment instrument is selected, applied, interpreted, and communicated can be a powerful initial intervention by itself.

READINESS ASSESSMENT DIMENSIONS

The leader and key stakeholders (who may include potential members of the resulting HPT team) gather data, diagnose, and assess the readiness for change of all key stakeholders. This is performed along several dimensions.

Activity: Customer assessment. This is the readiness for change from the customers' perspective. Are they ready for significant change? Depending where they are on the "readiness" curve, they could become obstacles or even "showstoppers" to change implementation. Should they be incorporated into the process or simply communicated with afterward? Strategic readiness may drive tactical decisions moving forward in HPT development.

Deliverable: Customer readiness assessment

Typical intervention level: Coach, SME

Activity: Shareholder analysis. This reviews the readiness of the organizational owners for change, including significant change. Although this is labeled "shareholder," this assessment is made of all key stakeholders who act in lieu of, or in the fiduciary capacity of, the stockholders. In practice, this typically includes the sponsoring executive and any budgetary or policy groups or committees that may be required for ultimate resource approval.

Deliverable: Stockholder readiness assessment, including readiness for significant change

Typical intervention level: Coach, SME

Activity: Operational assessment. This assessment is focused on the technical aspects of change and the readiness and flexibility of infrastructure and support services to change. What is the level of documentation and technical history? Are regulatory or customer-approval cycles required for change? Are long vendor cycles required to be overcome? Has there been custom tooling or long-term capital investments that have to be recouped before significant change is practical? What is involved with making process and procedural changes to the product or service?

Deliverable: Readiness assessment for technical change readiness

Typical intervention level: Facilitator, SME

Activity: Employee assessment. This is typically perceived as the most significant barrier to change. Although this barrier may vary from effort to effort, it is important to provide an assessment of employees involved with the work. Using a combination of assessment instruments (e.g., survey, focus group, interview), this activity provides a readiness assessment and corresponding detailed review as appropriate. This includes orientation and training on differing assessment instruments as well as the application and interpretation.

Deliverable: Employee readiness assessment

Typical intervention level: Coach, SME

LEADER ASSESSMENT

Though the leader's role in successful HPTs changes throughout the transition cycle, as does that of the team members, it is important to remember that the process of developing HPTs begins with a *transition* from conventional teams. In the conventional change strategies of DCM and BCM, the leader is the focal point of change. Therefore, in the initial stages of the transition to HPT, even in a Culture Change strategy, the readiness of the leader is key to the success of the overall effort.

Leaders are often more resistant to change than the workforce, yet may be more difficult to quantify in that resistance. In many organizations, value-added analysis leads to a decrease in organizational levels, directly threatening the future of intermediate leaders. Many leaders intuitively understand this threat. When combined with a sense of loss of direct control, leaders often comprise the most resistant stakeholder group in the change effort. *It is mission-critical to assess all levels of leaders for readiness to change.*

Activity: Leaders' capacity to lead change. Based on interviews and surveys, the leaders' ability to lead change is assessed, as well as their flexibility and resiliency. This should be performed at all levels affected by the change, *particularly the levels affected during the Implementation phase* of HPT development.

Critical deliverable: Assessment of key stakeholder leaders' ability to lead change

Typical intervention level: Catalyst

Activity: Leaders' desire to lead change. Based upon interviews and surveys, assess leaders' desire for significant change, and the willingness to

make personal changes to accommodate system-wide change. As with the capacity, this should be performed at all levels. This assessment may be performed coincident with the capacity instrument(s).

Critical deliverable: Assessment of key stakeholder leadership's desire to change

Typical intervention level: Catalyst

BUSINESS CASE REFINEMENT

Given the data and assessments determined to this point, it now remains to update the business case for change, including the following key components. This sets up a standard "business plan" for the HPT development.

Activity: Issues and drivers. What are the key pressures and constraints to change? What are the top three reasons to consider change? On a relative scale, itemize the barriers and enablers to significant change.

Deliverable: Itemize key issues and drivers to/against change

Typical intervention level: Coach, SME

Activity: Opportunities for change. What are the key opportunities for change? What advantages come from increased market share/profitability/new products/services, and the like? What corporate values are enhanced through achievement of key change? To the greatest degree possible, itemize the pro forma quantitative results that could be expected to be obtained.

Deliverable: Itemize key opportunities, both tangible and intangible

Typical intervention level: Coach, SME

Activity: Approach / Time line for change effort. What is the basic strategy to obtain the change? What is the project plan to achieve the high-level change? What are the key external factors that need to be factored into the time line?

Deliverable: Itemize basic strategy and time line for overall change.

Typical intervention level: Coach, SME

Activity: Resources required. Given the requirements and strategy shown here, what resources (including external consulting resources) are required to obtain significant change?

Deliverable: Itemize key resources required for effort

Typical intervention level: Coach, SME

VALUE ASSESSMENT

A comparative analysis can now be made. Given all the flash assessment and surveys completed to this point, a comparison of the estimated cost to the projected impact should be made. This is the "value proposition" and can be expressed in ROI, CVA, ROA, shareholder value, or other common metric. For validity, this computation of value should be made to other options open to the leadership (e.g., mandated change, outsourced analysis/sourcing, elimination of product/market share).

This is a key point of business decision: Do the benefits outweigh the costs, and is this approach an appropriate one for the business?

On an individual level, this may also be a point of significant intervention. This provides the opportunity for the catalyst to help the executive compare her or his *personal values* with the perceived *organizational values*. In most cases, these are not aligned; however, typically it is more important that the executive understand the dichotomy, rather than try to arbitrarily change and align the value sets.

Deliverable: Cost versus impact matrix

Deliverable: Comparison of change alternatives

Typical intervention level: Catalyst, SME

KEY GO/NO GO PROGRESS TEST, READINESS ASSESSMENT

This is a mission-critical decision point. Given all the potential advantages of HPT development and all the attendant opportunities, is the organization ready/willing/able to go through the significant challenge of change to get there? Is it worth it?

Template: Leaders' Preparation

> Education makes a people easy to lead, but difficult to drive; easy to govern, but impossible to enslave.
>
> —*Henry Peter Brougham*

In the HPT context, a leader is much more than simply an authority in the organization. It refers to all those who take a leadership stance, who are followed by others in the organization, and who have strong influence over others. This may include those who are in high-level positions in the company, but also might include supervisors, work crew leaders, managers, union leaders/organizers, social coordinators, and even local politicians.

Leaders' Preparation is much more than simply arming the leaders with planning schedules and Work Re/Design agendas. For HPT efforts initiated from within conventional cultures and workplaces, it is axiomatic that the leaders' support is key to a successful effort. It is mission-critical that the leaders want change, want the HPT approach, and are passionate about success.

This third set of activities continues the *Forging a Common Drive* phase of Culture Change and simultaneously provides an initial platform for assessment and intervention along the Individual Transition dimension.

HPT PURPOSE

The leader must understand the fundamentals of the HPT effort's purpose and be able to passionately explain and influence others to that charter. The leader should be able to explain in detail and persuade others in the following areas.

Activity: Charter of effort. The charter is the *reason to exist* for the HPT effort. It provides clarity to the team for their purpose and the "burning platform" for change.

Deliverable: Draft charter for HPT effort—establishes scope, purpose, and background for the HPT

Typical intervention level: Coach

Activity: Outcome. The leaders are clear about what the outcomes—both tangible and intangible—look like and what the general timeline is. The key success metrics are itemized and prioritized (although only qualitatively at this time).

Deliverable: Key success outcomes, tangible and intangible

Typical intervention level: Coach

Activity: Expectations. Expectations are more than just the specific results of the HPT effort. Leaders may also have expectations of *how* the HPT transition is implemented, independent of the HPT goals or metrics. For example, leaders may set clear expectations for the team members as well as for themselves and their organization—what generally will happen by when—and generally by whom. These expectations may extend to personal expectations of learning and discovery as well as more formal expectations of goals and deliverables.

For many efforts, this also begins to establish intangible goals for the transition of HPT; for example, that the HPT may be the first example of new thinking for the organization as a whole, or that the HPT effort would become the model of new team design. In short, expectations can set the platform for *culture shift* even beyond the scope of the instant team.

This can be built upon the vision expressed earlier in the Vision for Changed Organization activity.

This activity also has the potential for a significant intervention in the leader's transitionss and support for Culture Change.

Deliverable: Leaders' expectations

Typical intervention level: Coach, Catalyst

Activity: Business case review. The leader reviews the overall business case developed in the earlier Business Case Refinement and Value Assessment for clarity around all opportunities and challenges associated with the effort.

This is more than a follow-up or simple check-in. This begins to set the pattern of *integrating* new discoveries and new assessments into previously defined documents. This is particularly important in conventional cultures, where baselined documents tend to be static and inviolate. By

practicing continual review, revision, and clarification of key platforms and perspectives, the leaders begin to experience the opportunities and challenges of dynamic documents. With appropriate practice and intervention, the leaders begin to experience a continual-design environment.

Deliverable: Business case review: Update and clarify

Typical intervention level: Coach

Critical Activity: Resource commitment. This provides the determination of scope and resourcing required to support the HPT development effort. Not only are the direct resources identified (the leadership and the team) but also the direct support resources (facilitators, SMEs, facilities, etc.) and indirect support resources (customers, vendors, key stakeholders, etc.). As appropriate to the resource and the role requested of the resource(s), invitations/assignments are made with appropriate lead times for the Preparation, Work Re/Design, and Implementation phases of the effort.

There is also a key decision to be made about the scope of the team that will be performing the Work Re/Design. The most successful efforts have ensured end-to-end HPT transition teams: The entire implementation team is involved from the beginning. Clearly that requires "front loading" of resources, although it also provides the most rapid rate of return. Some organizations, believing that they are unable to have those resources offline for a significant period, focus on a smaller design team that is tightly integrated with the implementation team. (See the Communication Team integration activity) (chapter 35, day 6).

Critical deliverable: Resource commitment is made for the full HPT development effort.

Typical intervention level: Coach, Catalyst, SME

Activity: Project management / calendar development. An effort-specific project plan is developed for the HPT effort. This minimally includes a project plan and key event calendar.

Deliverable: Project plan and key event calendar are developed for the project with defined goals, time lines, and responsibilities.

Typical intervention level: Coach

ORGANIZATIONAL PREPARATION

The capability and capacity of the organization to embrace and support the new thinking of the HPT effort will be critical to the effort's ability to make necessary changes in business, technical, and social aspects. Preparing the overall organization for this change is a critical component of this capability. This will be necessary from all levels of the organization.

Activity: Organizational communication. The leader needs to communicate the basic intent, purpose, and expectations of the effort to the organization, tailored to the specific needs/pains of the target audience(s).

Deliverable: Communication outline to the organization, itemizing key target populations and key stakeholders, with key messages itemized for each major group. This plan includes who will be responsible for communicating what to whom by when.

Typical intervention level: Coach, SME

Activity: Key leader socialization. Although key leaders may already have been informed through conventional means, it will be important to socialize the advantages and needs of the organization for change. The key leaders need the "soak time" that socialization provides to internalize this need and understand how the changes will help/hinder their present efforts. This is not a "sales pitch" designed to sell the key leadership; rather, it is an integrated, overall look at the impact of the HPT effort so that the leaders can understand how they will deal with the challenges and benefit from the opportunities that this effort presents.

Deliverable: Key leaders have the purpose and the basic approach of the HPT socialized from their peers and executive leadership.

Typical intervention level: Coach, Catalyst, SME

Activity: Key leader capacity increase. The capacity to deal with changes that may be highly impactful and ambiguous can be critical to the success of the effort. Working with the key leaders to increase their ability to deal with those challenges will be key to the effort. This is the implementation phase of the potential barriers to change, identified in the earlier Readiness Assessment for leaders.

Critical deliverable: Implementation of plan to increase capacity and capability for change identified in the Readiness Assessment

Typical intervention level: Coach, Catalyst

Activity: Key event. To effectively communicate that the HPT effort is fundamentally different from other typical projects, it is important to provide a key event that demonstrates the passion for change that the organization needs. This may be range from "town hall meetings" to symbolically powerful organizational changes, but it always represents a "stake in the ground" that leadership provides to demonstrate the importance of the effort.

This event should be impactful and symbolic, providing a strong message that something fundamental has shifted. This is typically the most

visible activity of the *Forging a Common Identity* phase, and it clearly evokes the *Common Crisis, Common Drive* triggering pressures or events.

Critical deliverable: Key event, planned and executed

Typical intervention level: Catalyst

KEY GO/NO GO ASSESSMENT OF LEADERS' PREPARATION

- Are the organizational leaders in full support of the HPT effort, and do they understand the challenges and opportunities of the effort as it relates to their area of responsibility in the organization?
- Are all key stakeholders ready to experience change?
- Are there any groups that may offer "showstopper" resistance to the HPT effort?

Template: Data Collection

Histories make men wise.

—*Sir Francis Bacon*

Data Collection, the fourth set of activities, is key to the success of the overall effort. On one level, it provides the data-based underpinning of the new thinking and new designs to come. Without this grounding in benchmarking and fact, it is easy for the effort to end up a complex mix of personal agendas, entrenched beliefs, and self-fulfilling prophecies. Though it is mission critical to recognize and deal with the intangible beliefs, it is just as mission critical to deal with the business realities of the situation. Data collection provides the basis for grounding and understanding of those realities.

On another level, the data collection becomes an important intervention for those collecting and receiving the data. For many HPT participants, these activities often represent the first time they have seen this type of (often sensitive) data and may be the first time they have interacted with the other key stakeholders.

This data collection process continues the *Forging a Common Identity* phase of Culture Change, as the stakeholders are initially exposed to considerably more data from considerably more sources than ever before.

BENCHMARKING

An important source of data, benchmarking is used to help the team achieve an appropriate perspective on their overall performance and the

challenges they face. When faced with major improvement challenges, many teams simply believe the goals to be impossible and lose incentive. For these teams, it is very helpful to compare the "impossible" goals against current and historical performance levels, as well as competitive levels. Most teams quickly discover that someone *else* is already achieving at "impossible" levels.

Activity: Competitive benchmark. Given the success metrics and vision defined earlier, data is collected from competitors across all key dimensions. Methods to obtain this data may range from literature/Internet search to actual site visits and interviews. Generally, the level of detail is determined by the time available and the level of detail defined in the success metrics.

Deliverable: Benchmarking analysis of current relative position across key success dimensions (usually safety, performance, cost, customer, employee, and cultural). This includes the sources shown next.

Typical intervention level: Facilitator, SME

Direct Competition

This specifically includes present competitors, against whom the company does business or against whom the company is regularly compared (such as in monopolies).

Industry-wide Competition

This includes similar products and services provided domestically and worldwide and provides key dimension information across the benchmark.

"Core Competency" Competition

This includes noncompany industries, but where the core competencies of the company are matched in other industries. For example, electric utilities may be compared against wired telecommunication companies, as the core competencies of each are directly compatible.

Activity: Historical benchmarking. This is generally the bulk of the data collection effort, as it often has the most impact on the organization. From an internal perspective, what are the historical (to present) data on key areas related the HPT effort?

While varying somewhat with the operational nature of the product/service, these benchmarks include the following areas of performance.

Critical deliverable: Data collection on the present product/service, including specifics on performance, safety, cost, customer, employee, and cultural areas

Typical intervention level: Coach

Operational Performance

This is the key product or service that the company provides and is typically technically oriented. It is simply why the customer purchases the product/service. This is usually the most easily obtained data.

This specifically includes work plans (period-to-date, present year, etc.), or production schedules that have been defined.

Safety

What is the history of employee and public safety associated with the product/service? What are the documented dangers/hazards/safety provisions associated with the product/service?

Cost

What are the costs associated with the product/service? Wherever possible/practical, itemize the *total absorbed cost* of this so that "apples-to-apples" comparisons can be made outside the company. Where major cost areas are not known, it is important to note this and make an order-of-magnitude estimate. Note that productivity can be defined as simply the performance divided by the cost. In some companies, this may extend all the way to cost-benefit analysis and shareholder value contributions.

Customer

What are the customer expectations and satisfaction levels? Because this is not necessarily related to gross revenue levels, this is often difficult to obtain. The Data Collection team may have to collect some ad hoc data for present levels, such as preliminary assessment, random interviews, and/or surveys.

What are the specific customer needs for defined product/process needs? Often, there is a blanket customer order or work plan that specifies the delivery requirements; this may be covered through the Work Plan / Master Production Schedule, or it may be in separate customer documentation.

Employee

What are the tangible employee metrics? What are the basic skillsets and capabilities of employees? What certifications are necessary? What training is required? What has been the history of employee attendance, tardiness, and turnover rates? How does the overall compensation and

benefit rank? How has it changed? These are examples of tangible employee data.

Cultural

These are the organizational intangibles, and may include data determined from the Organizational Readiness Assessment. Typically, this data is obtained through employee surveys, focus groups, and interviews. If the Readiness Assessment did not include a cultural survey, this information should be collected at this time.

Activity: Vendor benchmarking. The vendors are often critical components in the HPT efforts and may often be full team members throughout the process. Because it will be important to back track the process by at least two full "state changes" later, it is important to obtain historical vendor information from the vendors' subprocesses.

Deliverable: Vendor benchmarking, itemizing key readiness instruments and historical information (such as performance, safety, cost, employee, and cultural dimensions—just as for the historical benchmarking).

Typical intervention level: Facilitator

Activity: Customer benchmarking. The Customer is a key reference and potential source of data—particularly about the customer. The customer is any stakeholder who receives the product/service of the team/company *and who makes the ultimate evaluation as to its success.* The customer may be internal or external and may include multiple layers (e.g., distribution and retail channels). Depending upon the customer and the organization's relationship with its customers, this may include any/all of surveys, focus groups, and/or direct data. For some teams, this may even include customer participation in the data collection or even the HPT effort.

Critical deliverable: Customer benchmarking

Typical intervention level: Coach

KEY GO/NO GO ASSESSMENT OF DATA COLLECTION

- Is there a basic understanding of the team/company's competitive position, and where performance has been to date?
- Is there sufficient level of detail to form the basis of evaluating the current state during the Work Re/Design phase? Is there sufficient scope of information (i.e., end-to-end in the expected process)?

Template: Team Preparation

Do not turn back when you are just at the goal.

—Syrus, Maxim 580

In this set of activities, the preparations for Work Re/Design are completed. It is important to note that this is much more than simply "being prepared" for the most visible phase of the HPT transition. If the preparations are inadequate, the Work Re/Design will *not* be successful. Effective interventions throughout the Work Re/Design phase are dependent upon full completion of these Team Preparation activities. In many HPT efforts, inadequate team preparation results in ineffective Work Re/Designs, in turn resulting in teams not achieving their HPT goals.

In Team Preparation, the leaders are expressing their commitment to change and their belief in the ability of the teams to achieve the impossible. This is the first *practical* commitment on the leaders' part, publicly demonstrating support and commitment for the effort. The nature, scope, and enthusiasm of the leaders' support is a key diagnostic to the authenticity of readiness for significant change.

As with the earlier Leaders' Preparation, this is often the first effective communication with key stakeholders (particularly the prospective HPT team members). As such, it represents the initial intervention on an individual level. For many, this is the *contextual connection* noted in the Awareness stage of Individual transition (see chapter 16). It is an important intervention point.

TEAM CHARTER

The executive leadership is now ready to prepare the basics of the "box" within which the design team will work. This includes goal setting, "sand-box," deliverables, and specific expectations.

Activity: "Impossible" stretch goals. HPTs work toward goals, finding new ways to achieve those goals, working hard to avoid the old thinking paradigms that may have contributed to obstacles in the past. To avoid these old patterns of thinking, it is critically important to *set goals that are not achievable by conventional means.* If the team should be given goals that are only 15 percent increased over present levels, for example, there would be a strong pressure to "simply do more the same way." It is the establishment of seemingly impossible goals, coupled with the shift in individual transition, that helps drive HPTs off of their previous thinking patterns.

Typically, HPTs are given goals that are at least 50 percent improved over present levels, to be accomplished in less than 12 months. This level is arbitrary, however, and is used to help propel the team past its initial self-imposed limitations.

An important factor in goal setting is the need for *timelines.* Having some stated timeline for each goal (or optionally, all the goals as a group), provides the team some planning room in their implementation. As noted later in the section Design: Transition Plan, the team needs to develop key transition strategies from the present to the new system design. Typically, teams are given 6 to 12 months to complete their goals.

The development of effective goals and their corresponding communication represent a significant intervention to Individual and Team Development dimensions.

Critical deliverable: Development of HPT goals, often at least 50% improved, within 12 months (with typical dimensions of performance, safety, cost, customer value and employee/cultural motivation, as shown next)

Typical intervention level: Coach, Catalyst

Goal: Safety

This is expressed in the value that the leaders *desire,* not merely expected levels of performance.

This first goal is the most significant; it is the first goal addressed in key presentations and communication plans. As such, it should represent the highest goals of the leader and the organization (not necessarily the most urgent). Although all goals should be treated equally throughout the Work Re/Design and Implementation phases, the first goal is thought of

first. This should represent the highest level of performance in terms of overall good of all stakeholders. Typically, this includes employee and customer safety, customer relationships, integrity, or other key success dimension.

It is important that this goal, as any other, have tangibly measurable metrics so that the team can routinely monitor its performance. Therefore, such high-level goals as community trust or goodwill should not be included, unless they have a corresponding real-world metric (they *can* and *should* be included under Expectations, later in this Section, however).

Goal: Operational Value

This is the key performance metric and may include several different goals; these should functionally determine what the customer is expecting/needing. This is the key *functional* dimension and defines whether or not the product or service is meeting its originally intended value to the customer.

Goal: Cost/ Shareholder Value

This is typically the total absorbed cost of the product/service and may be expressed as a productivity measure when combined with the performance metric(s).

Goal: Customer Value

This is the *perceived* value that the customer places on the product/service and should be measurable on a regular basis with the customers.

Goal: Employee Value

Though intangible, this should be specifically measurable (even if only a survey). This may be measured on an individual level (e.g., motivation and quality of work life) or may be captured on an organizational level (i.e., cultural).

Activity: Sandbox. HPT principle: People will achieve more when they understand what they are not allowed to do (see chapter 14).

The Sandbox, or list of constraints, is an itemization of actions that the HPT effort is *not* allowed to do; it sets up boundary conditions for the team.

By listing the items the team is not allowed to do, the "Sandbox" effectively defines the area that the team can work within, without automati-

cally being dismissed by the leaders. This list should be complete, but not unnecessarily long. This list is considered the "You can do anything *except…."* chart; if there is any recommendation that the team might make to the leaders that leaders simply cannot accept, it should be on this list. Conversely, if the leaders *could be* persuaded with data and presentation, then it should *not* be on this list.

The development of the Sandbox is an important intervention for leaders; properly defined, it helps them experience their own limits to radical change. When the interventionist compares the leaders' limitations to the team's creativity, with the original pressures for change, significant learnings and Individual Transition are possible. This activity is where the leaders' vision is integrated with their resistance to change; the result can be considerable growth.

As will be seen during the Work Re/Design phase, the application of the Sandbox is a critical intervention for the team members; the use of limited constraints on a creative team is a very effective re-enforcer of team identity.

Critical deliverable: Sandbox list of topics/recommendations that the team is not empowered to change. This may include both "cannot do" and "cannot do without approval items" (next).

Typical intervention level: Coach, Catalyst

Cannot Do

Most of the list includes items that the team simply is not empowered to pursue. These may include areas such as pay, compensation and benefits, or high-level organizational structure, but are not necessarily limited to any area. In some large-scale designs (such as start-ups), there may literally be no "cannot do's" at all.

"Cannot Do without Approval"

Some Sandbox items may be included, but deliberately encompass leadership into the recommendation loop. These items cannot be done independently, but could be done with appropriate (and specific) management approval.

Activity: Deliverables. The leader defines key *deliverables* for the Work Re/Design; those documents and/or presentations that communicate the team's new plans. Although these are typically common deliverables based upon the Work Re/Design process, they may vary from effort to effort. These deliverables are the formal assignment from the leader to the team; they represent the *tangible material* the team has been assigned to produce.

However, the deliverables are less important than the goals or the Sandbox. The deliverables may be negotiable with the leaders throughout the Work Re/Design process (and often are), yet the goals and Sandbox should remain firm.

Typical deliverables include the following:

- "To Be" Process Map
- Organization Chart
- Roles and Responsibilities
- Training Plan
- Integration Plan
- Change Management Plan
- Transition Plan
- Metrics/Monitoring Plan
- Contingency Plan

Deliverable: The Work Re/Design deliverables are defined by the leader.

Typical intervention level: Facilitator

Activity: Expectations. The leaders are clear about expectations. These will often include intangible "feels" about the team, sense of energy or interaction with the team, and perhaps personal goals.

Deliverable: Leader provides clear expectations of the team throughout the HPT effort. This may include professional and personal expectations next.

Typical intervention level: Coach

Professional Expectations

How does the leader expect the team to appear and behave with customers? with vendors? What is the general quality that the leader would like to see in the outcomes? What is the sense of motivation and excitement that the leadership would expect from the team?

Personal Expectations

This may include the leaders' personal expectations of themselves as well as personal expectations of the team. What personal growth is expected—from the team members and from the leaders? What learnings and opportunities to try new ways of interacting, new methods of leadership, and new group behaviors are possible that simply would not be practical in a typical setting?

TEAM LEADER PREPARATION

Activity: Selection and initial preparation, team leader. The leader of the HPT team is not necessarily the leader of the HPT effort to date; this team

leader will be working extensively with the team membership and the Work Re/Design effort, as well as the first weeks/months of the implementation rollout. There may be several team leaders, depending on the size and scope of the HPT effort.

It is important to remember that the team leader will be the initial focus of the High Performance Team. As a *transition* from typical team to High Performance, the leader needs to be competent in *both* cultures. This may require a careful consideration of the leader selection and preparation prior to any interaction with the HPT team members. In the initial phases of the HPT process, as the team follows its conventional culture, the leader is the most significant "success factor" in the transition. The ability of the leader to lead in this phase, transfer his or her authority to the team as the team demonstrates its maturation, and the desire and capacity of the leader to accept guidance from HPT interventionists are *mission critical criteria in the success of the HPT effort.*

Critical deliverable: Team leader is selected, notified, and supported well before the Work Re/Design phase. Team leader wants to be an active leader and desires to learn about and prepare for the HPT development process. Key components are listed next.

Typical intervention level: Coach, Catalyst

Selection

The team leaders will need to be selected sufficiently before the Work Re/Design to be prepared and to be emotionally ahead of the team members. Whether selection is by choice or by assignment, team leadership needs to (1) have the capacity and capability for the major shifts required by the team; (2) want to support the HPT effort; (3) desire to learn about the underlying HPT team-dynamic processes; and (4) be open to individual intervention.

Team Leader Notification and Preparation

The team leaders are notified and prepared for the Work Re/Design. Typically, this includes several half-day periods of orientation and preparation with the HPT SMEs. Individual coaching and preparation are also provided for each team leader.

Activity: Charter rollout meeting with organizational leaders. The organizational leaders meet directly with the team leadership, providing interactive communication and sponsorship. This includes both Sponsoring Executives and Non-Sponsoring Executives. This provides the initial phases of integration between the conventional organization and the

future HPT. It is important for both the initial *contextual connection* (see chapter 16) between the groups, as well as a key opportunity to establish a working relationship for the Work Re/Design. This will become important as the HPT effort needs (1) support during the Work Re/Design, and (2) work integration during implementation. For most HPT efforts, this is particularly important when the HPT culture is significantly different from the conventional culture.

Deliverable: Charter rollout integration meeting(s) with organizational leaders

Typical intervention level: Facilitator, Coach

TEAM SELECTION AND PREPARATION

Key Decision: Team Membership Scope:
Full or Phased Implementation

HPT principle (see chapter 14): All the people who do the work, actively design the work; everyone is involved who wants to be involved.

One of the difficult implementation decisions of HPT efforts is whether—and how—to involve all interested employees in the design of their own work. For many organizations, the belief that workers can *not* be taken "offline" precludes an effort that includes all team members in the initial Work Re/Design effort. This creates the real-world challenge of creating HPTs without the benefit of an intensive, end-to-end product review.

For most teams, the application of an intensive three-week period of orientation, education, analysis, and multidimensional design is *mission-critical* to the team's ability to achieve breakthrough results. Having all the team members actively involved in the design of their work is a critical common theme for successful teams.

Many traditional leaders review the agenda for Work Re/Design and confuse the detailed analysis with conventional redesign. The similarity of Work Re/Design activities to process optimization and re-engineering efforts often hides the true purpose of the Work Re/Design process.

The critical factor in team development is that the HPT functions of Work Re/Design be completed by the team as a whole. This includes the intensive exposure to, and analysis of, organizational change pressures and the opportunity for the team to eliminate those pressures.

Although the extensive review, analysis, and planning activities are important to creating real-world approaches, without the developmental processes the team will most likely fail to become High Performance.

These underlying process functions of team and individual development are critical to a successful HPT effort, yet they do not necessarily

require a structured, offline Work Re/Design activity to occur. With considerable support by effective, experienced interventionists, some teams have experienced team development in the field, as the product is being produced. This approach has been successful for some teams, yet it requires considerably greater intervention resources and typically takes longer for the teams to reach their performance levels.

A formal Work Re/Design environment, with all potential team members included, provides the most effective path to High Performance. In this implementation, there is considerable emphasis on team member selection, and the implementation of creative approaches is immediate. This is referred to as a "total immersion" implementation, or *Full Implementation*.

For those teams not including all team members in the original Work Re/Design, a *phased implementation* is possible. For this approach, a Work Re/Design includes members of a design team who then implement the new design in several phases, typically by function or geography. With this Phased Implementation plan, extensive communication and stakeholder enrollment are required throughout the Work Re/Design section, and significant *additional* intervention and support are required for each expansion phase.

For reference, both of these implementation approaches are included in the template.

In either approach, however, team member selection and preparation are key to the HPT effort's success. The right team members, with the right perspective, can make the difference between success and obstruction. However, there is no benchmark for "right" and "wrong," nor any checklist that can ensure that any given team member will be successful or not. By focusing on the *HPT values* and ensuring that team members understand and can support the underlying values of the process, however, the probability of success can be enhanced.

Diversity is highly valued in effective HPT efforts. Cultural and individual diversity offer a boost to creative and innovative approaches throughout the transition period.

Typically, a diverse team will display more conflict initially, then create firmer attachment bonds later in their development. With diversity of thought, perspective, and experience, these teams typically produce breakthrough results more quickly than do homogeneous teams.

Conversely, a team comprised of similar individuals will typically offer rapid compliance, minimal conflict, and conventional answers to their performance challenges.

By selecting a diverse group of people, *while still maintaining a minimum base of operational competence*, the leader can optimize the team's development and breakthrough achievements. It is *mission critical* that a basis of expertise exists for the operational perspective of the product; if the aggregate knowledge and experience of the team are insufficient to produce the

product, the team will most likely fail to achieve its objectives. In the event that a minimum competency base is unavailable to the team per se, it is important to fill in the gaps with SMEs as needed throughout the Work Re/Design and Implementation phases.

Different HPT efforts have used different selection criteria and application methods. One team asked for volunteers, and chose the most senior, whereas another team asked candidates to fill out an extensive questionnaire. There are many effective selection methods; the HPT Sponsoring Executive and team leader, supported by the interventionist, should design and implement the selection criteria that are aligned with both the existing and HPT cultures.

Key Consideration

In many highly successful HPTs, some of the most energetic and motivational team members were considered "negative influences" in their traditional originating organization. Although negative attitudes should not be a primary selection characteristic, attention should be paid to the environmental differences between the existing organization and the High Performance organization. For many HPT efforts that deliberately excluded those candidates considered negative, the time required to achieve High Performance was significantly increased.

Activity: Communication: Team selection. Communicating the team selection *process* to the organization is important and should be integrated with the other phases of communication. This communication should restate the purpose of the HPT effort, the importance/relevance of the effort to the organization, and general expectations as a result of the effort.

For many key stakeholders, including potential team members, this communication may represent the initial contextual connection. This is often aided by (again) communicating a short synopsis on the business pressures for change and why the organization needs to change.

Deliverable: Team selection process communication

Typical intervention level: Facilitator, Coach

Activity: Team selection. The team's selection criteria should be patterned along the HPT principles. Though all members should *want* to be part of the effort, the most successful team selection processes have included self-nomination and preselection interviews with effort leaders and/or team leaders.

Selection criteria should be specific, including both tangible and intangible dimensions. These dimensions should encompass HPT principles, success vision compatibility, and passion for change.

The selection process should have clear objectives and be communicated to all stakeholders. Whether selected by appointment or team vote, the results of the process should be communicated quickly to all stakeholders as well.

Deliverable: Selection process developed and implemented; team members selected

Typical intervention level: Facilitator, Coach

Activity: Team member notification and preparation. Once the team has been selected, they should be notified and be prepared for the Work Re/Design. This preparation will vary with each team, but minimally should include a one-on-one with the team members' present supervisor/manager to discuss the purpose of the HPT effort and the specific impact that it may have on the team member. Specific expectations about performance, opportunities, and principles should be discussed and understood prior to Work Re/Design start.

Note: If team members had not taken part in the organizational Cultural Survey earlier, this instrument is readministered for the team. This will be important to provide a baseline reference later on.

Facilitated deliverable: Team member is notified and prepared. Key expectations are set, by both (originating) manager and team member.

Typical intervention level: Facilitator

Activity: Nonselected candidate notification. Once the team members have been selected, the remaining candidates should be notified with an explanation for the decision. For most individuals, providing a candid, supportive assessment offers the greatest long-term support. The opportunity exists for the candidate to revolunteer for future HPT efforts and/or to work with her or his manager in a personal development plan to address any surfaced issues.

Facilitated deliverable: Nonselected candidate is notified and the decision explained. Opportunity exists to explore personal development with candidate's manager.

Typical intervention level: Facilitator

Activity: Team preparation: HPT background. Team members are provided preliminary background reading to prepare for the Work Re/Design phase; these may range from simple articles to video(s) to full reference books.

Deliverable: Background preparation, appropriate to study habits and capabilities of team members

Typical intervention level: Facilitator

Activity: Organizational communication: Prework Re/Design. This communication updates the organization since the original Organizational Preparation section and provides more detail. This may be part of the previous selection communication, but is most effective if provided separately. Key messages are included next.

Deliverable: Organizational communication update

Typical intervention level: Facilitator

Business Case for Change: Team Specific

This reaffirms the business case for change and details how this specific team/effort will support that business case. This is best done line-of-sight to the business case so that the organization is aware how achieving the team's specific goals will support the overall organizational business case.

Team Charter

This provides an outline of the team's charter, including the goals and constraints. It is emphasized that the goals are "stretch" goals and different from conventional, operational business goals.

HPT Effort Calendar and Key Events

This is often a high-level calendar of activities and focuses on those key events that may involve the organization, such as the "As Is" and "To Be" fairs. This also specifies the actions and inputs that the team is expecting from the rest of the organization.

This section also itemizes the backfill of resources necessary to support the Work Re/Design, if applicable. For many efforts, the Work Re/Design takes many people and resources from the actual work, requiring others to backfill the actual work. Recognition for those backfilling is often acknowledged here.

CONTINGENCY PLANNING

From one perspective, developing a High Performance Team is a unique, breakthrough strategy with special considerations, support, and requirements. From another perspective, however, it remains simply a *strategy for change*; like any change strategy, it has the potential for failure and work disruption.

Every effective strategy plan includes contingency planning as a risk mitigation. In the event of unplanned problems, the organization is able to

recover using a fallback plan that can be initiated even in the event of major failure on the part of the original plan.

Given the potential chaos and disruption that failed HPTs can cause, it is even more critical to have predeveloped contingency plans in place *prior to beginning any Work Re/Design.*

Activity: Develop contingency plan. Contingency planning is a *mission-critical* deliverable. The executive and leaders of the HPT effort need to define and develop contingency plans for the potential failure of the effort. Depending on the company culture and the comfort levels of the executive and the HPT leader, this plan may be formal and extensive or simple and straightforward. It should contain the minimum components listed next.

Mission-critical deliverable: Develop contingency plan

Typical intervention level: Facilitator, Coach

Contingency Actions

These detail the specific actions that will be taken in the event of catastrophic failure of the team. These actions are clear, concise, and not ambiguous.

Triggers That Initiate the Plan

This portion details the specific failure triggers that would initiate the plan. These may be tangible, such as the team's failure to meet minimum cost targets, or intangible, such as a team's active rebellion to authority.

These triggers are also referred to as the "circuit breakers" that engage in the event of serious failure.

If the trigger is minor, such as inadequate cost justification or poor presentation, the leader should consider whether this is appropriate to sidetrack the entire HPT effort. Often, retraining or redesign or increased intervention is appropriate to bringing the team back on track.

Roles and Responsibilities

The contingency plan should clearly define who does what by when to achieve which results. This may include stakeholders who are not currently part of the HPT effort; these external individuals should be part of the contingency plan preparation process.

Clearly Defined Timelines and Expectations

The plan should clearly identify specific dates by which results are expected. In most contingency plans, these are short-term dates in days or weeks. There should be clearly defined expectations and deliverables throughout the plan.

Impact and Potential Impact Mitigation Planning

The plan should outline the expected impact on the different stakeholders with its primary focus on the organization, the HPT members, leaders, and the executive. Activation of most contingency plans is a dramatic message to the organization with negative impacts. There may be impact mitigation efforts included in the plan.

Activity: Communicate the plan. The contingency plan, including the circuit breakers that trigger the plan, is communicated with all the appropriate stakeholders. In most cases, this is focused on the HPT members and not the overall organization. Though there may be negative reaction to the existence of the plan, in most cases the plan can be referred to in a simple, matter-of-fact approach that signals the business realities that underpin the HPT effort. The key message is that the HPT effort is no more immune to normal risk mitigation than any other strategic change approach.

Key deliverable: Contingency plan is communicated to key stakeholders.

Typical intervention level: Facilitator, Coach

Activity: Measure/Monitor/Revise contingency plan trigger. Measurement and monitoring of the key trigger indices should be performed on a regular basis. In the event of the contingency plan being initiated, it should not be a surprise to anyone directly involved in the HPT effort.

The triggers should be monitored on a regularly scheduled basis, and a means of reporting and communicating them should be implemented. When there is an apparent danger of initiating a trigger, there should be adequate warning through the monitoring and reporting mechanisms. This may be as simple as posting the monitored trigger in a public area with a green–yellow–red symbol or as sophisticated as real-time automated monitoring.

The key consideration is the ability of key stakeholders to jointly monitor the trigger state and to know whether there is an immediate danger of initiating the plan. There should be no ambiguity about the level or the current state.

Key deliverable: Regular monitoring and review of contingency triggers

Typical intervention level: Facilitator, Coach

FACILITY PREPARATION

Due to the intense nature of the Work Re/Design period, it is often difficult for teams to arrange for facilities and logistics support in the

moment, particularly during the intense periods of process creation. Prepared facilities, logistical support, and documentation can avoid minor crises during the Work Re/Design. Key areas include the following.

Activity: Facilities preparation. This should include a large common working room capable of all HPT members meeting at the same time. There should be enough display space to include the "As Is" process maps and the "To Be" process maps simultaneously. Although this can be displayed electronically, most teams elect to use standard flip-chart paper displayed along the wall. This often results in a key requirement being considerable wall space, free of doors or windows, that can be left in the same condition for the entire duration of the Work Re/Design. A general rule of thumb has been about four or five feet of linear wall length for each team member.

Breakout rooms should be available for teams to subdivide their work, allowing for subprocesses to be developed. Though it may be difficult to determine the number of processes until the work is actually performed, a common metric has been about one breakout room for each 5 to 10 team members. Breakout rooms should also have a linear wall length dimension to support simultaneous display of information.

Each team member should be prepared with background information, notepads or computers for detailed data review, calculators, and the like.

Standard facility support and logistics should also be included, such as food, communication, copy, and similar support items.

Deliverable: Preparation of adequate facility logistics, support, and location

Typical intervention level: Facilitator

Activity: Documentation support. There should be a real-time means of storing the information developed by the team; this will vary considerably with the style and culture of the team, leader, and facilitator. For those teams displaying all information electronically, it is a simple matter to make copies for all members and key stakeholders.

For those teams working by hand and displaying information on flip charts and paper, this can be a considerable task. Some teams have included support people to be real-time scribes, transcribing all the work simultaneously; others have used electronic means to capture the paperwork and then copy electronically.

Whichever way the teams elect to document their effort, it is very important to capture this information at the same time that the team is working on it.

Deliverable: Documentation support is defined and obtained prior to the start of Work Re/Design.

Typical intervention level: Facilitator

Activity: Support roles and responsibilities. Because the Work Re/Design effort is a transition from heavy dependence on external sources to more accountability and responsibility on the part of the team members, predefinition of support roles and responsibilities is helpful. It is helpful to request that the team take more and more accountability for routine facilities and logistics support throughout the effort.

Deliverable: Definition of roles and responsibilities for facilities and support logistics

Typical intervention level: Facilitator, Coach

KEY GO/NO GO ASSESSMENT
OF TEAM PREPARATION

- Are all members of the team ready to review all aspects of the HPT effort from start to finish? Is the team leadership ready, able, and prepared to spend continuous time with the team throughout the Work Re/Design phase? Is the leadership clear on what it cannot live with? Is the leadership ready to accept recommendations from the HPT Work Re/Design team on any aspects not specifically listed in the Sandbox?
- Does the organization know about the effort and what is expected of both the HPT effort and the rest of the organization?
- Is there a clearly defined contingency plan that itemizes the path in case of major problems? Does it include the specific triggers that would initiate it? Is it clear to the leaders?
- Is every key stakeholder ready to invest time, money, and effort into what some have called the hardest work of their career?

Template: Work Re/Design

I am the people . . . Do you know that all the great work of the world
Is done through me?

—Carl Sandburg

The Work Re/Design phase is often perceived as being synonymous with the overall HPT process; in fact, it is only the most visible intervention, intended to provide an environment that allows the team to shift its sense of identity in such a way as to integrate organization, team and individual. It is designed to create an entirely new business plan for new ways of thinking and new ways of obtaining traditional metrics. It requires new paradigms, new approaches, and often involves difficult adjustment from previous assumptions.

The sequence and duration of each portion of the process, as with other sections, will vary with each team. In most cases, the actual duration of each portion is compressed or elongated to accommodate the special needs of the team and the specific work process(es) defined. In some cases, there may be different interventions. In all cases, however, the approach is to obtain an integrated, comprehensive approach to reach the impossible goals within the Sandbox constraints. (See the sample calendar in Figure 35-1.)

A functional process outline is provided in Figures 35-2 and Figure 35-3.

Some HPT transition efforts do not appear to have a Work Re/Design; in the case of the defense power supply team (see chapter 2) and the utility team (see chapter 2), most of the team members did not

Work Re/Design

Sunday		Monday		Tuesday		Wednesday		Thursday		Friday		Saturday	
CHAPTER	35	34	36		37	34	38		39	34	40		41
EXECUTIVE		ORGANIZATIONAL COMMUNICATION		W		ORK RE/DESIGN PREPARATION		FI		NAL WORK RE/DESIGN PREPARATION			
TEAM		TEAM MEMBER PREPARATION				FACILITIES PREPARATION							
	42	35-1	43	35-2	44	35-3	45	35-4	46	35-5	47		48
INT		RODUCTION		**DETAILED INTRO**		CUSTOMER REVIEW		PROCESS MAPPING		CHILD PROCESS REVIEW			
		KICK-OFF		**GOALS - SANDBOX**						COMMUNICATION			
		WORK SIMULATION		EMPLOYEE DATA REVIEW		SHAREHOLDER VALUE REVIEW		DEVELOP CORE " AS – IS " MAP		PREP: AS-IS FAIR			
	49	35-6	50	35-6	51	35-7	52	35-8	53	35-9	54		55
		"AS-IS" FAIR		CONTROL CHART		CREATIVE THINKING		GOALS AND SANDBOX – PROCESS TEST		TO-BE ANALYSIS			
				PROCESS CONTROL DEVELOPMENT		PRELIMINARY "TO – BE " PROCESS MAP		REITERATIVE TO-BE MAPPING					
EXEC VISIT ->										PREP: TO-BE FAIR			
	56	35-10	57	35-10	58	35-11	59	35-13	60	35-13	61		62
		"TO-BE" FAIR		TRANSITION PLAN		SKILLS ASSESSMENT		CHANGE MANAGEMENT ANALYSIS		FINALIZE CM PLAN			
						GAP ANALYSIS		STAKEHOLDER ANALYSIS		PREP: TRANSITION PLAN FAIR			
EXEC VISIT ->						TRAINING PLAN							
	63	35-13	64	35-14	65	35-12, -15	66	35-12, -15	67	35-15	68		69
		"TRANSITION PLAN" FAIR		INTEGRATION PLAN		DETAILED WORK PLAN		DETAILED WORK PLAN		FINAL REPORT- OUT PREP			
										REPORT OUT			
EXEC VISIT ->				INITIAL PREP: REPORT-OUT		PREPARATION: REPORT-OUT		PREPARATION: REPORT-OUT		NEXT STEPS			

Figure 35-1 Template Calendar: Work Re/Design

experience a formal Work Re/Design. For these members, however, the *functions* of the Work Re/Design were performed, albeit as the team members were performing the work itself. The processes of individual transition, team development, and effective interventions were all present for these field Work Re/Design teams; they were simply done outside of a template environment. *There are many ways to achieve the same results* (see chapter 14).

For simplicity of illustration, this template uses an example of an HPT effort, in dedicated rooms, offline of work, focused on their goals, Sandbox, and deliverables. Based on a template of five-day weeks, eight-hour days, the team completes its Work Re/Design in four weeks. For simplicity of illustration, this template is separated into daily buckets of activity and work.

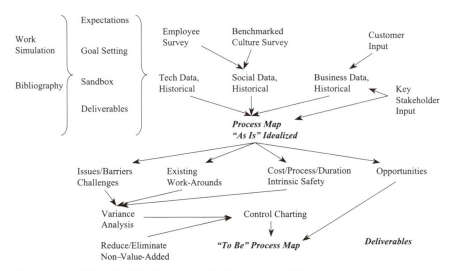

Figure 35-2 Work Re/Design: Data Gathering and Analysis

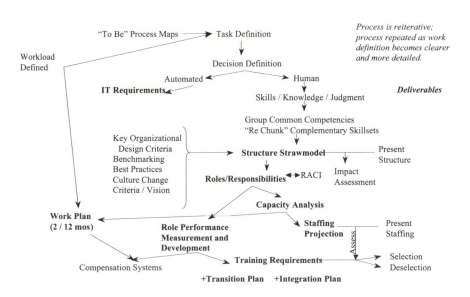

Figure 35-3 Work Re/Design: Design Synthesis and Integration

Each day, the overall agenda includes:

First 15 to 30 minutes	Daily agenda/daily deliverables
	Issue raising/addressing
Final 15 to 30 minutes	Review of learnings/accomplishments
	Review of progress against daily deliverables
	Review of progress against Work Re/Design schedule/deliverables
	Issues for next steps

1. KICKOFF: ENTIRE TEAM

Activity: Leader introduction. The Sponsoring Executive provides the basic business case for the HPT effort, stating passionately *why* the team has been brought together and presenting general expectations about the future. This may include personal motivations and commitments on the part of the executive, as well as asking the same from individual members. When several executive sponsors are included, they should each provide their own perspective. General statements about executive availability and specific support offered should be outlined at this time. Executives should demonstrate their support for the team leaders and the overall effort moving forward.

Deliverable: Executives should kickoff the Re/Design effort, with specific statements and passions about change and their own vision(s) for the future of the effort and the role that each member may have in that future.

Typical intervention level: Facilitator

Activity: Kickoff. Team leaders provide basic introduction (names, original organization, etc.) and state passionately why the team has been brought together. This may include more specific expectations and more specifics on the personal commitment of the team leadership.

Deliverable: Team leaders bridge from the executive's case for change, specifically stating personal commitments and expectations.

Typical intervention level: Facilitator

Activity: Work simulation. There are many different work simulation exercises available to the team. Typically simulating linear work, this full-day exercise provides a preview of the entire Work Re/Design process. In a single day, the team simulates a traditional workflow, learns and applies HPT principles to change its design, then applies its new learnings to its work. Although not a complete model, it provides an overview of the Work Re/Design process and, most significantly, typically demonstrates that breakthrough results *are* possible.

In the morning, the team creates simulated product, using common office tools. Laboring under traditional work rules and traditional design, the team practices, then has a formal production run to produce its product. After 30 minutes of production, typical teams have produced less than five acceptable products.

After some debriefing, the team reviews some basic HPT principles and design approaches, taking a very different perspective about performing work. By the afternoon, the team redesigns its original work, using the same overall objectives but no given work rules or traditional design. At the end of the exercise, the team reruns its work, using HPT techniques, and compares the HPT results with the traditional results. In most cases, there is a dramatic difference, typically of an order of magnitude, showcasing that HPT can have demonstrable results—quickly. In all cases, the exercises demonstrate many of the basic process steps that the team will be taking over the following three weeks.

Deliverable: Work simulation exercise is performed, requiring approximately six to eight hours. This includes work simulation, HPT overview, design guidelines, and practice designs. The team applies its new learnings and evaluates the results, comparing the "To Be" results with their original "As Is" results.

Typical intervention level: Facilitator

2. EMPLOYEE / KEY STAKEHOLDER REVIEW: ENTIRE TEAM

This day is designed to provide in-depth introduction and review of the Employee and Cultural data that has been collected in Readiness Assessment and Data Collection, Historical. The team should have a clear understanding of HPT principles and general expectations about the following three weeks.

Activity: Sponsors' purpose. This is the outline of the basic business purpose of the HPT effort. The sponsor and/or team leadership will lead the team through the basic drivers and success metrics of the business case, clearly outlining the business case of the Business Case Refinement.

Deliverable: Leaders communicate the business case—both tangible and intangible—to the membership, and expectations for the future. Key perspectives of the business case and real-world pressures and constraints are presented with passion.

Typical intervention level: Facilitator, Coach

Activity: Detailed introduction. Each team member is introduced, giving some indication of personal background and expectation for the Work Re/Design and/or HPT effort.

Deliverable: Personal introduction and expectation for Work the Re/Design

Typical intervention level: Facilitator

Activity: Goals and Sandbox. Leaders review the HPT goals in detail, presenting the dimensions and the specific goals developed earlier in Stretch Goals. Team should be allowed to react to the goals, particularly if the initial reaction is one of disbelief and rejection. Leaders should not take a defensive position, but should encourage open discussion of the goals' intent. Because these are non-negotiable, the goals should not be considered "soft"; the leader should not bargain with the members about what the goals are or why they were set at their levels. Rather, leaders should work with the team to increase clarity about the goals' metrics and dimensions.

Similarly, leaders review the Sandbox developed earlier in Sandbox and answer questions for clarity and understanding, without negotiating the actual sandbox items. There should be a caveat stated about the sandbox not necessarily being all-inclusive, but that it clearly outlines the best knowledge of the leaders as of this date.

Critical deliverable: Leaders present the HPT goals and HPT Sandbox without negotiation or defensiveness.

Typical intervention level: Coach, Catalyst

Activity: Deliverables. Leaders outline additional deliverables requested by the end of the Work Re/Design. This may include HPT process deliverables, such as Training Plan(s), as well as leadership-requested deliverables. Deliverables are defined as tangible, specific outcomes of the Work Re/Design phase, usually delivered to the leaders and executives as part of the Final Presentation.

Critical deliverable: Leaders present additional deliverables due by the end of the Work Re/Design phase.

Typical intervention level: Facilitator, Coach

Activity: Expectations for team. In addition to any specific expectations listed earlier in the Sponsors' Purpose, specific expectations about behaviors, interaction, learnings, or other areas are presented by the leaders. This may include personal and professional expectations, and may include both the team and the leaders.

Deliverable: Leaders present personal and/or professional expectations of the team.

Typical intervention level: Facilitator, Coach

Activity: Expectations for participants. Team participants discuss/disclose their individual expectations of the HPT effort, including what personal growth/learnings/experience they expect for themselves as well as what they might expect from the leaders.

Deliverable: Participants present individual expectations for the HPT effort overall and the Work Re/Design in particular.

Typical intervention level: Facilitator, Coach

Activity: Ground rules. Common rules of behavior and meeting rules are presented in effect throughout the Work Re/Design phase. These may be developed by the team leaders earlier and presented to the team, or may be developed ad hoc by the team. In either event, complete team *consensus* is required for Ground Rules to be in effect; this is one of the few times when everyone must be able to live with the rules.

Deliverable: Either (1) leaders present and obtain consensus for Ground Rules; or (2) the team and the leaders develop consensus-driven Ground Rules in the moment.

Typical intervention level: Coach

Activity: HPT Outline and cases. A basic outline of High Performance Team efforts is presented, indicating an overview of opportunities and challenges. Case histories are discussed, including successful and less-than-successful efforts. Understanding the critical areas and critical success factors (CSFs) are key to understanding HPT potential.

An outline of the proposed calendar for this effort's Work Re/Design is provided, with corresponding caveats about flexibility and each team being different.

Deliverable: HPT SME provides background of HPT, including principles, case histories, and critical success factors. An overview of this effort's calendar, with emphasis on the Work Re/Design phase, is provided.

Typical intervention level: Catalyst (as HPT SME)

Activity: Social/Cultural survey results review. Results of previous cultural/employee survey is provided, with context setting and benchmarking, if available. Team reaction and preliminary interpretation is sought and reviewed. Wherever possible, competitive comparisons should be made.

For many teams in stressful, pressured organizations, this data review may present information that is not positive. In some HPT efforts, this is the first presentation of potentially negative data that hits home to the

team. Because this data is the result of the team members' own input, identification of social and cultural issues can trigger resentment and resistance. Having appropriate interventionists present during this presentation is often helpful.

Critical deliverable: Results of social survey are presented, with benchmarked competitive review (if possible). Team reacts and flash assessment performed.

Typical intervention level: Coach, Catalyst, Social/Cultural SME

Activity: Previous HPT efforts' membership interaction. If possible, members of other HPT teams are present for individual case history discussion and interaction of personal/team challenges and accomplishments.

Optional deliverable: Previous HPT efforts' member interaction/panel

Typical intervention level: Facilitator

3. CUSTOMER / SHAREHOLDER DATA REVIEW

This day presents an overview of Customer Value and Stockholder Value reviews. For many teams, this provides focus on areas that traditionally have been invisible to the team. There are several potential areas of individual and team intervention required during these activities, depending upon the team's reaction to the data presented.

Customer Value Review

The Customer Value Review provides for personal interaction between the team and the HPT effort's key customers. As indicated in Customer Data Collection, the customer is any stakeholder who receives the product/service of the team/company and who makes the ultimate evaluation as to its success. The customer may be internal or external and may include multiple layers (e.g., distribution and retail channels).

The customers are invited (well in advance) to interact with the team and are provided basic information as to the general process that the team will be addressing. The customers may be offered honoraria or simply thanks.

Activity: Key Customers Identified and Invited

Deliverable: Customers are invited to meet with the HPT to share their experiences, perspectives, and opinions on the key process(es) being reviewed by the team.

Note: This should be performed sufficiently in advance of the panel date to accommodate customer needs.

Typical intervention level: Facilitator

Activity: Customer preparation

Context Setting

Setting the stage for the customer interaction is critical, particularly with teams that have typically had little direct contact with key customers. Similarly, customers must be prepared to understand that this is not a typical focus group or complaint session.

Customer Context

Customers are prepared, often with a half-hour warm-up before the panel, to understand what they will be participating in and what kinds of questions to expect. Customers are invited to ask their own questions, within the scope supported by the moderator of the panel.

Deliverable: Customers on the customer panel are prepared and coached prior to the panel.

Typical intervention level: Facilitator

Activity: Team context setting. Team members are prepared prior to the panel interaction, including coaching on customer interaction basics; in some cases, this may include specific directions as to inappropriate actions and/or questions. A moderator is selected as the "master of ceremonies" for the panel discussion, and team members are requested to follow the moderator's lead. Depending upon the development of the team and the team members at this time, the moderator role may be filled by either a team leader or team member.

Facilitated deliverable: Team members are prepared and coached prior to the panel discussion.

Typical intervention level: Facilitator, Coach

Activity: Panel interaction. The panel of customers meets with the team members, with the designated moderator presiding. The moderator serves to focus participants' attention to the agenda and matter at hand.

Deliverable: A moderator is designated beforehand and keeps the attention of the customers and team members on track. The moderator understands that the customers are critical to the success of the HPT effort and continuously works to support the customers' communication needs while keeping the meeting on time and on track. Individual team members are designated beforehand to scribe the customers' input on flip charts as the customers describe their perspectives.

Typical intervention level: Facilitator

Activity: Customer requirements discussed. The customers' basic requirements are discussed and itemized. This answers the basic questions,
"What do you need [from the HPT team] to meet your minimum daily
needs?" and "What do we do that is critical to your success?" Very simply, if the team does not provide these minimum requirements, the customer cannot be successful.

Deliverable: Customers describe their minimum requirements of the team,
which the team scribes.

Typical intervention level: Facilitator

Activity: Customer expectations discussed. This defines the customers' ongoing expectations. This answers the basic question, "What are you
expecting [from the HPT team] on a regular basis?"

Deliverable: Customers describe their on-going expectations of the team,
which the team scribes.

Typical intervention level: Facilitator

Activity: Customer ideal desires discussed. The customers' "best of all
worlds" hopes for the HPT effort. This answers the basic question,
"What would you like to see from us in the best of all worlds?"

Deliverable: Customers describe their ideal vision for the team, which the
team scribes.

Typical intervention level: Facilitator

Activity: Customers' other comments discussed and understood.

Deliverable: Customers describe any other input/suggestions for the team
that they may have, which the team scribes.

Typical intervention level: Facilitator

Team's Active Listening

During a break for the customers, the team reviews what it has scribed
and summarizes its key "listenings," providing that feedback to the customers. It is important that the team *clearly state only* what it heard from
the customers, and not place its own interpretation and/or make promises to the customers. *This is only about active listening.*

Activity: Team feedback to customers

Deliverable: Team restates to the customers what it heard, without commitments or promises for change. Checking back with the customers to

ensure that what the team heard was, in fact, what the customers had intended to communicate is important to avoid placing interpretive analysis on the customer panel. Once the customers have confirmed the key points, they are thanked and the session ended.

Typical intervention level: Facilitator

Activity: Team review/reaction. The team reviews its own scribed comments and provides key reaction to itself and leadership. Are there any key issues that need to be addressed in the final presentation? What are the key learnings and reactions to the customer panel that need to be captured and highlighted? Is there any additional information that we may need in the near future to build on what we heard with the customer panel?

Deliverable: Team reacts to the leader and to the team about the impact of the customer panel, and highlights key learnings/gaps to be addressed throughout the Work Re/Design.

Typical intervention level: Facilitator

Business Case for Change

Leadership reviews the business case for change in more detail than previously. Reviewing all aspects as outlined earlier in the Business Case Refinement, the basics and the data collection leading to the Business Case for Change are presented. Reaction is solicited from the team, with interaction following.

Facilitated deliverable: Leaders present details of business case for change, and team/leaders review relative impacts and learnings from the Business Case.

Typical intervention level: Facilitator

Shareholder Value Review

Activity: Business review

Key Deliverable Decision: Leaders and executives decide, beforehand, the level of information available to the team. Understanding that the team should have at least as much information as a manager would have in the same position, most HPTs are offered open information excluding Company Secret and Personnel data. This may be decided separately or presented in the Sandbox. The level of information afforded the team will be directly proportional to the validity of recommendation that the team is able to make.

Typical intervention level: Coach, Catalyst

The team reviews the cost side of the HPT effort, including cost histories detailed in the Cost History Data Collection. Because this often requires interpretation, a Business Review SME is usually invited to present the data and to offer the basics of budgeting, cost structures, and workplans.

Facilitated Deliverable: An outline of the business data collection is made by a Business SME, usually including cost information, budgeting, workplans, and key political realities. This typically includes the following components.

Typical intervention level: Coach, Business/Financial SME

Budget

The budget of the originating company departments is reviewed, historically as well as year-to-date. Discussion is provided to ensure basic conceptual understanding of the budget compartments and constraints by the team members. Where necessary, offline tutoring and orientation may be offered.

Work Plan

The workplan or production schedule or work schedule for the financial period (usually year) is provided at an overview level, with resourcing, so that the team understands the level of work presently committed to the customer(s).

Activity: Key Stakeholder/Stakeholder Analysis. Key stakeholders are listed and outlined. Where a formal Stakeholder Analysis has been performed, the frequency, influence, and impact of key stakeholders may be listed. At the minimum, leadership reviews the politics surrounding the HPT effort.

Deliverable: Stakeholder Analysis review or flash assessment of key stakeholders.

Typical intervention level: Facilitator, Coach

Activity: Vendor subteam selected

Deliverable: The first of the breakout teams, the Vendor team will be meeting with key vendors in parallel with the primary Work Re/Design process work. This team is formed with volunteers and may include SMEs from purchasing/procurement to assist the team.

Typical intervention level: Facilitator, Coach

Activity: Request to vendors

Deliverable: An ad hoc list of vendors is drawn up and invited to meet with the Vendor Team. *Note:* If longer lead time is required for key vendors,

this step will need to be completed adequately before the onset of the Work Re/Design phase.

Typical intervention level: Facilitator

Activity: Communication subteam selected

Deliverable: The Communications Team, a breakout team, will be responsible for providing initial and ongoing communications with key stakeholders throughout the Work Re/Design process. This team is formed with volunteers and may include SMEs from corporate communications or other group to assist the team.

Typical intervention level: Facilitator

Activity: Plans for organizational communication. The Communications Team should discuss plans and approaches to communicate status and solicit feedback from key stakeholders. This may include voicemail, email, Web pages, newsletters, and the like.

The Communications Team should also discuss plans and approaches to communicate "As Is" process maps and "To Be" process maps and designs to key stakeholders as well as means of obtaining stakeholder feedback.

Deliverable: Communications Team outlines initial plans for communicating with key stakeholders throughout the Work Re/Design process.

Typical intervention level: Facilitator, Coach

Activity: Ad Hoc Teams Formed / Selected / Chartered. Any additional breakout teams that need to address key needs are begun at this time.

4. OPERATIONAL REVIEW: "AS IS" PROCESS MAP: ENTIRE TEAM

"Process mapping" is used as the key mechanism to integrate various perspectives of the HPT effort, and to integrate the old "As Is" design with the new "To Be" design. Process mapping is a standard quality-management tool and can be referenced in many QM manuals.

Critical Note: It is important to have as many key stakeholders as practical during the "As Is" process mapping phase(s), particularly those who have strong process knowledge and real-world situation experience. Because the validity of the overall process is driven by the validity of the errors/variances discovered, it is vital that input to process mapping be as complete as practical. This is an excellent time to include SMEs who might otherwise not be supportive of the HPT effort/process.

Throughout the "As Is" process map steps, team members typically begin to assert their *individual* beliefs about the proper paths forward for the team as a whole. This is a natural assertion of individual desire and need, and the individual should be recognized and acknowledged for his or her contribution. However, it is very important that individuals *not* assert themselves onto the team at this time. The use of a "parking lot" or other intervention can be used to capture the idea, yet not allow it to dominate the team at this time.

There are two major purposes for the "As Is" process mapping phase: analysis and team integration. From an analytical perspective, having a detailed "As Is" map—complete with work definitions, costs, and impacts—allows for an effective *baseline* against which to compare future changes; this will later become critical to the teams' acceptance of accountability.

From a team development perspective, it offers the opportunity for all team members to contribute, interact, and *integrate* their experiences on a single media, visible to everyone, *without the domination of a single team member*. Because the team members are not allowed to describe new design ideas on this process map, they are not offered the opportunity to assert personal agendas. The overall team is given the opportunity to practice interaction, integration, and cooperation. This is critical at this stage of their identity. The decision-making processes they undergo to create the "As Is" map enhance and re-enforce the *Forging of a Common Identity*. In this case, a visibly mapped common experience represents a significant common identity.

These dynamics are recognized, encouraged, and supported by the interventionists throughout the "As Is" process mapping phase.

In the "child process" phase, these dynamics are repeated for the sub-team level.

Activity: Process mapping basics. A process mapping SME demonstrates the basics of process mapping, using common experiences as an example (e.g., making coffee or driving to the store). A high-level sample map is provided, then more detailed maps as appropriate.

Process map SME deliverable: Presentation of process mapping basics, including high-level generic process map, and subsequent sample detailed maps, including examples of cost, time, duration, safety, and work-arounds. Review comments are also displayed.

Typical intervention level: Facilitator, SME

Activity: Generic process map. A generic, high-level map is displayed, walking the team through a simple example. Time estimates are provided, yielding cost estimates, including major queues and conditional

branching. Intrinsic safety analysis is provided, if applicable, as well as informal work-arounds (a.k.a. Contingent Process Paths). Finally, team reaction is encouraged, and review comments are made on the process map.

"Child" process maps, or more detailed sample maps, are drilled down from the generic process map, demonstrating how the high-level map can be extended to full working detail.

Deliverable: A generic process map is demonstrated, with corresponding child maps, to illustrate how any process can be mapped graphically.

Typical intervention level: Facilitator, SME

Activity: Core "As Is" process map

A high-level map is developed, the core process that defines the HPT effort's scope. This includes several key components described next.

Activity: Idealized process map. The initial process map is the idealized process—the way the process is supposed to work. According to procedures and/or training and/or management direction, this process describes the way the process is expected to work on paper.

Critical facilitated deliverable: A designated team member acts as scribe, another as moderator, to collect the team's input on synthesizing a core process map. These are drawn on a wall visible to the entire team, either on hardcopy or computer projection (hardcopy preferred so that the map can remain visible throughout the Work Re/Design).

Typical intervention level: Facilitator

Activity: Cost/Time/Duration/Queues identified. For each segment on the process map, costs, times, durations, queues, and other time/cost-related information is itemized. Where possible, standardized units of measure are used (e.g., standard hours, standard labor), although each will ultimately have to be converted to "total absorbed cost" for uniform comparison. Where times/costs vary considerably, an average should be used or an average with deviation limits.

Deliverable: The process map is itemized with time and cost information for each segment of the map.

Typical intervention level: Facilitator, SME

Activity: Intrinsic safety value assigned (for those processes involving a potential hazard to stakeholders). A Safety SME provides basic information about assigning an intrinsic hazard value to each segment, and orients the team to its usage. The team then assigns a hazard value to each

segment of the process map; the higher the value, the more hazardous the process.

This may also represent a key intervention point for team members. Personal safety is often one area where the process *directly affects the team member*. Depending upon individual resistance, this may offer the team member the opportunity to explore the relevance of the process map—and the work—to his or her routine work.

It is important to note that physical safety is not the only key metric for safety and hazards. Emotional safety, mental health, and other dimensions are also critically important in today's working environment, and *all* safety dimensions need to be examined as part of this intrinsic safety value assignment/review.

Deliverable: A Safety SME orients the team to intrinsic safety value analysis, and guides the team through an assignment of value for each segment.

Typical intervention level: Facilitator, Catalyst, SME

Activity: "As Is" Initial Process Review. The team now reviews the idealized process for its correlation to real-world work, and makes comments and changes accordingly.

Deliverable: Sanity check review of process map by overall team

Typical intervention level: Facilitator

Activity: Contingent process paths identified

Deliverable: The team's designated moderator and designated scribe mark the real-world process map segments that really occur during problems. These segments and paths are marked in different inks to readily separate them from the idealized paths.

Typical intervention level: Facilitator

Activity: Problem/Issue/Opportunities identified. The team provides specific input on problems, issues, and opportunities through adhesive note information adhered to appropriate portions of the process map. Color-coded notes include red/pink (problems), blue/green (issues), and yellow (opportunities). Problems are defined as potential barriers and showstoppers to the process; issues are defined as things that might increase costs/times but would not potentially stop the process; and opportunities are those items that could be done to make a considerable difference in output.

Deliverable: Team provides overall review by adhesive notes on process map indicating key problems, issues, and/or opportunities.

Typical intervention level: Facilitator

5. OPERATIONAL REVIEW: "AS IS"—
BREAKOUT TEAMS

Having itemized the core process map and, as an integrated team having created, reviewed, and provided feedback on it, breakout teams are ready to drill down to the next level of detail. This may include separate key processes or more detail on key segments of the core processes; however selected and determined by the team, the breakout teams are formed and the "As Is" Process Map and "As Is" Process Review are repeated for the breakouts. The selection of key processes to be analyzed and the drill-down detail required is simple: What is required to make quantum changes in the overall results? For example, drilling down a segment of the core process that only consists of 8 percent of process time and 5 percent of process costs would probably not make a quantum change in overall results (unless it significantly impacted other areas).

Activity: Key "child" "As Is" process map created. Derived from the higher-level core process map, the child process map further defines a specific scope of work. Typically, the child process is a subset of the core process map, and includes the following components.

Activity: Idealized process map (child). The initial child process map is the idealized process; the way the process is supposed to work. According to procedures and/or training and/or management direction, this process describes the way the process is expected to work "on paper."

Critical facilitated deliverable: A designated team member acts as scribe, another as moderator, to collect the team's input on synthesizing a core process map. These are drawn on a wall visible to the entire team, either on hardcopy or computer projection (hardcopy preferred so that the map can remain visible throughout the Work Re/Design).

Typical intervention level: Facilitator, Coach, SME

Activity: Cost/Time/Duration/Queues identified (child). For each segment on the process map, costs, times, durations, queues, and other time/cost-related information is itemized. Where possible, standardized units of measure are used (standard hours, standard labor, etc.), although each will ultimately have to be converted to "total absorbed cost" for uniform comparison. Where times/costs vary considerably, an average should be used or an average with deviation limits.

Deliverable: The child process map is itemized with time and cost information for each segment of the map.

Typical intervention level: Facilitator, SME

Activity: Intrinsic safety value assigned. A Safety SME provides basic information about assigning an intrinsic hazard value to each segment and orients the team to its usage. The team then assigns a hazard value to each segment of the process map; the higher the value, the more hazardous the process.

Deliverable: A Safety SME orients the team to intrinsic safety value analysis and guides the team through an assignment of value for each segment.

Typical intervention level: Facilitator, SME

Activity: "As Is" initial process review (child). The team now reviews the idealized process for its correlation to real-world work and makes comments and changes accordingly.

Deliverable: "Sanity check" review of process map by overall team

Typical intervention level: Facilitator

Activity: Contingent process paths identified (child)

Deliverable: The team's designated moderator and designated scribe mark the real-world process map segments that really occur during problems. These segments and paths are marked in different inks to readily separate them from the idealized paths.

Typical intervention level: Facilitator

Activity: Problem/Issue/Opportunities identified (child). The team provides specific input on problems, issues, and opportunities through adhesive note information adhered to appropriate portions of the process map. Color-coded notes include red/pink (problems), blue/green (issues), and yellow (opportunities). Problems are defined as potential barriers and showstoppers to the process; issues are defined as things that might increase costs/times but would not potentially stop the process; and opportunities are those items that could be done to make a considerable difference in output.

Deliverable: Team provides overall review by adhesive notes on process map indicating key problems, issues, and/or opportunities.

Typical intervention level: Facilitator

Activity: Integration review of all child process maps. Depending upon the number of child processes and their interdependence, the overall team reviews all child process maps for understanding and identification of key integration points. This may vary from a generic presentation of each child map to a detailed itemization of interdependencies and work flow linkages.

Deliverable: A comprehensive review of all child process maps, potentially including specific interdependencies, by all team members.

Typical intervention level: Facilitator, Coach

Communication

Continuing communication is critical to the success of the effort; key stakeholders must be kept "in the loop" during the Work Re/Design, and the organization needs to be updated. Also highly recommended are Process Map Fairs or Road Shows that take the "As Is" maps and then the "To Be" maps to the organization, asking for input, feedback, and opinions; this can be very helpful in enrolling the organization in the change management process. Though this is often coordinated by the Communications Team, it needs to be actively supported by all members of the HPT effort.

Activity: Summary to the organization (Week 1). The Communications Team should decide on the best media to use to communicate to the affected organization(s); this often includes newsletters, voice mail, and internal company documentation. However, at a minimum, the team should be communicating once a week to the organization as to its progress, its learnings, and its plans. This includes the following items (next).

Facilitated deliverable: Communication is made to the organization and to key stakeholders as to the progress, learnings, and plans of the Work Re/Design effort to date.

Typical intervention level: Facilitator

Learnings

What are the key learnings so far this week? Any surprises? What were the reactions to what the team heard—from customers to leaders to SMEs to key stakeholders?

Accomplishments

What did the team get done this week? Were there any unanticipated results from the data reviews or the review of the "As Is" process maps? What were the intangible accomplishments of the team?

Plans for Next Week

In outline form, what are the plans for the following week? What will affect the rest of the organization and the key stakeholders? Will there be an "As Is" process fair? How will the HPT team continue to communicate

with the rest of the organization? How does the team want the rest of the organization to communicate with itself?

6. OPERATIONAL REVIEW: CONTROL CHARTING—ENTIRE TEAM / BREAKOUT TEAMS

Having completed the initial data review via process mapping and graphical problem identification, the team now begins to analyze its data. In this series of activities, the team prioritizes its barriers and develops an initial problem mitigation strategy.

When Control Charting is used, the team identifies the leading issues and barriers based upon overall stakeholder review of the detailed "As Is" process maps. The top issues are identified, and a framework for their elimination or reduction is developed. This method is relatively straight-forward; it offers a platform for consensus building and decision making that will be critical to the team moving forward.

A technical concern with problem mitigation is its underlying assumption that the barriers *require* actionable mitigation. Some barriers are self-enforcing; they only exist as team members *believe* they exist. Some technical and perspective interventions may be helpful for the teams to explore this.

Another expansion of Control Charting is Variance Analysis, where the team analyzes each problem occurrence (i.e., process variance) and performs an in-depth review of its causations throughout the entire end-to-end process. Variance Analysis can be very effective, particularly when there are many different contributing factors to the product variance, and particularly when there are cascading variances where problems create problems that may create problems. For most teams at this stage, however, the detail and patience required to complete the Variance Analysis is excessive. These teams often feel ready to make decisions; they may feel they have been precluded from asserting their own individual answers, and are impatient to get to the actual design phase. The use of an abbreviated Control Charting analysis can be effective in addressing both the teams' impatience and the need for effective problem mitigation.

In either Control Charting or Variance Analysis, some team members may attempt to assert their own agendas at this point. It is helpful for the interventionists to recognize that behavior and offer a structure that diminishes it at this time.

Activity: Control Charting of key variances: Core process. The control chart itemizes the variances that occur in a process, and specify *where* they occur, *where* they are first noticed, *how* they impact/affect the overall process results, and *what* can be done to eliminate them. If they cannot

be eliminated, then they need to be reduced at least to the level where they do not significantly impact the overall results of the process. The key components of this activity are shown later.

Deliverable: The team completes control chart for the core process defined in the core "As Is" process map.

Typical intervention level: Facilitator, SME

Activity: Control charting basics: Entire team. The team reviews basics of Control Charting and is walked through a sample development.

Deliverable: Orientation of Control Charting and development of example.

Typical intervention level: Facilitator, SME

Selection of Top "Errors/Problems/Variances" by Team: Core Process: Entire Team

Using the core process As-Is process map, the team determines the top variances. This can be from multivote, consensus, or other nominal group technique. These variances are those that have the most impact on the overall process results (including intangible impacts on the organization).

Identification of "Showstoppers": Entire Team

The team identifies all potential issues/barriers that could bring the entire process to a halt. There may be prioritization required to make this a realistic list of major showstoppers.

Reduction/Elimination Strategies: Entire Team

The team takes each specific variance and develops a specific strategy to reduce or eliminate the variance. These strategies need to be specific.

Process Changes

For each strategy developed, identify the specific process changes that are required. What are the process steps to be added/eliminated, and what critical paths are needed to accomplish this?

Resource Requirements

For each strategy developed, identify the specific resource requirements to implement this. At an overall level, what costs are associated with this variance reduction/elimination? Are additional people required? Are less people required? What equipment is needed? Are outside resources required? Note that this is only an estimate; as appropriate, more detail will be developed later.

Impact on the Organization

For each strategy developed, the impact should be assessed. As the variance is reduced/eliminated, what is the *impact* on the organization? on the key stakeholders? Will this be a major or minor impact? What would change in customer expectations? Will present vendors be impacted?

Potential Barriers and Opportunities

For each strategy developed, itemize the potential barriers to getting this accomplished. Are policies in place to preclude this from happening? Would the change be too great for specific people in the organization to support it? Would it take too much money?

Similarly, what are the *opportunities* should this variance be eliminated? What would happen to customer satisfaction and employee motivation? Would new product or service areas be possible? Would this free up other resources to do needed work?

The only negative criterion—a case where the strategy is out of bounds—is where it violates the Sandbox.

Activity: Control Charting of key variances: Child processes: Breakout teams. The process of Control Charting is repeated for each of the child processes developed earlier. This also includes the following key components.

Deliverable: Each breakout team completes a control chart for each child "As Is" process defined earlier.

Typical intervention level: Facilitator, SME

Selection of Top Errors/Problems/Variances" by Team: Child Processes: Breakout

Using the child process(es) "As-Is" process map, the team determines the top variances. This can be from multivote, consensus, or other nominal group technique. These variances are those that have the most impact on the overall process results (including intangible impacts on the organization).

Identification of "Showstoppers": Breakout Teams

The team identifies all potential issues/barriers that could bring the entire process to a halt. There may be prioritization required to make this a realistic list of major "showstoppers."

Reduction/Elimination Strategies: Breakout Teams

The team takes each specific variance and develops a specific strategy to reduce or eliminate the variance. These strategies need to be specific.

Process Changes

For each strategy developed, identify the specific process changes that are required. What are the process steps to be added/eliminated, and what critical paths are needed to accomplish this?

Resource Requirements

For each strategy developed, identify the specific resource requirements to implement this. At an overall level, what costs are associated with this variance reduction/elimination? Are additional people required? Are fewer people required? What equipment is needed? Are outside resources required? Note that this is only an estimate; as appropriate, more detail will be developed later.

Impact on the Organization

For each strategy developed, the impact should be assessed. As the variance is reduced/eliminated, what is the *impact* on the organization? on the key stakeholders? Will this be a major or minor impact? What would change in customer expectations? Will present vendors be impacted?

Potential Barriers and Opportunities

For each strategy developed, itemize the potential barriers to getting this accomplished. Are policies in place to preclude this from happening? Would the change be too great for specific people in the organization to support it? Would it take too much money?

Similarly, what are the *opportunities* should this variance be eliminated? What would happen to customer satisfaction and employee motivation? Would new product or service areas be possible? Would this free up other resources to do needed work?

The only negative criterion—a case where the strategy is out of bounds—is where it violates the Sandbox.

Activity: Child process Control Charting: Report-out to entire team. Each break-out team reports back to the entire team, providing the results and learnings. Key areas of active listening and interaction include specific points of integration, conflict, and potential leveraging between processes. Where do the strategies complement each other? Where could they build upon each other? Where are there potential conflicts between the strategies and/or resources?

It is strongly noted that these strategies are not necessarily the key strategies moving forward; though many may be incorporated into the

final presentation to Executive Leadership, at the moment they are only potential strategies to address the issues.

Deliverable: Report-out of child process control charts; includes integration of these potential strategies and identification of areas of potential leverage and potential conflict

Typical intervention level: Facilitator, SME

Activity: Vendor Team report-back to entire team. The Vendor Team has been working in parallel to the overall Work Re/Design effort, working with vendors to determine new ideas and potential product areas. This report-back is a status update to the entire team.

Potentially Critical Activity: Communication Team solicits input and feedback on "As Is" The Communication Team coordinates the communication of the "As Is" processes (both core and child) to the rest of the affected organization. This may be in the form of Process Fairs or simply email; whichever media is chosen, the Communication Team solicits active input and feedback from the organization, including those specific inputs identified in earlier analysis steps: Contingent Process Paths Identified and the Problems/Issues/Opportunities. This is repeated for the child processes.

Note: Depending upon the team and the overall organization, this can be a mission-critical activity.

The level of de facto integration between the working team and its surrounding organization may determine the effectiveness of this activity.

For those HPT efforts that are relatively self-contained (i.e., where the Work Re/Design team comprises all the team members that will actually be performing the work), this activity serves to foster support and integration. For these efforts, communication is typically in the form of newsletters, broadcast voicemails or emails, or Webcasting. It provides an important communication link and is typically biased from the team; that is, although the team wants and needs feedback, it is more focused on output rather than input.

For those efforts that may be facing phased implementation, where the future team members may not be included in the formal Work Re/Design, the effective integration of these potential team members into the real-time deliberations of the Work Re/Design team is critical. In this type of Work Re/Design, it will be *mission-critical* for the interventionist to support the team and the leader in creating a continuous integration that links the Work Re/Design team with the potential team members. For many HPT efforts, this consists of regular updates and field data collection, informing key stakeholders of the teams' progress, and soliciting input.

Potentially Critical Deliverable: Communicating the Work Re/Design teams' discoveries and decisions, and integrating key stakeholder input into the teams' design

Typical intervention level: Facilitator, Catalyst, SME

7. DESIGN: "TO BE" PROCESS MAPPING

Throughout the Work Re/Design so far, the team has been undergoing significant change. In the initial days of Work Re/Design, the team was forging a common sense of identity through *the common experience of impact*. For many teams, this impact began as soon as they were introduced to their "impossible" goals. Continuing throughout the data review and analysis phases, the team has typically been impacted by all success dimensions: employee value, customer value, stockholder value, and operational value.

As the team progresses through the template activities, they have also been encouraged to *forge a common identity*. This is a natural outcome of their common reaction experience to the organizational challenges, but also is practiced through the activities. Throughout the first half of the Work Re/Design, the team has been called upon to make decisions with increasing frequency and intensity. As the team attempts many different decision-making mechanisms and formats, it is inherently forging and displaying its new sense of self. This is continually reinforced by the leader and interventionist.

Similarly, individuals have typically been asserting their own agendas and testing their own position within the team throughout the "As Is" mapping and analysis phases. Different individuals typically assert themselves through a variety of behaviors: resistance, aggressiveness, and even withdrawal. The leader and interventionist can help these individuals discover effective ways of asserting their own ideas and identity within the team. When these interventions are effectively applied, all individuals discover appropriate ways to achieve their own desires and needs while supporting the overall direction of the team.

By this point in the Work Re/Design process, an important strategy of *responsibility* and *accountability* has also been applied. In the first few days, the team was provided a structured agenda; activities were preplanned to provide a predictable format for the day's work. Over the following week, however, this structure was deliberately lessened; the team was provided fewer and fewer *tasks* and more and more *goals* to achieve the day's deliverables. There was decreasing emphasis on *specific work* and more emphasis on *accountability for results*. This follows the natural progression of team development.

Since the beginning of the Work Re/Design, this increase of accountability and decrease of structure is also supported by the leader and inter-

ventionist. Teams and team members are expected to produce more and more of their support services as the Work Re/Design phase increases. By the middle of the second week, the team is expected to be arranging all its key support activities. For most teams, even rudimentary meeting facilitation is expected to be performed by team members.

These dynamics support the team's rapid development and re-enforces their formation of an *integrated* team built upon the needs of its individuals in a way that addresses the organizational needs.

Now, the team begins the phase that allows them to design a new system; the team members apply their identity to the issues and challenges that face them.

In the design phase of Work Re/Design, the team is now ready to start making decisions about the new system and how it will achieve the goals without violating the Sandbox. Their own change in perspective and perception will allow them to view the problems with a new level of creativity.

Having been discouraged from making design choices to date, the team is now expected to make many different design decisions. This will increase toward the final date of the Work Re/Design phase, the "Final Presentation."

Activity: Creative thinking. To change the paradigm from "what is" to "what could be," a series of creative thinking exercises are often performed. This may range from simple creative video review to interactive exercises to more extended experiential interventions.

Although this activity may assist in creative thinking, it does not typically induce creativity per se. As shown earlier, creativity is the result of a shift in perspective and perception; all the previous activities may contribute to this shift.

However, this exercise can be effective in reminding the team to look for creative approaches and can provide a change of pace to the brisk "As Is" activities that preceded it.

Deliverable: Creative thinking exercise

Typical intervention level: Facilitator, Coach

Activity: Goal/Sandbox/Deliverables/Expectation review. Leadership reviews the original goals, expectations, deliverables, as well as the Sandbox limitations for the team. Discussion is held for clarity of understanding but not for renegotiation of the goals or sandbox items. This provides a reminder of the high-level goals and constraints that the new "To Be" process must achieve.

Deliverable: Review of the charter goals and constraints

Typical intervention level: Facilitator, Coach

Initial "To Be" Process Map

The team now determines how it will split up into breakout teams (if at all) and create the first "To Be" process map, which will become the basis for the recommendations of the Final Presentation.

The team is now asked to come up with a process map, and *process only* suggestions are made. This is a critical time for the team to take responsibility; allow the natural leaders of the team to move the team forward to an answer. It is often helpful to encourage the team to diagram *something* on the process map, even if it is not their vision of the final recommendation.

Note: The period required for this activity may vary from hours to days.

Critical deliverable: Team provides first draft of "To Be" process map. This may be a single core process or several child processes or several integrated processes (this is determined by the team).

Critical note: The team may try very hard to resist being given the responsibility to develop this process map and may react negatively to the apparent lack of support provided by facilitators and leadership in developing their first draft of the process map. It is critical that the team be supported in the process, without being directed in the content.

Typical intervention level: Catalyst

Activity: Initial test against goals/Sandbox/deliverables/expectations. The team reviews its first draft against the goals/Sandbox. Will this achieve the specified goals? Does it fit within the Sandbox given earlier? How does it need to be modified or changed or scrapped to achieve the goals?
Deliverable: Test of initial "To Be" process against charter
Typical intervention level: Facilitator, Coach

8. DESIGN: "TO BE" PROCESS MAP

Activity: Team reaction. The team reviews its first day of open design. The team reviews its progress, accomplishments, and frustrations.

Typically, the team's first iteration of "To Be" process map does *not* achieve the goals and may violate some of the Sandbox. A truly critical review of the process is important; an effective partnering of the leader (as content expert) and interventionist (as developmental process expert) is needed to help the team become self-critical.

Deliverable: General reaction to increase self-checking and peer review. What can the team do moving forward to enhance the learnings and reduce the frustrations? What progress checks need to be made on a regular basis? What would the team like to see more of / less of?

Typical intervention level: Facilitator, Coach

Activity: Reiteration: "To Be" process mapping. As almost all initial "To Be" designs do not achieve the HPT goals, it now becomes a reiterative process to continually redesign the initial draft process into a process that meets the goals and stays within the Sandbox. The teams break out or stay integrated as they design, but the organization of the team is focused around the process map design.

Deliverable: Reiterated process map of "To Be" process, continually checked against the goals and the Sandbox.

Typical intervention level: Facilitator, Coach

Activity: Test against variance/challenge criteria. As a continuing part of the reiterative process, the team checks the validity of the reiterated process design against the variances noted and described in the control charting.

Deliverable: Reiterative check of the current "To Be" process map against the variances identified in Control Charting.

Typical intervention level: Facilitator, Coach

Activity: Communication Team: "As Is" report-out. The Communication Team has coordinated the communication of the "As Is" process map to the organization, and has coordinated the collection of feedback back to the team. This information is summarized. Any surprises or significant differences between the organizational feedback and the HPT team are highlighted and reviewed. The entire team then determines if significant changes need to be made in the HPT "As Is," and whether additional control charting needs to be done to accommodate the organizational feedback.

As noted earlier, in the Phased Implementation, this process becomes critical to the eventual team. For this approach, considerable focus and resource support should be provided to the Communication Team activities.

Deliverable: Communication Team reports back on "As Is" feedback from the organization.

Typical intervention level: Facilitator, Coach

9. DESIGN: "TO BE" PROCESS MAPPING REVIEW

The "To Be" process map is now reviewed in the same manner as the "As Is" process maps were reviewed earlier in the Operational Review. This includes costs, time, and safety reviews.

Activity: Cost/Duration/Queues defined and reviewed. Each segment of the "To Be" process map is reviewed and quantified for cost, time (duration

and process), and queues. Wherever possible, costs are "total absorbed cost," and include all applicable overheads and indirect costs.

Deliverable: Team quantifies costs and times of each segment of "To Be" process and totals for overall process. Total resources are compared to goals and Sandbox for applicability.

Typical intervention level: Facilitator, Coach

Activity: Intrinsic safety value assigned (for those processes involving a potential hazard to stakeholders). As performed earlier in the "As Is" phase, an intrinsic safety/hazard value is defined for each segment of the "To Be" process map, and an overall value is determined for the process. Should this value be greater (i.e., more hazardous) than the "As Is" value, the process should be re-examined and redefined until it contains more intrinsically safe activities and/or exposures.

Deliverable: Intrinsic safety analysis of the "To Be" process map is completed, and an overall value is assigned. This safety value should be less than the value determined for the "As Is" process.

Typical intervention level: Facilitator, Coach, SME

Activity: Barriers/Issues identified. Because the new process is new, it offers the opportunity to create new barriers and issues as it is implemented. As with the "As Is," these need to be identified, and strategies/tactics are required to be developed to address these issues. These are itemized next.

Deliverable: Team identified key issues, develops strategies to reduce the issues and barriers, and enrolls key stakeholders to provide a platform of support moving forward.

Typical intervention level: Facilitator

Potential Issues/Barriers Identified

The team brainstorms potential areas of issues and potential barriers to the implementation and success of the new process. These are itemized, listing key stakeholders, specific potential issues, and the nature of potential barriers.

Strategy to Reduce Barriers

As with the Control Charting in the Operational Review, the team develops specific strategies and tactics to reduce or eliminate the potential for barriers to occur during the implementation process. These strategies should be specific, including any group of key stakeholders that may require assistance in the move to the new state/process.

Key Stakeholders Enrolled

In addition to specific actions to reduce barriers, strategies for all key stakeholders is developed (at a high level) to enroll these stakeholders into the success of the HPT effort.

Activity: Impacts identified. The team reviews the overall process and itemizes the potential impacts on the organization as a whole and the existing process specifically. These are itemized next.

Deliverable: Team identifies key impacts on the existing organization and processes and develops the framework for a transition strategy to ease the impact.

Typical intervention level: Facilitator, Coach

Activity: Impact on organization (qualitative). The team reviews the potential impact on key areas of the organization and predicts the qualitative level of impact. This may include sampling of key individuals within the affected organization, as well as individual team members' assessment of the impact. Qualitative review is performed on local portions of the organization, as well as an overall qualitative assessment of the impact on the general organization. Specific attention is paid to customers.

Impact on Process (Quantitative)

The team quantitatively assesses the impact on present processes, particularly those that either feed the core process or are fed by the core process.

Transition Strategy Developed

Given the qualitative and quantitative impacts identified, the team now develops general strategies to ease the impact and ensure the successful implementation of the "To Be." This specifically recognizes that the "To Be" *cannot* be simply implemented; there must be a transition period from the "As Is" to the "To Be" process.

Reports-Out

If the team had performed the Reviews through Breakout teams, the team reports back and integrates its learnings.

10. DESIGN: TRANSITION PLAN

One of the critical success themes of High Performance Teams is: All key success dimensions are addressed.

HPTs are not less accountable for developing real-world answers to their problems; in fact, most successful HPTs have higher levels of expectations for the business validity of their approach. Successful teams include effective business plans for change.

It is important to note that the team's activity assignments are less task specific and more project specific. As the team progresses toward its Final Presentation deliverable, the team has increasing flexibility in its approaches and corresponding increasing accountability for its outcomes. This increases the team's natural tendency to leverage its own team culture to achieve its goals, and re-enforces the *Application of Common Identity to the Common Outcome.*

Critical Activity: Transition Plan development. Following the outline of standard business plans, the *Transition Plan* simply states the means of getting from here—the "As Is"—to there (the "To Be"). Many traditional implementations fail because they do not pay attention to this step; teams are too eager to implement their new designs and management is often impatient for results: The results are typically chaotic in these instances.

The team must acknowledge and deal with the here and now and *transition* to the new system design within the time frame stated in the goals. This requires deliberation and consideration of which actions are needed by whom with whom to make the permanent changes happen.

Critical Deliverable: Team develops a Transition Plan that details not only the changes needed to achieve the goals, but also the path to get those changes implemented. This includes cost justification, barrier removal, and risk mitigation. This deliverable is one of several delivered during the Final Presentation. These include the following areas next.

Typical intervention level: Facilitator, Coach

Financial Costs / Impacts

Total absorbed [investment] costs are itemized for each major change. Impacts, both tangible and intangible are itemized, and risk mitigation tactics are described for each major change. The team is clearly able to describe the new costs, and any contingent liabilities, in outlining the outlays required to make the changes.

Financial Benefits / Returns

Short-term (less than 12 months) and long-term (multiyear) benefits are calculated for tangible benefits, and intangible benefits are itemized.

Goal Benefits / Returns

The contribution of each key/major change to the goals is itemized and, where possible, quantified for its impact on specific goal achievement. Rate(s) of return are also calculated where practical, include Return on Investment (ROI), Return on Asset (ROA), and Return on Sales/Revenue (ROS).

Net Value of Major Changes

All the quantitative rates of return and benefits are calculated and totaled. Intangible benefits are itemized and described. Where possible, an overall increase in Shareholder Value calculation should be made.

Summary of Transition Strategy

Given all the changes itemized in the section, Design: "To Be" Process Mapping and the barrier/impact transition strategy highlighted earlier, the team summarizes the transition strategy for key areas. This becomes the basis for the transition project plan moving forward. Standard project-management elements are included in this plan.

Critical: Roles/Responsibilities/Action Plan(s)

Individuals are identified for each major section of the transition plan, including *who* will do *what* by *when*. Action plans are outlined in this section, providing the basis for individual project plan elements as the transition phase is begun.

As noted in the Culture Change section, the ability of individual team members to assert their own identity within the team's framework is critical to their mutual development. This allows the team members to *Apply their Individual Identity to Specific Roles and Responsibilities*. By ensuring that this is explicitly stated as part of the Transition Plan, individuals' ability to assert themselves within the team is enhanced.

Key Stakeholders' Action Plan(s)

The team itemizes a listing of key stakeholders and the action plan(s) required to enroll their support for the transition. If a formal Stakeholder Analysis was performed in the earlier activity, Stakeholder Analysis, this would include specific action plans to support the stakeholders' move to the desired internalization level.

Note: This may be included in the specific Change Management and Stakeholder Communication Plan, later, rather than as an explicit part of the Transition Plan.

Milestones Required

Specific milestones required by due date by responsible party to achieve the transition are necessary. This may involve significant support from outside the HPT effort.

Time Line for Transition

A full Gantt chart is prepared for the transition itself that ends up supporting the goal timeline. This includes all milestones indicated in the previous note.

Metrics for Success

Key monitoring and measurement metrics are defined to evaluate the transition plan's success. Note that this is not the monitoring metrics for the team as itemized later in Metric Development, but rather the metrics for the *transition*.

Reports-Out to Entire Team

If the team has developed the Transition Plan in segmented parts (e.g., following separated process maps), it is necessary to report out to the entire team and integrate the effort, including potential leverage and conflict areas.

Communication Team Report-Out

Continuing communication remains critical, even with all the different media channels being used simultaneously.

Activity: Summary to organization. As itemized in Summary to Organization, a report summary to the organization is made, including learnings, accomplishments, and plans for the following week.

Deliverable: Summary to the organization

Typical intervention level: Facilitator

Activity: Communication Team solicits input and feedback on "To Be." As shown in the earlier section, Communication Team Solicits Input and Feedback on "As Is," the Communication Team now needs to coordinate the same with the "To Be" process maps. The Communication Team coordinates the communication of the "To Be" processes (both core and child) to the rest of the affected organization. This may be in the form of Process Fairs or simply email; whichever media is chosen, the Communication Team solicits active input and feedback from the organization, including those specific inputs identified in Barriers/

Issues Identified and Impacts Identified. This is repeated for any child or dependent processes. A timetable is developed to summarize this information back to the team.

Also as with the earlier section, in the Phased Implementation plan, this step is critical to the eventual success of the effort.

Deliverable: "To Be" feedback and interaction

Typical intervention level: Facilitator, Coach

Critical Activity: Executive input and feedback on "To Be." Whether coordinated through the Communications Team, the leader, Sponsoring Executive, or other key stakeholder, it is critically important that *all* key executives are integrated into the design process. Despite the Final Presentation deliverable, there should be no surprises at that time; all critical review and feedback should take place well before the end of the Work Re/Design phase.

From the perspective of the executive—both Sponsoring and Non-Sponsoring—it is an important sanity check to ensure that the team's approach does not violate the Sandbox. For those approaches that are difficult to accept or represent political challenges to the external organization, the executive should take the time to consider whether the approach is *possible*; this may require considerable interaction with team members.

From the team's perspective, although the executive should not be directing a specific approach, the executive does have valid input and guidance to the team. This expertise should not be excluded.

For all key stakeholders, there should be sufficient ongoing communication and interaction so that the team has an opportunity to work through difficult issues with the executives and the executives are able to truly understand the new approaches of the team. Practically, this typically involves several hours per week of interaction between the team and the key executives.

Critical deliverable: Executives interact and understand team's new processes.

Typical facilitation level: Coach, Catalyst

11. DESIGN: TRAINING AND PERFORMANCE

Given the new key processes, the team now defines the training and performance requirements, and develops plans to support that, moving forward. Where skillset gaps exist between the old and new processes, training is used to support the team's transition to the new state.

In almost all cases, performance is a function of training and experience. Although the team may elect to define positive and negative conse-

quences for behavioral performance, this section deals with the *ability* of the team members to perform the work.

Activity: Profile of revised skills/training/competencies. Given the new core process map and the key child processes (Design: "To Be" Process Mapping), the team needs to define the skillsets required for the new processes. What are the specific skills needed to accomplish each segment of the new process?

Deliverable: Skillsets required to perform the "To Be" processes are defined; this may be a complete definition or just those that are different from the previous "As Is" process. Skillsets should include specific competencies, task capabilities, and capacity and should be specific, measurable, and testable.

Typical intervention level: Facilitator

Activity: Organizational assessment of baseline skills. The team provides an assessment of the organization's ability to perform the new skillsets, focusing on those skillsets/competencies that are different from the "As Is" process map. (Technical Review: "As Is" Process Mapping). This may be qualitative in parts, but should be as comprehensive and as complete as practical. Specifically, what is the general baseline of skillsets ? What targeted segments of the population are identified?

Deliverable: Assessment of organizational baseline skillsets. This may be combined with the earlier profile of revised skills.

Typical intervention level: Facilitator, Coach

Activity: Gap analysis. Reviewing and comparing the Profile of Revised Skillsets and Organizational Assessment of Baseline Skillsets, the team determines the specific gaps in skillsets, competencies, and orientation/education that exist as a direct result of the "To Be" process. This gap analysis is specific to target populations and in critical situations may even be specific to individuals.

Deliverable: A gap analysis is derived that identifies the skillset gaps created as a result of the transition to the "To Be" process. This specifies the gaps and the populations.

Optional deliverable: In the event of critical resources and/or critical-path process steps, a skills chart may be developed, by process step, by individual, to identify critical gaps.

Typical intervention level: Facilitator, Coach

Activity: Training required. Coincident with the gap analysis, the team determines the specific training required. What training is required to

fill the gaps? What target populations are required to undergo the training?

Deliverable: A list of training requirements are defined.

Typical intervention level: Facilitator, Coach

Activity: Training plan developed. The training requirements are compared with the gap analysis and a new training plan is developed. What training is to be delivered to which group by when and how will its success be measured? How long will it take to deliver the training, and what is the period of time required for the training to take hold (i.e., what will be the positive and negative impacts on output effectiveness)? Who will deliver the training (i.e., what resources are required)?

Deliverable: Training plan is developed to transition the present workforce/team members to the new state, supporting the new key process requirements and the new goals.

Typical intervention level: Facilitator, Coach

12. DESIGN: WORK PLAN DEVELOPMENT

As the team increases its work definition, it increasingly discovers that it needs to provide *conventional* deliverables. Though the actual work plan may vary from a simple level-of-effort" work assignment to a more complex Master Production Schedule, it is an important planning vehicle for the team.

When producing this deliverable, many HPTs discover that they can produce *conventional* documents as a result of their *unconventional* approach. This is an important learning; not only does this allow the team to leverage their own traditional skillsets, they are also more readily integrated into their surrounding organization.

Activity: Work plan development. The work plan is the master scheduling plan for the team in terms of overall inputs and outputs. It defines the customer expectations of when to expect what. Most organizations already maintain a detailed scheduled of planned output, whether called a Work Plan or Master Production Schedule or Job Plan Sheet. This provides a comprehensive plan of output, detailed for the next 2 months after the Work Re/Design, and a planning horizon of 12 months after the Work Re/Design.

Note: In most cases, the team will need to create its own schedule inside the overall work plan, to allow for its own development and its own free time to continue redesign, training, and so on, while still meeting cus-

tomer demand. Whether or not to do this team schedule is decided by the team, but most teams will find this is a "critical path" to their success.

Deliverable: A Work Plan is developed in detail, by day for 2 months proceeding Work Re/Design, and a Planning Horizon by week for 12 months proceeding Work Re/Design.

Typical intervention level: Facilitator, Coach, SME

Activity: Work plan detailed review by organization. Each organization/child process reviews the detailed process requirements of the "To Be" process and compares this with customer requirements of delivery/service. Using the old estimates of resources (labor, materials, equipment, etc.), a capacity estimate is made of the resources necessary to produce the services required (high-level summary only).

Next, a resource plan is developed, using the new process, and a capacity estimate is made, also stating the labor, materials, and other resources required.

This plan provides specific job/product output that matches with customer need and requires a particular capacity. Key capacity bottlenecks are identified, specifically including skillsets, capital investment, special equipment, and the like.

Note that there may be a significant difference (delta) between the old capacity level and the new one. The new capacity level may not necessarily be less than the old, particularly in those areas that may have new bottlenecks of new equipment, new skillsets (training), and the like.

Deliverable: (1) Draft Work Plan and capacity analysis for customer needs using the "As Is" process; (2) Draft Work Plan and capacity analysis for customer needs using the new "To Be" process, without transition factored in.

Typical intervention level: Facilitator, SME

Activity: Required transition support. The transition plan identified earlier is now used to define the ramp-up period that transition items will require to become effective. The transition plan will be used to define the phasing in of the new work plan to the old work plan, to develop an overall work plan that supports transition needs. In most cases, the transition period will impact the speed with which the team can implement new safety/performance/productivity levels; it some cases, it may even *decrease* the team's levels while new equipment/training is brought in. It is the team's responsibility to predict this bubble of reduced effectiveness and to account for it in the overall business case for change.

Deliverable: Transition support requirements (resources and effectiveness impact) are itemized. The timeline for these requirements is identified,

as well as the impact (enhancing or diminishing) of output effectiveness. These include the components described next.

Typical intervention level: Facilitator, Coach, SME

Resources

The team reviews the transition plan itemization of resources required for transition, and incorporates the need for these resources into a new Transition Work Plan.

Work Plan Impacts/Opportunities

The team reviews the Transition Plan predictions and timeframes for improvement, and estimates the net impact of the improvement on the new Transition Work Plan.

Activity: Revised work plan by organization. Each child/key process team develops a separate work plan for the process, given the customer requirements developed earlier in the Work Plan/Production Schedule, the Draft Work Plans, the Work Plan Detailed Review by Organization, and the Required Transition Support. This revised work plan integrates these efforts and develops a comprehensive work plan per key process.

Deliverable: Integrated work plan, 2-month detailed/12-month planning horizon, that provides a net output plan for the process/team, given the transition requirements and effectiveness impacts.

Typical intervention level: Facilitator, Coach, SME

Activity: Reports-out by organization to entire team. Each work plan is presented and outlined to the entire team, with discussions around potential leverage and conflict points. Areas of common interest as well as areas of critical resource(s) are identified.

Deliverable: Each process's work plan is presented to the HPT effort team, with attention to potential points of leverage and conflict.

Typical intervention level: Facilitator, Coach, SME

Activity: Revised HPT effort work plan. Given the integration issues and opportunities identified in the earlier Reports-Out By Organization to Entire Team, an integrated, comprehensive work plan is developed, with 2-month detailed planning and a 12-month planning horizon that incorporates all key transition and customer requirements.

Deliverable: Final work plan

Typical intervention level: Facilitator, SME

Note: The actual placement of work plan design may vary in different efforts. For some efforts, with a fixed production or service schedule, the work plan can be quantified and reviewed after the transition plan. In other efforts, particularly where the work plan is flexible and may be contingent on other stakeholders, it is necessary to review the work plan after other plans are completed. It is important to remember that this template is intended to be shifted, modified, and rearranged as appropriate for the individual team.

13. DESIGN: CHANGE MANAGEMENT AND KEY STAKEHOLDER COMMUNICATION

To be successful in their High Performance approach to work, almost all HPTs' success depends upon the motivation and support of their key stakeholders. To be able to change a manufacturing process, for example, an HPT may require the customer to approve a product design change. In a distribution organization, another HPT may require engineering and documentation change approval. For most HPTs, the support and integration of their key stakeholders is required, but the stakeholders' culture shift is not.

Thus, whereas High Performance Teams are an example of Culture Change and depend upon culture-shifting interventions to become successful, their own strategies to address change are typically limited to Behavioral Change Management.

For those teams that *do* require breakthrough changes on the part of their key stakeholders, a *coincident HPT effort* is often undertaken. In these efforts, the team members of all key stakeholders are included. This may include members of other organizations, vendors, and even customers. For the purposes of this template, however, the key stakeholders are assumed to require incremental or significant change to support the HPT.

Activity: Change Management Orientation: Entire Team. Basics in Change Management are outlined for the team, from the tangible communication strategies to the intangible effects of leadership and motivation. Basic concepts of resistance, reaction, and motivation are outlined, as well as tenets of successful change management efforts.

Deliverable: Change Management orientation: The basics and sample case histories; how to develop a typical change management strategy for the HPT effort

Typical intervention level: Coach

Activity: Communication Team: Report-back on "To Be." The results of the feedback and input coordinated by the Communication Team is provided to the team. Given the change management orientation in the Social Data Review, Employee Data Review, and the Organization

Readiness Assessment, the team evaluates the feedback and input in the context of the organization's overall change management state.

Deliverable: Communication Team reports back on the organizational response to the "To Be" processes. Entire team reviews feedback in change management context.

Typical intervention level: Facilitator, Coach

Activity: Change management strategy development. The team (as a whole or in breakout teams—per stakeholder or per process) develops a specific change management strategy. These include the following components.

Deliverable: Change management plan

Typical intervention level: Coach

Key Stakeholders

The key stakeholders list itemized in Business Driver Stakeholders, Stakeholder Analysis, and/or Business Review Stakeholder Analysis is updated and includes new information from Communication Team report-back on "To Be." This may include specificity on level of influence and frequency of interaction, as well as level of internationalization, if included in the stakeholder analysis.

Major Impact Areas

Given the new "To Be" design, identify the major areas (process, organizational, stakeholder, etc.) to be impacted the greatest from the change to the new design. How will this impact the technical aspects? Cost? Customer? Employees? Vendors? What are the tangible impacts? The intangible?

Stakeholder Analysis Update

Update the stakeholder analysis to include the major impacts itemized earlier.

Strategy to Ease Impact

For each of the major impact areas and key stakeholders, develop strategy to ease the impact and change management of the new processes. What tangible strategies need to be employed by whom, for whom, and by when to make this a success? What intangible strategies are needed?

Roles and Responsibilities: Change Management Actions

The team now assigns roles, responsibilities, and time lines to the actions needed to support the change management strategies developed

in the Strategy to Ease Impact. This is project-oriented, providing clear direction moving forward and specifying follow-up requirements as soon as implementation is begun.

Activity: Communication Team solicits input and feedback on transition plan. As shown earlier in the template, just as the Communication Team solicited input and feedback on the "As Is" and "To Be" process maps, the Communication Team now needs to coordinate the same with the transition plan. This may be in the form of Process Fairs or simple email; whichever media is chosen, the Communication Team solicits active input and feedback from the organization. A timetable is developed to summarize this information back to the team.

Also as with the earlier section, in the Phased Implementation plan, this step is critical to the eventual success of the effort.

Deliverable: "To Be" feedback and interaction

Typical intervention level: Facilitator, Coach

(Continuing) Critical Activity: Executive input and feedback on the transition plan. Whether coordinated through the Communication Team, the leader, Sponsoring Executive, or other key stakeholder, it is critically important that *all* key executives are integrated into the design process. Despite the Final Presentation deliverable, there should be no surprises at that time; all critical review and feedback should take place well before the end of the Work Re/Design phase.

From the perspective of the executive—both Sponsoring and Non-Sponsoring—it is an important sanity check to ensure that the team's approach does not violate the Sandbox. For those approaches that are difficult to accept or represent political challenges to the external organization, the executive should take the time to consider whether the approach is possible; this may require considerable interaction with team members.

From the team's perspective, although the executive should not be directing a specific approach, the executive does have valid input and guidance to the team. This expertise should not be excluded.

For all key stakeholders, there should be sufficient ongoing communication and interaction so that the team has an opportunity to work through difficult issues with the executives, and the executives are able to truly understand the new approaches of the team. Practically, this typically involves several hours per week of interaction between the team and the key executives.

Critical deliverable: Executives interact and understand team's new plans for transition to the new process.

Typical facilitation level: Coach, Catalyst

14. DESIGN: INTEGRATION

Having developed many (apparently) disparate deliverables, it remains to integrate all these strategies into a comprehensive, cohesive business plan package. Not only is integration of the HPT effort team's deliverables required, but also integration with other HPT teams may be necessary at this point. Note that *resolution* all of these items may not be practical in a single day, but at least the *plan* to resolve these leverage/conflict points needs to be completed.

By this point in the Work Re/Design, the teams should be highly motivated and highly energetic; most efforts include multiple teams working in parallel to achieve their deliverables. There may even be some resentment toward the interventionists for "getting in the way."

Overall, the team's outputs are typical of HPTs: considerable invisible work early, then explosive output at the end. The final days of Work Re/Design follow this pattern: Many plans are finalized at once.

Activity: Integration plan. This plan provides the strategy for integrating the work of the HPT with those of other key stakeholders. Where the Change Management plan provides for the alignment and motivation of key stakeholders, the Integration Plan provides the work flow integration and information and decision flows.

The Integration Plan may include *previous* and *future* HPTs, as well as "external" stakeholders. This is particularly important in the Phased Implementation approach.

Deliverable: An integration plan is developed, including all key stakeholder and integration points external to the HPT effort, including specific process interdependencies. For each unique item, itemize strategy to integrate overall, including specific roles, responsibilities, and action plan(s). These include the following areas (next).

Typical intervention level: Facilitator, Coach, Catalyst, SME

Key Stakeholder Groups and Integration Points Identified

The team reviews all applicable groups and efforts potentially affected by the process changes and develops specific strategies to integrate with the teams/stakeholders. *Note:* This may overlap the Strategies to Ease Impact, although this specifically includes any external dependencies for the process not already captured.

Gaps Identified

What are the integration requirements (either for this HPT effort or for other efforts that must feed/be fed by this effort) for each key stake-

holder/process interdependency identified in Key Stakeholder Groups and Integration Points Identified? From a process perspective, itemize the specific gaps that must be eliminated/mitigated for overall success. From a change management perspective, itemize any potential missing issues/stakeholders not identified in Strategies to Ease Impact.

Strategies Developed to Integrate

For each unique item not identified in Strategies to Ease Impact, the team develops a strategy to successfully complete the integration. Whether this is a simple "memo of understanding" between varying efforts/organizations or as complex as a new organizational design, the integration plan outlines the strategy, tactics, and action plans required for successful integration.

Final Team Report(s)-Out to Entire Team

Where breakout teams have been developing and interfacing with external teams, all teams report out the strategies and plans to the entire team.

Metric Development

Although the original success metrics and the stretch goals outlined the high-level goals for the HPT effort, they are usually of insufficient detail for the team to be using on an *operational* basis. What are the key indices that the team should be measuring, monitoring, and basing course correction upon, on a frequent basis? How can the team determine the critical measures that would predict progress against the high-level metrics before it was too late? How and who will measure, monitor, and report out those metrics? How will the team make any necessary changes to the process? How will the team integrate all of its information? All these issues need to be determined *before* the plan becomes operational.

Metrics Defined for All Key Processes

There are three key levels of metrics defined that the team needs to determine for each key process and/or subprocess: minimum, planned, and stretch.

Activity: Minimum required metrics/levels of performance. What are the absolute minimum levels of performance (or lack thereof) that would dictate that the project would have to be dramatically changed immediately? This is not a de facto definition of the effort's failure, but rather an *emergency indicator that something must be changed – immediately.*

Deliverable: Minimum required metric/performance level for all key processes and subprocesses.

Typical intervention level: Facilitator, Coach

Activity: Planned metrics/levels of performance. What are the expected, routine levels of performance? What are most of the budgets and resource allocations made around? What is the basis of typical planning levels moving forward?

Deliverable: Planned levels of performance metrics for all key processes and subprocesses.

Typical intervention level: Facilitator, Coach

Activity: Stretch/HPT levels of performance. What are the greatest "impossible" levels of performance? These metrics are those levels that could be achieved, when everything goes right with the "To Be" process, after all transitions and integrations are completed. Contingency plans may need to be made for this eventuality. *Note:* Many teams achieve this level well before their estimated timeline!

Deliverable: Stretch levels of performance metrics for all key processes and subprocesses.

Typical intervention level: Facilitator, Coach

Activity: Timelines defined. Comparing the metrics defined in Metrics Defined with the Timeline for Transition, a ramp up or ramp down is made to the baseline metrics, defining an overall metric timeline.

Deliverable: Metric timeline defined for minimum, planned, and stretch metrics for all key processes and subprocesses

Typical intervention level: Facilitator, Coach

Activity: Metrics baselined. Defined metrics are baselined against "As Is" levels, if possible, to establish the baseline against which future progress is monitored. If present levels are not available, progress is monitored against the first week's monitoring metrics.

Deliverable: Metrics defined in Metrics Defined are baselined against "As Is" or initial implementation levels.

Typical intervention level: Facilitator, Coach

Activity: Monitoring methods defined. Specific means and methods of monitoring the key process/subprocess metrics are defined, including any specific equipment/training/orientation to obtain the measurements. Frequency of measurement is also defined.

Deliverable: Methods of measuring key metrics are defined.

Typical intervention level: Facilitator, Coach

Activity: Roles and responsibilities and action plans defined. Who will do what by when to obtain the metrics required is itemized in detail.

Deliverable: Action plan(s) for obtaining metric measurements and monitoring is (are) developed and defined.

Typical intervention level: Facilitator, Coach

Activity: Metric summary presentation: Entire team. Report-out of metrics definition, measurement, and monitoring is made to the entire team, and integration made to rest of the HPT plan.

Deliverable: Summary of metrics plan presented to entire team

Typical intervention level: Facilitator, Coach

Draft Presentation of HPT Recommendation

Activity: First draft presentation: Practice to entire team. Team prepares draft presentation of overall HPT effort recommendations, including charter, learnings, recommendations, and plans of action moving forward. This can be in varied formats; whichever format provides the most effective communication to the leadership and the executive leadership is recommended. The first presentation is made to the entire team, with each team member providing support and critical review.

Deliverable: Draft presentation of HPT recommendations to entire team

Typical intervention level: Facilitator, Coach, Catalyst, SME

Activity: Informal leader review of HPT recommendations. Key stakeholder/leader is provided draft presentation, with opportunity for reaction, support, and critical input/review. This not only may include the re-enforcing of socializing critical issues, but also may highlight final gaps or opportunities that need to be addressed prior to the formal presentation.

As noted earlier, it is critically important that the leaders and executives be involved with the team's designs; this should *not* be their first exposure to the team's draft recommendations.

Deliverable: Informal leader review of HPT recommendations

Typical intervention level: Facilitator, Coach, Catalyst

Activity: Presentation review/revision. Any last-minute changes are made at this time. Additional presentations/resources are also revised.

Deliverable: A formal rehearsal presentation is completed; all final revisions are made.

Typical intervention level: Facilitator, Coach, Catalyst, SME

15. FINAL PRESENTATION

This is the apparent culmination of the Work Re/Design phase of the HPT effort. Although the team may be focused on making the presentation, it is important to remember that the purpose of the effort is to develop alternative paths to achieving the goals, not necessarily to "make a pitch" to executive leadership.

It also represents a point of celebration for the team. As part of the executive review, the team typically receives intangible recognition and reward for its work in developing High Performance recommendations.

For the HPT, it is also a demonstration of the ability to *Apply Common Identity to their Common Output*, as well as *Applying Individual Identity to Specific Roles and Responsibilities*. In the Final Presentation, the team demonstrates to itself that a Culture Change, integrated with individual desires and organizational needs, can achieve "impossible results." This is a significant milestone.

Activity: Final preparations/resources required for presentation. The team defines and obtains whatever last-minute resources and preparation are required for the presentation.

Deliverable: Final preparation

Typical intervention level: Facilitator, Coach, Catalyst, SME

Activity: Initial presentation to line leadership (optional). Depending upon the planned attendance at the final presentation, it may be very effective for individual teams to present to their parochial key stakeholder. By providing a heads-up to the individual leadership, the team cannot only increase the enrollment of that leader in the process but also reduce potential conflict/issues during the actual final presentation. Of course, it is most effective when the line leadership is continuously communicated with during the Work Re/Design so that this step is redundant, but that may not be practical in all cases.

Optional deliverable: Initial presentation to line/local leadership

Typical intervention level: Facilitator, Coach, Catalyst, SME

Activity: Final presentation. The team presents its overall recommendations of change, meeting the goals while staying within the Sandbox. This summarizes the work, effort, learnings, and growth of the Work Re/Design phase and prepares the team and the organization for the first phase of implementation.

Critical deliverable: Final presentation to (executive) leadership

Typical intervention level: Facilitator, Coach, Catalyst, SME

Activity: Feedback/Reactions/Opportunities. The team actively solicits reaction and feedback from the leadership/key stakeholders and works to actively listen and check back with the audience to ensure that they understood the issue/feedback.

Deliverable: Team actively listens and confirms feedback and direction received from the executives and leaders.

Typical intervention level: Facilitator, Coach

Activity: Next steps. If appropriate, given the feedback and reaction noted in Feedback/Reactions/Opportunities, the team may need to define immediate next steps, revising any proposed next steps shown in the final presentation.

Deliverable: Team defines immediate next steps for its activities, typically for next working day.

Typical intervention level: Facilitator, Coach

Key Go/No Go Progress Test, Work Re/Design

This is a mission-critical decision point. Given all the work that culminates in the final presentation, the leadership must make a decision about next steps. If the leadership accepts some/all of the recommendations, approval/sanction must be given to move forward the next business day. If leadership cannot accept the recommendations, direction/agreement must be achieved on the next steps.

Leadership should be sufficiently in the loop to have no surprises during the final presentation; the leadership should be communicating with the team leadership and meeting with the team prior to the final presentation. Similarly, the team should be socializing the informally briefing key stakeholders prior to the final presentation. In sum, all key players should be ready for implementation the next business day.

Mission-Critical Issue

If the team perceives that everything is "business as usual," and everything returns to normal the next business day, considerable negative sentiment will be generated and significant negative impact can occur on the workforce. Even if leadership does not accept *any* of the recommendations, plans for adjustment/review/reassessment should be outlined *at this time.*

Template:
Implementation

Knowledge must come through action; you can have no test which is
not fanciful, save by trial.

—Sophocles

For each HPT effort, the actual implementation will vary dramatically
with organization, product, team, and culture. For some self-contained
efforts, implementation is straightforward and conflict minimal; the team
is provided the time and resources to achieve their goals. For other efforts,
particularly those contained within traditional surrounding organizations, this period can be very difficult.

THE IMPLEMENTATION PHASE:
ACTIVITY SUPPORT

As a generic implementation description, it is presumed that the teams
are following the detailed plan deliverables outlined in the Work
Re/Design section. The *Transition Plan* should detail the preparation and
conversion work required to implement the new processes and ideas. The
Change Management Plan should provide a road map for communicating
with and involving key stakeholders in the team's new changes. The
Training Plan should outline the resources and training schedules for the
team members. The *Integration Plan* should detail the workflow interactions with supplier and vendor stakeholders. All these plans should be
integrated with the *Work Plan* so that the team is converting to its new

processes while still producing product. The activities of implementation should, in fact, be the activities specified in these plans. For this reason, this section includes few discrete activities.

There are several activities, in addition to those itemized in the team's plans, that can help the team to be more effective more quickly. For the most effective teams, these activities are already part of their implementation plans.

METRICS MONITORING AND REPORTING

The metrics defined in the Work Re/Design are now critical to monitor and measure. Any deviation from the original metric baseline must be evaluated and reviewed, to be understood as to *why* the deviation(s) occurred. The metrics were defined to allow the team to predict and anticipate potential problem areas before the problems impact the work plan or original goals. The team should be measuring and monitoring these real-time so that all team members understand the learnings and the implementation of the new process.

Activity: Key metrics monitored/measured/reported. As defined in the Work Re/Design, all key metrics are monitored and evaluated. These may range from real-time process measurements to semiannual cultural surveys. Frequency per se is less significant than the information and the perspective that the instrument provides the team.

Deliverable: Key metrics are monitored as appropriate, and all team members know the real-time metrics.

Frequency: Continuous (at least daily)

Typical intervention level: Facilitator, SME

Activity: Projected results tracked against baseline.

Deliverable: Metric performance is tracked against the original baseline, and deviations are understood. Impacts of significant deviations are understood by the team, and necessary corrections/adjustments in process and/or approach are made/implemented.

Frequency: First month: twice weekly; thereafter: weekly or as required

Typical intervention level: Facilitator, SME

Activity: Projected results tracked against original projections

Deliverable: Team tracks metric performance against the impact on original goals and evaluates significant deviations for necessary correction/adjustment. Team continually tracks projected goal per-

formance and makes/recommends necessary correction to achieve the goals.

Frequency: First month: twice weekly; thereafter: weekly or as required.

Typical intervention level: Facilitator, SME

Activity: Metrics reporting to management

Deliverable: Team reports metrics performance to management in a way that is integrated with management's typical performance reviews.

Frequency: First month: twice weekly; thereafter: weekly or as required

Typical intervention level: Facilitator, SME

PERFORMANCE REVIEW AND EVALUATION

As the team implements its many new ideas and transition activities, it is common for team members to be *too* focused on their individual tasks at hand and not focus on their overall performance goals and expectations. These reviews are intended to provide both an appropriate focus on overall goals and increased communication and interaction with key stakeholders.

Activity: Team performance review

Deliverable: Team reviews its overall HPT goal performance to date, integrating the key metric results into the goal status. Projection of timeline for goal achievement is included with itemization of key issues, challenges, and opportunities. For each issue, the reduction/elimination strategy is outlined and current status provided.

Frequency: First month: daily; thereafter: weekly or as appropriate

Typical intervention level: Facilitator

Activity: Management performance review

Deliverable: Team reviews its overall HPT goal performance to date with key leaders, integrating the key metric results into the goal status. Projection of timeline for goal achievement is included with itemization of key issues, challenges, and opportunities. For each issue, the reduction/elimination strategy is outlined and current status provided.

Frequency: First month: weekly; thereafter: monthly or as appropriate

Typical intervention level: Facilitator, Coach

Activity: Executive performance review

Deliverable: Team reviews its overall HPT goal performance to date, with emphasis on integration of the HPT goals with organizational strategy.

Team outlines its learnings and cultural progression as well as discrete goal achievement.

Frequency: First three months: monthly; thereafter: quarterly, or as appropriate.

Typical intervention level: Facilitator, Coach, Catalyst

Activity: Key stakeholder performance review

Deliverable: Team reviews its overall HPT goal performance to date, similar to "To Be" Fair provided during Work Re/Design. Individual team members are ready to discuss detailed progress and issues as appropriate with any key stakeholder.

Frequency: First three months: monthly; thereafter: quarterly, or as appropriate

Typical intervention level: Facilitator, Coach, Catalyst

THE IMPLEMENTATION PHASE: TEAM DYNAMICS

The Implementation Phase is the most critical phase of the team's transition to High Performance. In addition to the real-world requirement of *performance*, the typical team is now faced with some of its most difficult *cultural* challenges as well.

During this phase, team members will be trying their many new ideas, testing their new relationships, and driving to achieve their performance goals. They remain focused on their common goals, re-enforcing the Culture Change phases of *Applying Common Identity to Common Output* and *Applying Individual Identity to Specific Roles and Responsibilities*. The team re-enforces its own identity as it begins to achieve High Performance; previously impossible goals are now being achieved.

This is typically a period of high motivation, high achievement, and high frustration as the team tries to do its work within the rest of the organization.

In theory, there should be no issues or challenges for the team. Throughout the Work Re/Design, the team has worked with its key stakeholders and developed detailed plans for its effective implementation. For the teams that worked to develop their integration and transition strategies, implementation should be a practical application of their ideas and agreements.

In practice, where the team's new identity and culture are significantly different from its surrounding organization, implementation can be one of the most difficult and challenging phases of the entire HPT transition.

New Teams: Emerging from Work Re/Design

Team Expectations

Teams emerging from the Work Re/Design phase are typically still in celebratory mode: motivated and tired. Most are physically tired from the previous weeks; though they typically attribute that to the intense last-minute work for the final presentation, many individuals are depleted from the *emotional* changes they have just experienced. It is important to allow the individuals time to catch up, and to allow each person her or his own time to transition. For many team members, this slow pace is simply a return to their typical working pace, for a short period.

Motivation is high in new HPTs; there is a strong desire to put their ideas into practice; to "finally do real work." Though they are ready to begin implementing their ideas, they may have unrealistic expectations of the level of their support.

Throughout Work Re/Design, the team's visibility was very high, ending with a final presentation that had even higher visibility. Typical support barriers, such as information gathering or product change approval, were lowered during this time, due to that high visibility. During its formation, the team became accustomed to the high level of support and visibility and low barriers. In the typical Work Re/Design phase, if the team wanted it, it received it—and quickly. The team's typical reaction is to expect the same level of support and recognition during implementation.

Cultural Reality of Key Stakeholders

As the team reintegrates into the "normal" organization, it is often met with stakeholder resentment and supplier reticence. This has a double impact on the team; not only is the level of implementation support significantly different from that of Work Re/Design support, the level of active resistance may increase as well.

To address these external issues, the team should be revisiting its Change Management and Integration Plans, ensuring that it has commitment and motivation from its key stakeholders. For many teams in this phase, additional work with the stakeholders is required to achieve an effective working relationship.

Internally, the team needs to focus on its own development and work to separate its own cultural expectations from those of its stakeholders. This may involve additional intervention time at the coach and catalyst levels, as the team norms its expectations.

Increased internal accountability and ownership for stakeholder relationships are key to a successful transition as well as reducing the incidence of runaway empowerment (see chapter 3). This may include

extended sessions and interventions with leaders, executives, and key stakeholder representatives.

The Pressure of the Old Culture

For many HPTs emerging from Work Re/Design back into a traditional organizational culture, there is considerable pressure for team members to "return to the right way of doing things." From a physical perspective, the team members may look forward to the slower pace of routine work after the intensity of Work Re/Design; their previous positions may seem attractive. More potently, however, the *emotional comfort* of returning to a familiar culture and known problems can be a very powerful draw.

There is often considerable pressure on the team members from peer and stakeholder groups to return to their original culture. Convincing team members to abandon their new ideas and new ways of doing work can be a very effective means of reducing coincident demand on the stakeholders.

This overall pressure to return to normal is a key reason why non–culture-shifted HPTs fail. When the team members have not shifted their sense of self, and when they are relatively unsupported at the end of the Work Re/Design phase, the pressure to return to a traditional culture can be overwhelming. It is only when the team members have formed a new culture for themselves that their sense of self is more powerful than that of the surrounding organization.

For those teams facing this pressure, they are helped by a strong focus on their own plans. By concentrating on the work that needs to occur, the changes they need to implement, and their own focus on implementation, the teams can re-enforce their own sense of purpose and desire for change.

Accountability and Responsibility

As noted in several earlier case histories (see chapter 2 and chapter 3), holding a team *accountable* is an important step to the team's development. HPTs, however, can benefit from a different type of accountability than conventional teams.

Multidimensional Accountability

Most conventional teams are held accountable to the performance of job tasks, rather than to overall goals. For most teams, the status of specific project tasks is compared against an expected performance timeline (e.g., Gantt chart), and the team's progress is noted. If the tasks or jobs are late, the team may have negative consequences. If there is a consistent pattern of incomplete or late tasks, the team may even be reassigned.

For High Performance Teams, accountability is best focused on *achievements, learnings, and projected goals*. Through continuous metrics monitoring and measurement, the team should be constantly providing real-time achievement status. At any given time, any member of the team should be aware of the team's metrics performance. Team members should be able to directly relate the team's metrics performance to its overall goals, and the overall goals to organizational objectives. With the team members' knowledge of the work processes, each member should also be able to predict the team's HPT goal achievement. This combination of detailed process knowledge and the "big picture" goal status is a hallmark of HPTs.

In the event of a projected goal not meeting original objectives, the HPT should be exploring alternative means of achieving the goal, along with any recovery plan to get back on track. Because HPTs have invested a considerable effort in *understanding* their processes, they are generally able to determine the underlying *cause* of their missed goals. The team should be expected to determine the cause, recommend corrections or changes, and present new paths forward to management for approval (if needed). If the team is not readily able to determine the cause, it should present an investigation plan to determine the cause and then develop a new plan forward. This is similar to the original Work Re/Design process; the team has experience in discovering new ways to address difficult barriers.

Similarly, the team members should be sharing key learnings of the implementation, including which ideas worked and which did not. Everyone on the team should be aware of the creative paths being attempted and the lessons learned of the unsuccessful alternatives.

HPTs are also accountable for their intangible behaviors and impacts and for their relationships among themselves and with their key stakeholders. More than conventional teams, HPTs are held accountable for all their key success dimensions, including employee value and cultural foundation.

In summary, HPTs are held accountable for many more dimensions than conventional teams; they are typically held to management level objectives rather than to work team tasks.

Choice versus Consequence

With conventional teams, accountability is often equated with consequence; if the team meets its goals, it may be rewarded; if the team misses its goals, it may be punished. Though maybe effective in the short term, this response may not be effective when dealing with High Performance goals; attempting to manage an HPT with consequences is a common theme of failed HPT efforts.

For High Performance Teams, successful goal achievement is a *choice*. Throughout Work Re/Design, the team made numerous design choices to

achieve their results; they also *chose* to join and stay with the HPT. For team members, not achieving their goals is also a choice; if they do not meet their original objectives, there may be no further organizational advantage to the High Performance Team. Most team members enjoy their work and want the team to continue; their personal future is dependent upon the success of the team. These members will work to find the new creative solutions that solve the "impossible" problem.

To be effective, the leaders are often required to change the way they hold team members accountable. By offering the team a choice and supporting the team in the choices they make, the leaders can help the team take personal accountability.

In one HPT effort, the leader was describing the new levels of empowerment for team members. The team would be responsible for its own job scheduling and work hours; the team members would have the ability to obtain materials directly and be able to directly interface with vendors. This new level of authority and empowerment was very desirable; workers were quickly volunteering for team membership. The leader summarized the accountability by saying, "The price of admission for this is performance. In order for you to have increased empowerment and authority, you have to demonstrate increased results. We will help you find new ways to do your work, but you must achieve the goals." For those individuals, the choice was clear; within a short period of time, they actually *doubled* their impossible goals.

To help the HPTs make choices, and to find new, creative alternatives to traditional challenges, both team members and leaders may need to adjust their preconceptions of accountability and consequence. To accelerate this process, intervention can be very effective. Intervention levels vary with the team and the leader, but typically require catalyst level interaction to help the team members, leaders, and executives change the way teams are held accountable.

Celebration

Many organizations celebrate the completion of phases or objectives; this is normal and appropriate. For High Performance Teams, however, celebration takes on additional levels; teams not only celebrate their objectives, they also celebrate *the work they did*. For some advanced teams, there is even celebration of "failed" objectives, as long as considerable learning was achieved.

To the casual observer, this may seem excessive and serve to re-enforce the perception of pampered teams. It is important for the leader and interventionist to understand the *reason* for the celebration and support it appropriately.

For mature HPTs, celebration is not an event; it is a continuing process.

Full Implementation: Formal High Performance Teams

For those HPT efforts resourcing the Work Re/Design at its full level, implementation is straightforward. Most of the transition interventions have been completed, and individual development has been integrated into the overall team development. Each team member has been actively, intensively, designing her or his own work and has been very involved since the first day of Work Re/Design. For these team members, they are ready to perform. This is the "full immersion" implementation plan.

For those organizations requiring rapid results and breakthrough performance, this is the recommended template for change.

These teams can benefit from a rapid focus on their work and executing their Work Re/Design Plans.

A sample full implementation calendar is shown in Figure 36-1.

Implement: Full

Sunday	Monday	Tuesday	Wednesday	Thursday	Friday	Saturday
CHAPTER **70**	36 **71** IMPLEMENTATION	36 **72** IMPLEMENTATION	36 **73** TEAM RVW TEAM UPDATE METRICS RVW ISSUES/CORRECT	36 **74** IMPLEMENTATION	7.1 **75** *MGMNT RVW* METRICS UPDATE ISSUE STATUS LEARNINGS	**76**
77	36 **78** IMPLEMENTATION	36 **79** IMPLEMENTATION	9.0. **80** TEAM RVW TEAM UPDATE METRICS RVW R/O PREP	36 **81** IMPLEMENTATION	36 **82** *MGMNT RVW* METRICS UPDATE ISSUE STATUS LEARNINGS	**83**
84	36 **85** IMPLEMENTATION	36 **86** IMPLEMENTATION	36 **87** TEAM RVW TEAM UPDATE METRICS RVW	36 **88** IMPLEMENTATION	36 **89** *MGMNT REVIEW* METRICS RVW PROCESS RVW CORRECTIONS	**90**
91	36 **92** IMPLEMENTATION	36 **93** IMPLEMENTATION	36 **94** TEAM REVIEW TEAM UPDATE *MGMNT PREP* TEAM R/O PREP	36 **95** IMPLEMENTATION	36 **96** **EXEC RVW** **EXECUTIVE MANAGEMENT REVIEW** PATHS FORWARD	**97**
98	36 **99** IMPLEMENTATION	36 **100** IMPLEMENTATION	36 **101** IMPLEMENTATION	36 **102** IMPLEMENTATION	36 **103** *STAKEHOLDER REVIEW* TEAM REVIEW	**104**

Left column labels (row 1): EXECUTIVE LEADERS, KEY STAKEHOLDERS, TEAM

Note: "IMPLEMENTATION" includes all of the key plans developed during the Work Re/Design, such as the Transition Plan, Work Plan, Training Plan, Integration Plan, and Change Management Plan.

Figure 36-1   Template Calendar: Implementation—Full

Phased Implementation: Design Teams and Implementation Teams

For some HPT efforts, however, a full immersion may not be possible. For some organizations, the perception of offline employees is negative. For others, a full immersion implementation is not practical for customer or regulatory constraints. In these cases, a phased rollout is required for the overall HPT effort, with expanding teams being phased in over time.

The Phased Implementation typically includes a pilot period, followed by increasing rollout phases until the overall objectives are achieved.

[For convenience of illustration, "field" refers to any implementation team. In practice, these teams have ranged from collocated teams on the same manufacturing floor to highly distributed teams across the country.]

Pilot: Conceptual Testing

During the pilot phase, the original Work Re/Design team members staff the working team and implement the new processes within a small controlled environment. Minimizing the variables, the team works to test the *concept* of its new ideas. The purpose of the pilot is to demonstrate *practicality* of the ideas, rather than their actual implementation; it is not a replacement for the actual rollouts. The pilot testing is typically performed in parallel with existing systems; it does not replace any of the old practices.

For HPT efforts initiating the pilot phase, the Work Re/Design team members test their new ideas and processes. Working closely with key stakeholders, the team members implement as many of the change recommendations as practical. For most teams, there are typically still additional transition issues to be completed, such as capital equipment and longer lead time items. These are completed in parallel to the pilot testing.

This is also a period of *role modeling* behavior by the executives and team leaders, demonstrating appropriate reactions to Pilot Phase discoveries. For those ideas not achieving expectations, leaders can demonstrate an appreciation of the new learnings, celebration of the hard work, and expectation of continued creativity. By helping the team to understand that it is okay to fail, the leaders can guide the team to accept their discovery, develop new ideas, and quickly pilot new alternative paths. This approach will become critical as the team drives toward its overall goal achievement.

During this pilot phase, with team members focused on testing the new ideas, team leaders are typically focused on new team member selection. As part of the original team selection (see chapter 34), and Communication Team work during the Work Re/Design (see chapter 35), the new team member selection process had already begun. During the pilot phase, these team members are identified and selected. Led by the team

Implement: Phased

Sunday	Monday	Tuesday	Wednesday	Thursday	Friday	Saturday
CHAPTER **70**	36 **71**	36 **72**	36 **73**	36 **74**	36 **75**	**76**
LEADER TEAM PILOT PHASE->	IMPLEMENTATION	IMPLEMENTATION	TEAM REVIEW: TEAM UPDATE METRICS RVW ISSUES/CORRECT	IMPLEMENTATION	MANAGEMENT REVIEW: METRICS UPDATE ISSUE STATUS LEARNINGS	
91	36 **92**	36 **93**	36 **94**	36 **95**	36 **96**	**97**
PILOT PHASE->	IMPLEMENTATION FIRST ROLLOUT TEAM SELECTION BEGUN	IMPLEMENTATION	TEAM REVIEW: TEAM UPDATE METRICS RVW R/O PREP	IMPLEMENTATION	EXECUTIVE REVIEW: GOAL UPDATE ROLLOUT APPROVAL	
105	36 **106**	36 **107**	36 **108**	36 **109**	36 **110**	**111**
FIRST ROLLOUT->	LEADER PREP PILOT TEAM PREP NEW MEMBER PREP	LEADER PREP	ORIENTATION – FIRST ROLLOUT LEADER PILOT TEAM INTERVENTIONIST	ORIENTATION – FIRST ROLLOUT LEADER PILOT TEAM INTERVENTIONIST	ORIENTATION – FIRST ROLLOUT LEADER PILOT TEAM INTERVENTIONIST	
112	36 **113**	36 **114**	36 **115**	36 **116**	36 **117**	**118**
FIRST ROLLOUT->	FIRST ROLLOUT TEAM BEGUN LEADER SUPPORT INTRVNTN SUPPRT	FIRST ROLLOUT TEAM BEGUN LEADER SUPPORT INTRVNTN SUPPRT	FIRST ROLLOUT TEAM BEGUN LEADER SUPPORT INTRVNTN SUPPRT	IMPLEMENTATION	MANAGEMENT REVIEW: METRICS REVIEW PROCESS UPDATE PATHS FORWARD	
133	36 **134**	36 **135**	36 **136**	36 **137**	36 **138**	**139**
FIRST ROLLOUT->	IMPLEMENTATION ROLLOUT #2 TEAM SELECTN BEGUN LEADER SUPPORT INTRVNTN SUPPRT	IMPLEMENTATION	MANAGEMENT REVIEW: METRICS REVIEW PROCESS UPDATE PATHS FORWARD	IMPLEMENTATION	EXECUTIVE REVIEW: GOAL UPDATE ISSUE UPDATE 2ND ROLLOUT OK	

NOTE: THIS IS A PARTIAL CALENDAR FOR ILLUSTRATION ONLY; KEY WEEKS ONLY ARE LISTED. THIS PATTERN IS REITERATIVE; IT IS REPEATED FOR EACH ADDITIONAL ROLLOUT. 'INTEGRATION TEAM' ACTIVITY IS INCREASED FOR EACH ADDITIONAL ROLLOUT

Note: "IMPLEMENTATION" includes all of the key plans developed during the Work Re/Design, such as the Transition Plan, Work Plan, Training Plan, Integration Plan, and Change Management Plan.

Figure 36-2 Template Calendar: Implementation—Phased

leaders, this selection process typically includes team members and key stakeholders, as well.

At the end of the pilot, the team provides a report-out to the team leader and executives, confirms or modifies its original plans, and requests permission to advance to the first formal implementation phase.

A sample phased implementation calendar is shown in Figure 36-20.

Phased Implementation: First Rollout

In the first rollout phase, a portion of the overall implementation is considered, typically a geographical area for distributed operations or a func-

tional group for product operations. It is important that the rollout portion still have end-to-end ownership; to be most effective, the teams need to have responsibility for their overall process.

New Teams: Integrated Additions, Not Separate Teams

For each rollout phase, there is an additional group of team members to be integrated into the original team. It is critical that the new team members be considered as an *integrated addition* rather than as a separate team; they need to be viewed as *building onto* the original process and structure. This reduces the creation of competing cultures and teams.

In one HPT effort, two identical teams were created, separate from each other. Though they began with the same ideas, they maintained separate facilities, separate staffs, and separate responsibilities. Although creative in concept, internal competition and political manipulation quickly reduced both teams' effectiveness and delayed the period required to achieve their goals.

In this case, the separation re-enforced the teams' *separate identities*, creating two separate cultures, rather than developing a single, diverse culture. This was a critical factor that diverted their creative energies and reduced their effectiveness.

For a phased implementation to be successful, additional teams need to be integrated into the existing Work Re/Design team with the perspective that they are learning from the original team. For this reason, they should be considered *new team members* rather than separate teams. This should be an integral part of the selection process; the team members should understand that they are *joining* an existing team rather than creating a new one.

First Rollout Implementation: Orientation and Training

Prior to actual start of work, the new team members undergo a High Performance Team orientation and training in the new processes and skilling of the Work Re/Design. Although this may appear as conventional training to the casual observer, it is critically important that the team members actually begin their *assimilation into the new culture* at this time.

For most teams using phased implementation, there is a short period of time allowed for orientation and training (else the team members would have been included in the Work Re/Design); this precludes extensive interventions at this time. However, there should be a definite structure to initial interventions, particularly around the *Common Crisis, Common Drive* need for organizational change. During the entire orientation and training period (typically three to five days), there is a need for Catalyst intervention supporting the team leader and original team members.

For many leaders having recently worked with transformed team members, it is often difficult to remember that the new team members *are still in their original culture*; they have not yet transitioned. Because of this, leaders need to return to their traditional leader roles, establishing firm, effective boundaries and providing detailed directions to the new members.

It is important to note that the new team members *have the same emotional need for transition* as the original team members did. Though that may be evident in retrospect, it can be very difficult for leaders and original team members to remember during the Rollout phases. Without the advantage of a controlled, structured series of interventions to accelerate that transition (i.e., the Work Re/Design), it takes more time and resources to support the new team members' transition. However, this is mission critical if the phased implementation is to be successful.

The orientation and training period is used to provide operational training and new process skilling. However, its key function is to *begin* the transition process for the additional team members. This period does not *replace* the Work Re/Design functional intervention; it only initiates it.

The leader and original team members should work closely with the interventionist, developing a structured agenda and intervention plan for the new team members. This begins with the orientation and training and extends throughout the rollout phases.

First Rollout Implementation: The Work Performed

After the orientation and training are completed, the team members are added to the pilot teams and the work plan is executed. For those efforts where the pilot team is small compared to the new team members, the pilot team members may be "seeded" into the new teams. In these cases, however, it is important that the pilot team members be considered de facto leaders; the new team members must be formed around the pilot team, not vice versa.

Although the new team members are part of the High Performance Team, they are not yet part of a High Performance Culture. It is critically important that these new members be supported in their transition and growth. Typically, this requires continuing contact with team leaders and interventionists to accelerate their transition. *Without this transition, the High Performance Team will most likely fail to achieve its goals.*

A key difference between the Work Re/Design team members and the Rollout team members is the work they are created around. Whereas the original team members were focused on creative alternatives to an existing process, the new team members are focused around actually performing the new work. This requires interventions to be designed around the performance of work, *without fundamentally challenging the new work*. In the Work Re/Design, part of the common culture shift came from the chal-

lenge of the "As Is" process and commonly developing a new work process. In the rollout phase, the common culture shift comes from a common drive for results and dealing with implementation challenges.

The continuing attention of the leader and interventionist is critical to the success of the phased implementation. The mix of individual perspectives in the new team is much greater than the mix during Work Re/Design. New team members are still oriented in the traditional culture, whereas the original team members have transitioned to a different perspective. The challenge for the leader and interventionist is to help the team develop its new integrated culture while retaining key High Performance traits.

As the team develops and admits new team members, its own culture shifts and adapts, creating new a new team culture as it grows. This is a normal and healthy pattern for High Performance Teams. Ultimately, the original team members' individual identities shift as a result of their interaction with the new team members as well.

The need for attention and effective HPT leadership places unique requirements on the leader and interventionist. The experience, knowledge, and competencies of the leader and interventionist are typically much greater than those in the full implementation strategy. This is one of the reasons why the required resources are much greater in the phased implementation than in the full implementation.

As the first rollout phase achieves its performance levels and the operational objectives are complete, the second rollout phase is begun, overlapping the first.

Phased Implementation: Second Rollout

The process of the second rollout phase is similar to the first, with the exception of scope. New team members are added to the existing team members, and first rollout team members are used to seed the new second rollout teams. Leader involvement and intervention levels remain high.

In this phase, leaders continue to emphasize the overall High Performance goals. Although the individual teams' results are important, the leader is holding *each* team accountable for the overall HPT goals. Typically, there is a tendency for each team to be solely focused on their own goals; when there is a gap, a single team may claim, "That's not our fault." It is important for the leader to refocus the team on the original Work Re/Design goals and to ensure that *every* team member is accountable for all team goals.

With the second rollout, there are now even more team members in differing phases of individual and team development; the interventions needed to accelerate transition are correspondingly complex. This may be eased by extending the period of the first rollout, until most or all of the team mem-

bers have transitioned to High Performance. In some HPT efforts, however, organizational constraints may limit this option; for these efforts, even more intensive leader involvement and intervention are required.

Interteam Integration

As the team increases in size and scope, there is an increasing challenge of keeping everyone connected. With each team developing new learnings and new trials, it is important for *all* team members to be in constant communication. Depending upon the operational needs, as well, there may be functional requirements of constant communication and integration.

This should be developed as part of the Work Re/Design's transition plan and integration plan. Many teams design an *Integration Team* that is responsible for regular communication and interteam decision-making. For one successful effort, this Integration Team was comprised of representatives of each team, on a rotating basis, meeting every day. Part of every team member's responsibility was to serve on the Integration Team; within a few months, all team members had rotated through the Integration Team; this helped to preclude it from becoming a de facto leader.

However the team designs its communication and integration, it is critically important that all team members are connected with each other, regularly exchanging learnings and information and providing real-time support for each other. This is more than simply convenient; it is critical to re-enforcing the sense of *overall team identity.* By keeping a sense of High Performance Team culture alive for each member, the Culture Change shift becomes *self-re-enforcing.*

Phased Implementation: Additional Rollouts

The process continues, with additional rollouts being completed. Overall, the teams are accountable for their HPT goals across the affected organization. Rewards and recognition may accompany the teams' achievement of the originally impossible goals; however, celebration should have been continuous throughout the transition.

As the teams achieve their goals, they begin the transition to the next levels of High Performance Teams.

Key Go/No Go Assessment of Implementation

The team needs to be monitoring its overall HPT performance, as well as monitoring and understanding its metrics. The team needs to be shifting from a dependency mode that requires support to an interdependency mode that takes responsibility for their own performance while working closely with key stakeholders.

It is critical that all dimensions of performance be monitored and understood, including employee and customer value. The team needs to be held accountable for all their original goals and objectives.

Very simply, the team needs to be doing what they committed to do, else major course correction is required.

V

Beyond High Performance Teams

A Natural Progression
of HPTs

The future enters into us, in order to transform itself in us, long before
it happens.

—*Rainer Maria Rilke*, Letters to a Young Poet

As seen throughout this text, HPTs can be a natural consequence of a
workgroup's shift in identity around their natural work. Although this
can occur naturally, particularly with unique leaders, most successful
efforts require an effective integration of real-world experience, cognitive
understanding, and appropriate intervention.

Once teams are in place, producing results, self-defining their own
approach, what is next? By definition, each team is different, each effort is
unique, and each cultural development is uniquely that of the team and its
stakeholders.

However, there are some common themes that advanced HPTs
encounter as they move forward.

THE SECOND CYCLE: MORE OF . . .

Having had major breakthroughs from their first cycle of progression,
many High Performance Teams want to extend that breakthrough. Typically, their experience has been modeled around the business case, Work
Re/Design, and implementation. In order to take it to the next level, the
team's first reaction is typically to repeat what has already worked: more
of the same.

This phase typically occurs in successful HPT efforts between 6 and 12 months after the team's initial implementation. The team has generally received recognition for its breakthrough results, it has been able to repeat and consolidate its performance, and there is often a sense of anxiousness to do it again. For most teams, this restlessness is often experienced as a general feeling that it is time to make changes again, rather than a response to a specific business change pressure.

More Scope: More Work Re/Design

Having had an experiential model of business process review, analysis, and design, many HPTs will repeat their success, using the same transition model. Most teams either expand on the ends of their work processes (i.e., increasing their process scope to include their customers or their suppliers) or work to expand the depth of their processes (i.e., increasing the detail and analysis for specific portions of their work process).

After about one year as an HPT, the team typically creates a subteam of its membership and charters them to go off-line for several days to several weeks, repeating the original team's Work Re/Design. They often use the same templates and the same general processes that helped them to achieve success originally.

For many HPTs, however, this Work Re/Design is not visible to many stakeholders; many teams prefer to covertly redesign portions of their work, inviting only key stakeholders and SMEs as required for their review. In fact, for many HPTs undergoing their second round of Work Re/Design, there is no outward sign that the activity is going on; there is no disruption of output and no major resource expenditure. In implementing their own Work Re/Design, the HPTs typically discover and develop quiet ways for their own members to be offline; it is rarely visible to customers and management.

More Team: Admission and Attrition

Within the two years of team maturation, there are often many changes to the team membership. Normal workplace cycles of attrition also impact themselves on HPTs; the teams can experience considerable loss as their team members move on to other organizations, other jobs, and other places. When this occurs in the early phases of the HPT maturation, this impact can be great; coach and catalyst interventions may be required to help the team member and the team continue forward. When attrition occurs later in a mature High Performance Team, there is often much greater acceptance; frequently, the departing team member will work with the team to allow for a transitioned exit.

Similarly, as new members are admitted into the team, the on-boarding processes described in chapter 34 are used to ease the transition for all key stakeholders. As with the attrition process, if admission occurs early in the team's maturation, intervention may be required to help the team and the new member acclimate to each other. As the team matures, however, it is increasingly able to adapt itself.

For many teams that have been in existence for one to two years, considerable interest and accountability are taken for member selection and deselection. The team is often very concerned about the type of member that would be on-boarding and the future of the team when someone leaves. These teams often ask for increased autonomy and decision making in the process, and interventions may be helpful when the teams first attempt to control the admission process. These teams have frequently benefited by a *transitioned* process of increased autonomy in admission and attrition, and may need considerable integration and interaction with management and union leaders.

A common approach among multiple, co-located HPTs is to provide team member rotation on a regular basis. This is particularly true in product-ownership environments, where the HPTs are created around specific product areas. For these teams, regular rotation is used to increase diversity of thinking and to provide skilling across multiple product areas. These teams are often highly resistant to rotation early in their maturation cycle and can be helped by effective intervention and support.

More Efforts: Evangelism

As High Performance Team members experience new autonomy, new responsibilities, and new relationships with each other, they typically want to share their success with others; they encourage other areas to consider a High Performance culture.

After the first year of operation, HPT team members' desire to evangelize often increases significantly. These team members readily encourage other groups to ask for High Performance, and often talk about their positive experiences even outside of work.

This is a very natural extension of Culture Change and can be very beneficial to an organization desiring an expansion of High Performance culture. At the same time, as with many evangelists, the people listening to the message may not have the same context as the team member. Orientation, intervention, and management guidance can be very helpful in helping the team discover appropriate means of spreading the word.

More Money: Compensation

A very common question early in HPT development is, "If the company is making all this money from my efforts, where is my portion of it?" The

underlying assumption of this question is that the company and employee are being adequately compensated for their products and services to begin with, and that any improvement warrants a corresponding increase in pay or benefits. As the employee learns of the financial and marketing realities of the product, she or he soon discovers that the company is often not being adequately compensated; in some cases, the company may be losing money in the marketplace. Part of the development cycle of HPTs is that the team members work hard to increase the organizational benefits as well as their own.

After two to three years, however, this question is often asked again, with a very different context. By this time, the HPT has typically been producing improvements and profits for the organization, and the individuals on the team are now looking for their own tangible compensation. This is not to infer that all teams become self-focused and greedy after a period of time. Rather, their new perspective on providing value-added services to all key success dimensions does not exclude the employees' compensation per se.

This is one of the reasons why early sociotechnical plant design included extensive compensation redesign as well as workflow changes. Whether pay-for-performance, pay-for-knowledge, or other alternative compensation systems, many 1980s sociotechnical systems designs included new means of compensation. However, this approach required a great deal of executive approvals and stakeholder involvement; in general, it fell out of favor by the 1990s. Consequently, many HPTs sought conventional compensation improvements as they achieved their breakthrough goals.

Working with High Performance Teams is often difficult, particularly when the HPT is surrounded by a conventional organization. For most organizations, it remains for the executives to develop and implement creative compensation programs that address employees' concerns. The most effective teams have partnered with executive management to develop special cases—ways in which existing, conventional compensation systems can be leveraged to recognize the breakthrough results of the HPTs.

It is important to note that the most effective HPTs are those that achieve breakthrough performance and productivity first, and demonstrate the ability to continuously perform at the breakthrough level. After the team has demonstrated this ability, some form of overall compensation is typically required to help keep the team incentivized. In rare cases, some High Performance Teams have left the organization after not being compensated for their results. This re-enforces the organization's need to provide overall employee value.

During the first and second years of a High Performance Team, the team works to consolidate its own processes, solidify its political position-

ing within the organization, and expand its influence. Typically, it also repeats the original processes that helped it become successful in the first place.

THE THIRD CYCLE: CONTINUOUS RE/DESIGN

As HPTs consolidate their internal and external relationships, they discover that their original processes are no longer as effective as they were. Typically, the initial visibility and attention paid to the team by executive management is much less as the team matures; key stakeholders now begin to expect the breakthrough results. Attrition and admission begin to fundamentally shift the team, as its group identity shifts with the member changes.

In the third cycle of change for the typical performing HPT, often in the second and third year of performance, the team is beginning to lose its feel of being special. This can have a profound impact on the team dynamics. Without guidance and intervention, this may influence the team to decrease its performance and motivation; some teams have even chosen to disband in this phase. With appropriate guidance, however, many teams have found a new level of drive and vision and are able to fundamentally shift their identity yet again.

Internal Changes and Expectations

Internally, the identity of the team shifts when the team members' identity shifts. By the third cycle, there are often several key members who have left the team, and some new members admitted. In typical HPTs, the most visible members leave the team at this time, often motivated to start new HPTs elsewhere in the organization. The remaining members often are still expecting the dynamics of the HPT to be the same, even though the individual identity and overall team identity have shifted.

In many unaided and unsupported HPTs—some teams lose their HPT SME support along with the decline in visibility—the team members' expectations do not shift as their team culture shifts. Despite the change in membership, many of the team members expect the team culture to remain the same; they still expect the high performance, the high rewards, and the high recognition. When the culture does not meet their expectations, these team members may feel a sense of betrayal and resentment.

In properly supported HPTs, education and intervention are used to help the team members understand their own natural processes of growth and maturation. For these teams, members are provided the opportunity to view their own changes as positive growth and to allow the team's growth to support their own individual growth. This is analogous to their

original paradigm shift, where they viewed the organizational goals as being able to be integrated with their individual goals. Now, they are able to view their own team as the organization, and can integrate both needs and desires.

External Relationships

In the third cycle of change, typical HPTs have a very different relationship with their key stakeholders. By this time, the uniqueness of the team has diminished, and routine has set in. As the management spotlight has shifted away from the team, the team has been dealing with other teams and key stakeholders as a perceived equal rather than as a special team. By the second year, there have been many routine situations that have been jointly resolved with key stakeholders; this has helped to improve relationships and solidify working bonds. The performing HPT and other teams have learned to work together on a regular basis, and their own instantaneous culture has shifted to incorporate all of the different working styles.

Though some HPTs experience a backlash from some stakeholders during this time, most have developed an effective, ongoing working relationship. This level of cooperation can be very effective and satisfying to the team members, but it also has the tendency to re-enforce complacency in some teams.

More of the Same Is Not Enough

Appropriately managed and guided HPTs continue to drive for more improvement in all of their key success dimensions. Having tried doing more of the same, they discover that this approach simply does not achieve the level of performance they want. In unsupported teams, disappointment typically results when the change processes that worked for them originally no longer produce the same results.

Supported teams continue to try new ways of obtaining breakthrough results, even when they had already achieved breakthroughs in their early development. These teams are not satisfied with their own status quo, and want more improvement, more discovery, and more challenge.

When their original change processes no longer produce breakthroughs, effective HPTs look for other processes that will.

Continuous Re/Design

As performing HPTs repeat their earlier cycles, they typically repeat Work Re/Design as well. They soon discover, however, that the sequential cycle of collecting data, analyzing work, designing new work, and imple-

menting new ideas is inadequate for their new level of performance. These teams typically transition to a continuous process of reviewing and redesigning their work, coincident with the work itself.

For these teams, a new level of integration of work and culture is achieved. The team members typically realize that the design of their work—in all key dimensions—is not a process that necessarily precedes the work. Rather, it is practical for all phases of work design to be considered an integrated, parallel process; the workflow changes dynamically as the work design changes.

Nonlinear Work: New Scope and Charters

Most HPTs are chartered to review their linear work; that is, the repetitive, routine work that provides the primary service or product of the organization. Linear work is typically discrete, quantifiable, and easily packaged into charters for analysis and change. Because this typically also represents the core product of the organization, most HPT efforts initially focus on the linear work required to produce their key product.

Although the core product is important—and typically includes opportunity for rapid achievement of breakthrough results—it is typically the *nonlinear work* that drives the long-term success of the organization. All of the key deliberation, planning, and intangible processes of the organization do not have a predefined outcome; they are not easily quantifiable or analyzable. Yet they have a pre-eminent impact on the core product of the organization. For these functions, the process of work becomes more similar to executive management work than traditional product- or service-related work.

Teams who extend their charter to include their nonlinear work soon discover that High Performance Teams and principles are applicable to both linear and nonlinear work, albeit with different processes and procedures. They find new levels of opportunity and performance and are able to discover "breakthroughs on top of breakthroughs." For these teams, powerful changes in organizational capacity and capability are possible, as the *enabling processes* are reviewed and changed.

This is one example where the organizational change processes themselves are shifted; not only are the enabling processes changed, but some executive teams even work to design how they change the enabling process. This becomes an infinitely recursive process, allowing the overall organization to achieve greater and greater change over a long period of time.

For convenience and simplicity of illustration, the template section of this book is focused on linear work. For nonlinear work charters, the underlying transformation processes remain the same, whereas the analytical and design processes change accordingly.

BEYOND CULTURE CHANGE

As teams grow, mature, split, and form new teams, the individuals on the teams continue to grow and develop as well. The team identity shift is transitory, but the individual identity shift is not, and individuals begin to influence the overall organizational culture more than the impact of performing teams.

As their own experience and influence grow, "High Performing Individuals" form new teams with new processes and new hopes and visions for their own future. They often try many different approaches, continually learning and growing from each approach.

Many individuals try cross-organizational or cross-cultural teams, forming working relationships with others in different organizations ("strategic alliance" HPTs) and even in different countries ("global" HPTs). All these have their own characteristics and their own approaches, yet all have commonality in HPT principles and identity.

As the teams develop and individuals grow, many team members are surprised to discover corresponding growth in their personal lives. As one team member said after a particularly intense Work Re/Design, "My wife says that I am easier to talk to, and that I listen more than any other time she's known me." Another said, "I just spent last night talking about work to my friends. I *never* talk about work to my friends—it was fun!" This reaction is not surprising to experienced HPT interventionists; for true growth, work life is not separate from personal life. From the perspective of many team members, however, they begin to experience a new level of fulfillment and excitement from their working life. For these fulfilled team members, their organizational value increased along with their personal growth.

For these people, work takes on entirely new dimensions of accomplishment, creativity, legacy, and enrichment.

Some team members have even discovered that fulfillment did not lie in their chosen occupation; they changed careers as a result of their individual growth.

For one group of HPTs, having a reunion years after corporate mergers had closed their plant and transferred its operations, most had been transformed by their High Performance Team experience. Many had advanced in their careers, doing jobs they never expected to be able to do, at performance levels they did not believe they were capable of. A few had changed careers, finding fulfillment in other paths. Each was profoundly impacted by their work experience. Each had made a profound impact on their work. Each was a lot happier in life.

Annotated Bibliography

The purpose of this bibliography is to provide the reader with access to additional resources. In addition to the conventional advantage of problem-solving or further subject investigation, the opportunity for group learning and discovery is very helpful for HPT development.

At the beginning of some early HPT efforts, the only initial advice provided to the leaders and participants was "get ready to read, read, read, and then read some more." Though no text can guarantee HPT success (including this one), reviewing many different perspectives on business, culture, change, and leadership can be very helpful to all key stakeholders.

It is important to note that all these texts have a great deal to contribute in their own right. A full study of HPTs would include all the referenced texts—and many more. Separated by corresponding text sections, these texts are divided into three categories: Highly Recommended, Suggested Reading, and Reference.

Highly Recommended includes those books that have had significant impact on HPT stakeholders. In many HPT efforts, some or all of these books were provided to all key stakeholders for reading before the start of the effort.

Suggested Reading includes titles that may be of interest for readers desiring more information about the Section. This additional reading often provides more detail, or examples, of topics outlined in the Section.

Reference includes titles that have been noted in the Section text, or provide general background information.

There are many more effective, excellent titles for the interested reader. A recent survey of HPT-related titles yielded more than 2,000 books, articles, newsletters, and Web sites. (Though very effective, Web sites are not included in this listing, due to their transient URLs.) As a practical matter, this bibliography is focused on those texts that have had the most impact on key HPT stakeholders. Exploring new ideas and new bibliographic references remains an opportunity for all effective HPT efforts.

SECTION I: INTRODUCTION AND BACKGROUND / CASE HISTORIES

Highly Recommended

Katzenbach, Jon R., and Smith, Douglas K. *The Wisdom of Teams.* New York: HarperBusiness, 2003, 1993.

Katzenbach and Smith leverage their McKinsey & Company background to provide an excellent qualitative reference to the success of team-based initiatives in the 1980s and early 1990s. Several chapters are focused on "high performance teams," including the significant impact on individual team members. A very good background read. Their subsequent book, *The Discipline of Teams*, builds on their premise that successful teams require a discipline of "team basics."

Note: In their Second Edition, Katzenbach and Smith review and update their learnings, including a revision of "high performance" to "extra-ordinary" teams; still an excellent reference.

Weisbord, Marvin R. *Productive Workplaces Revisited: Dignity, Meaning and Community in the 21st Century.* 2nd ed. San Francisco: Jossey-Bass, 2004.

This is an excellent history of sociotechnical workplaces, as well as a personal journey of learning by one of the leading consultants and thought leaders. This book is highly recommended for anyone interested in the evolution of alternative workplaces. Part 1, in particular ("The Search for Productive Workplaces"), gives the reader an excellent grounding in productivity and sociotechnical thinking in the twentieth century.

The second edition updates Weisbord's earlier work with additional perspectives and relevant cases. Weisbord's wisdom is unmatched.

Wellins, Richard S., and Byham, William C., and Wilson, Jeanne M. *Empowered Teams: Creating Self-Directed Work Groups that Improve Quality, Productivity, and Participation.* San Francisco: Jossey-Bass, 1991.

A compilation of surveys of self-directed teams, including some HPTs, this text provides a very good "benchmark listing" of team practices. Built upon the authors' experience at Development Dimensions International, the text reviews the differing approaches of self-directed teams in the 1980s.

Suggested Reading

Carter, Louis, Gilber, David, and Goldsmith, Marshall, eds. *Best Practices in Organization Development and Change.* San Francisco: Jossey-Bass, 2001.

Passmore, William A. *Designing Effective Organizations: The Sociotechnical Systems Perspective.* New York: John Wiley & Sons, 1988.

Wellins, Richard S., and Byham, William C., and Dixon, George R. *Inside Teams: How 20 World-Class Organizations are Winning through Teamwork.* San Francisco: Jossey-Bass, 1994.

Reference

Trist, Eric L. *The Social Engagement of Social Science: A Tavistock Anthology: The Socio-Ecological Perspective (Tavistock Anthology).* Philadelphia: University of Pennsylvania Press, 1997.

SECTION II: CONTEXT OF HPT / CHANGE STRATEGIES

Highly Recommended

Adams, Scott. *Dogbert's Top Secret Management Handbook.* New York: Harper-Business: 1996.
For many comedians, "Humor is simply telling the truth in ways that no one would site still for." Adams' satire of business, particularly in section 2, Motivating Employees, showcases many of the negative behaviors displayed in failed HPT efforts.
Although not often acknowledged, humor can also be an *essential survival skill* in major change efforts.

Anderson, Dean, and Anderson, Linda Ackerman. *Beyond Change Management.* San Francisco: Jossey-Bass, 2001.
The Andersons explore "mindset" as an important perspective in changing workplaces and build upon their successful history of change consulting in a wide variety of industries. The integration of mindset shift into BCM strategies is outlined and explained well. A very good reference for organizations undergoing major change, particularly for the leaders.

Blanchard, Ken, and O'Connor, Michael. *Managing by Values.* San Francisco: Berret-Koehler, 1997.
The most successful HPTs are *principle-based* teams. In addition to measuring and understanding their conventional metrics, HPTs are also sensitive to their own alignment of beliefs, values, and principles. Blanchard and O'Connor provide a brief look at how value-based management can work. A good framework to view the important, intangible values shared among the HPT team and leaders.

Champy, James. *Reengineering Management: The Mandate for New Leadership.* New York: HarperBusiness, 1996.
Building on the original Reengineering concept, Champy discussed real world issues of major change, and the leaders' role within that upheaval. A very good reference for those attempting Business Process Redesign. Champy's focus on managerial and workforce challenges provides excellent guidance to those in the trenches.

Hamel, Gary, and Prahalad, C.K. *Competing for the Future.* Boston: Harvard Business School Press, 1994.

An excellent reference for strategic thinking and creative strategies. Along with Hamel's book, *Leading the Revolution*, this text provides a good starting point for determining core competencies and future potential. In developing their business plan for the future, HPTs benefit most from an effective, creative, and integrated strategy. Hamel helps to guide the way.

Hammer, Michael, and Champy, James. *Reengineering the Corporation: A Manifesto for Business Revolution*. New York: HarperBusiness, 1993.
The text often cited as the catalyst for corporate self-examination and Business Process Redesign in the 1990s. Hammer and Champy do an excellent job of outlining the need and advantage of major corporate revision, and pose fundamental questions and challenges to the leaders of the organization. An excellent set of questions to re-ask and re-read as organizations proceed through their own challenges.

Klein, Eric, and Izzo, John B., Ph.D. *Awakening Corporate Soul: Four Paths to Unleash the Power of People at Work*. Gloucester, MA: Fair Winds Press, 1999.
It is very easy to talk about organizational change in the abstract, defining it as it were disconnected from the people that comprise it. This book helps all team members, particularly the leaders, connect with their passions and release their energy for change. While focusing on shifts in culture, at times it is far more important to deal with *soul*.

Kotter, John P., Strebel, Paul, and Augustine, Norman R. *Harvard Business Review on Change*. Boston: Harvard Business School Press, 1998.
A compilation of key HBR articles, the book contains several articles that are particularly helpful for those considering HPTs, including:

Leading Change: Why Transformation Efforts Fail, Kotter, John P.
Why do Employees Resist Change? Strebel, Paul.
Reshaping an Industry: Lockheed Martin's Survival Story, Augustine, Norman R.

Robbins, Harvey, and Finely, Michael. *Why Change Doesn't Work: Why Initiatives Go Wrong and How to Try Again – and Succeed*. Princeton, NJ: Peterson's Press, 1996.
Robbins and Finely, also the authors of *Why Teams Don't Work*, outline many of the common frustrations and challenges in attempting wide-scale change in an organization. While the text focuses more on the identification of resistance than techniques to overcome those barriers, it does provide suggestions on new approaches to move forward. A good book to help identify social and cultural barriers to change.

Ulrich, Dave, and Lake, Dale. *Organizational Capability: Competing from the Inside Out*. New York: John Wiley & Sons, 1990.
The concept of organizational capability as a competitive force is long established, and outlined well in this text. Ulrich and Lake outline the advantages of increasing the organization's capability and capacity, and discuss some methods to achieve it. The discussion of a (shifted) shared mindset and its impact on the organizational culture, can be very helpful to leaders and teams attempting wide-scale change.

Suggested Reading

Dunlap, Albert J. *Mean Business: How I Save Bad Companies and Make Good Companies Great*. New York: Simon & Schuster, 1996.

Gerstner, Louis, Jr. *Who Says Elephants Can't Dance? Inside IBM's Historic Turn-around*. New York: HarperBusiness, 2002.

Koch, Richard. *The Financial Times Guide to Strategy: How to Create and Deliver a Useful Strategy*. London: Financial Times-Prentice Hall, 2000.

Krames, Jeffrey A. *What the Best CEOs Know: Seven Exceptional Leaders and Their Lessons for Transforming any Business*. New York: McGraw-Hill, 2003.

Oden, Howard. *Transforming the Organization: A Socio-Technical Approach*. Westport, CT: Quorum Books, 1999.

Slater, Robert. *The New GE: How Jack Welch Revived an American Institution*. Homewood, IL: Business One, 1993.

Tichy, Noel, and Sherman, Stratford. *Control Your Destiny of Someone Else Will: Lessons in Mastering Change – The Principles Jack Welch is Using to Revolutionize General Electric*. New York: Doubleday, 1993.

Vietor, Richard H. K., *Contrived Competition: Regulation and Deregulation in America*. Cambridge, MA: Belknap Publishing, 1994.

Walton, Sam. *Sam Walton: Made in America*. New York: Doubleday, 1992.

Welch, Jack, and Byrne, John A. *Jack: Straight from the Gut*. New York: Warner Books, 2001.

Reference

Amelio, Gil, and Simon, William L. *On the Firing Line: My 500 Days at Apple*. New York: HarperBusiness, 1998.

Appel, Martin. *Now Pitching for the Yankees: Spinning the News for Mickey, Billy and George*. Kingston, NY: Total Sports, 2001.

Freiberger, Paul, and Swaine, Michael. *Fire in the Valley: the Making of the Personal Computer*. New York: McGraw-Hill, 1999.

Iacocca, Lee, and Novak, William. *Iacocca: An Autobiography*. New York: Bantam Books, 1988.

Mathews, Chris. *Hardball: How Politics is Played Told By One Who Knows the Game*. New York: Simon & Schuster, 1999.

Mayo, Elton, and Thompson, Kenneth. *The Human Problems of an Industrial Civilization*. New York: Routledge, 2003.

Treacy, Mchael, and Wiersma, Fred. *The Discipline of Market Leaders: Choose Your Customers, Narrow Your Focus, Dominate Your Market*. Reading, MA: Addison-Wesley, 1995.

SECTION III: TRANSITION AND PROCESSES

Highly Recommended

Block, Peter. *Flawless Consulting: A Guide to Getting Your Expertise Used*. San Francisco: Jossey-Bass, 1981, 2000.

This book helps to define whether internal or external to the organization. As a facilitator, coach, or catalyst, the interventionist is often set in the role of consultant to the team and its leader. Block's book addresses many of the real-world considerations involved in that role. Highly recommended for the HPT interventionist.

Bridges, William. *Transitions: Making Sense of Life's Changes*. Cambridge, MA: Perseus Publishing, 1980.

Bridges, William. *Managing Transitions: Making the Most of Change.* Cambridge, MA: Perseus Publishing, 2003.

Bridges' original distinction between *change* (an external shift) and *transition* (the internal process of shifting in response to change), was helpful to many who found themselves struggling with changing jobs, environments, and organizational rules. His use of analogies and mythologies, combined with his personal experiences, allowed many to recognize and understand *why* people struggle with change.

His later book applies those learnings to organizational change. Building upon his consulting work, Bridges reviews the organizational turmoil and chaos that can occur with unmanaged change, and outlines several helpful approaches.

Both books are excellent reads from a very authentic and candid writer.

Bynner, Witter. *The Way of Life According to Lao Tzu.* New York: Berkley Books, 1944.

A very early interventionist, Lao Tzu's writings ask some of the most fundamental and difficult-to-answer questions. Leaders and interventionists of some of the most successful HPT efforts read and quote from Lao Tzu's writings.

Fisher, Kimball. *Leading Self-Directed Work Teams: A Guide to Developing New Team Leadership Skills.* New York: McGraw-Hill, 1993.

While "Self-Directed Work Teams" are not necessarily High Performance (and vice-versa), many HPTs *do* select a self-directed or self-managed design for their organization. This text provides an excellent description of the development and transition of teams toward self-direction. Fisher's focus on the changing role and required skillsets of the leader is particularly helpful for potential HPT team leaders. Very good advice and perspective.

Kotter, John P., and Heskett, James L. *Corporate Culture and Performance.* New York: Simon & Schuster, 1992.

Kotter and Heskett compare the perceived "strength" of a corporate culture with its performance results, based upon surveys of top officers in 207 market leaders. While their working definition of culture is based upon conventional meaning, their results demonstrate an excellent correlation between culture and performance at the enterprise level. A very good reference.

Schein, Edgar H. *Organizational Culture and Leadership.* 2nd Ed. San Francisco: Jossey-Bass, 1992.

Schein's original edition in 1985 helped to redefine the concept of organizational culture, providing a foundation for analyzing, understanding, and dealing with group culture. While Schein's definition of culture is somewhat different than that used in this overall text, the two definitions are not necessarily incompatible—merely different aspects of the same phenomenon. Schein's extensive review of cultural diagnostics, culture change, and leadership within an organization is a "must read" for any interventionist working with High Performance Teams.

Schein, Edgar H. *Process Consultation Revisited: Building the Helping Relationship.* Reading, MA: Addison-Wesley, 1999.

There are many "how to" books on *process consulting*; however, most discuss the *actions* of the process consultant, rather than the actual process. Schein reviews the "why" of process consultation, combining theory with practical advice. A "must read" for serious process consultants, and strongly recommended for any HPT interventionist.

Suggested Reading

De Vries, Manfred E. R. Kets, and Miller, Danny. *The Neurotic Organization: Diagnosing and Revitalizing Unhealthy Companies.* San Francisco: Jossey-Bass, 1984.

Gilliland, Burl E., and James, Richard K. *Crisis Intervention Strategies.* Pacific Grove, CA: Brooks/Cole Publishing, 1988.

Hunter, Dale, and Bailey, Anne, and Taylor, Bill. *The Art of Facilitation: How to Create Group Synergy.* Tucson: Fisher Books, 1995.

Whitfield, Charles L., M.D. *Boundaries and Relationships.* Deerfield, FL: Health Communications, 1993.

Reference

Houghton Mifflin Company, *American Heritage Dictionary*, © 2000. Boston.

Philadelphia Daily News, *Hundreds Swarm Bank in Fear,* Page 29, Philadelphia Daily News, April 23, 2003.

Philadelphia Inquirer, *Rarely Seen Run on Bank*, Page 1, Philadelphia Inquirer, April 24, 2003.

SECTION IV: HPT TEMPLATE

Highly Recommended

Block, Peter. *The Empowered Manager: Positive Political Skills at Work.* San Francisco: Jossey-Bass, 1987.

While Block focuses on the empowered "manager," many emergent HPTs face similar stakeholder challenges. By reviewing the issues discussed in this book, and following Block's guidance for stakeholder relationships, new HPTs can become more effective, more quickly.

Conner, Daryl R. *Managing at the Speed of Change: How Resilient Managers Succeed and Prosper Where Others Fail.* New York: Random House, 1992.

This text has been a "must read" for many organizations undergoing major change. Particularly helpful in the "readiness for change" phases, Conner outlines major factors regarding the organizational resilience. An excellence reference, with very helpful analysis.

Mager, Robert F. *The Mager Six-Pack.* Belmont, CA: Lake Publishing, 1984.

These include several key modules:
Developing Attitude Toward Learning
Goal Analysis
Making Instruction Work
Preparing Instructional Objectives
Measuring Instructional Results
Analyzing Performance Problems

Mager provides a strong set of "how to" training books; in short, the "Six Pack" provides a "how to . . . how to train." Taken together, these texts provide a rapid means of integrated training planning and implementation that have helped many HPT efforts achieve rapid on boarding and implementation ramp-up.

Stewart, G. Bennett, III. *The Quest for Value.* New York: HarperCollins, 1991.

Throughout the HPT effort, "shareholder value" is discussed as a generic term, including factors such as return on investment, profitability, cash flows, goodwill, and community respect. In conventional terms, shareholder value is equated with EVA (economic value-added) that can be quantified, calculated, and predicted. While the depth of this text is beyond the scope of many HPT efforts, the ability to calculate and predict EVA can be key to the consideration of major activity and capital expenditures. For those HPT efforts having a major impact on the overall corporation, or considering major investment expenditures, EVA is often far more compatible with the *integrated* nature of HPTs. This reference text is very helpful to those teams considering major investment as part of their "To Be" process.

Suggested Reading

Boxwell, Robert J., Jr. *Benchmarking for Competitive Advantage.* New York: McGraw-Hill, 1994.

Brown, Steve. *Manufacturing for the Future: Strategic Resonance for Enlightened Manufacturing.* London: Financial Times/Prentice Hall, 2000.

Cohen, Allan R., and Bradford, David L. *Influence Without Authority.* New York: John Wiley and Sons, 1989, 1991.

Goldratt, Eliyahu M., and Cox, Jeff. *The Goal: A Process of Ongoing Improvement.* Great Barrington, MA: North River Press, 1984.

Goleman, Daniel (introduction). *Business: The Ultimate Resource.* Cambridge, MA: Perseus Publishing, 2002.

Hiebeler, Robert, and Kelly, Thomas B., and Ketteman, Charles. *Best Practices: Building Your Business with Customer-Focused Solutions.* New York: Simon & Schuster, 1998.

Hitchcock, Darcy. *The Work Redesign Team Handbook: A Step-by-Step Guide to Creating Self-Directed Teams.* New York: Quality Resources, 1994.

Moody, Patricia E. *Strategic Manufacturing: Dynamics New Directions for the 1990s.* New York: Dow Jones-Irwin, 1990.

Rappaport, Alfred. *Creating Shareholder Value: A Guide for Managers and Investors.* New York: The Free Press, 1986, 1998.

Seybold, Patricia B. *Customers.Com: How to Create a Profitable Business Strategy for the Internet and Beyond.* New York: Random House, 1998.

Slywotzky, Adrian J. *Value Migration: How to Think Several Moves Ahead of the Competition.* Boston: Harvard Business School Press, 1996.

Verity Consulting Group. *A Hands-On Guide to Competitive Benchmarking: The Path to Continuous Quality and Productivity Improvement.*

Glossary

Given the highly eclectic backgrounds of those involved in High Performance Team efforts, the use of any given word or phrase may be unfamiliar or confusing. This abbreviated glossary is intended to provide context-based definitions to words and phrases used throughout this work.

Accountability. Being answerable for actions and results of self or team. Accepts consequences of actions.

Active listening. Technique of being actively engaged with the partner or audience; may include the repeating of key words or paraphrasing to ensure clarity and understanding.

Alignment, behavioral (individual). The synchronization of verbal and nonverbal cues—for example, facial expressions or affect that match the words of the individual.

As-Is. A description of the present state of the process or organization.

Attitude. A state of mind or feeling; a (generally) transitory emotional state of mind.

Authenticity (individual). Fully aligned within self; external behaviors and interactions match inner attitudes and feelings.

Authority. The established placement of power and influence of a position or role within an organization; may or may not be related to a specific individual.

Autonomy. The degree of self-reliance and independence from the surrounding organization; typically focused on areas of deliberation and empowerment.

Basic Value Imperative. The idea that all organizations must provide unique, perceived, value-added services and products in order to survive.

Behavior. The actions of an individual or organization (not necessarily her or his thoughts, intents, or feelings).

Behavioral Change Management (BCM). A specific change strategy involving the alignment of attitudes within an organization. See chapter 9.

Beliefs. Mental acceptance or conviction in the validity of a person, concept, or value.

Benchmark. A standard against which performance or activity is compared and judged. Commonly used with competitive benchmarking.

Boundary. A border or limit between people and behaviors, typically described in terms of differing roles.

Business case for change. An outline of the key business pressures for change, and potential consequences for action or inaction.

Business Process Redesign. The study of evaluating business an enterprise processes in a straightforward and linear way. Synonymous with *Re-engineering*.

Cash flows. The actual monies flowing into or out of the business. This may be significantly different from budget or profit/loss.

Catalyst. A level of intervention that has the ability to accelerate the HPT transition process. See chapter 27.

CEO perspective. A "big picture" view of the organization, its strengths and weaknesses, and the pressures for change; not necessarily held uniquely by the CEO (Chief Executive Officer).

Change, breakthrough. Revolutionary organizational change, typically involving more than 50 percent performance improvement in key success dimensions.

Change, culture. The shift in the group sense of self.

Change drivers. Those environmental conditions that generally influence the organization. These may or may not become actual change pressures. Examples may include government regulation, competitive markets, and technology.

Change, incremental. Minor organizational change, typically involving less than 10 percent performance improvement in key success dimensions.

Change Management. The deliberate strategy of aligning organizational behaviors and/or attitudes.

Change Management (CM) plan. The Change Management Plan provides the CM strategy for the HPT moving forward; may be included in the transition plan and/or implementation plan.

Change pressures. Those internal or external factors that create a significant impact on the organization (for change).

Change, significant. Moderate organizational change, typically involving 10 to 50 percent performance improvement in key success dimensions.

Change strategy. A series of deliberate actions and processes designed to eliminate or reduce specific change pressures.

Charter. The overall purpose of the team or organization, including the mission, constraints, and sometimes the future vision.

Coach. A level of intervention that has the ability to accelerate the team development process. See chapter 26.

Command and control. An organizational structure and culture that supports a strict hierarchical distribution of power. See chapter 7.

Common experience. A very significant event or environment, simultaneously experienced by the team/organization.

Common impact. A common experience, with significant individual impact, commonly shared by the members of the team/organization.

Constraints. The actions and tasks that the team is not allowed to change. Typically, these areas are out of bounds for the team. Also see **Sandbox.**

Consultant—internal/external. Support resources that are not part of the actual HPT; may include those from within the organization (internal) or outside (external).

Context. The circumstances, environment, or setting of an action or concept. Typically, context imparts meaning to the action; typically varies considerably from individual to individual.

Contextual connection. The context surrounding the communication or contact. Particularly important during the initial phases, this context may define expectations and beliefs for future interactions.

Contingency plan. An alternative strategy, typically including a series of actions designed to correct a problem situation.

Control chart. A qualitatively analytical process to reduce or eliminate process variances.

Creativity. The process of creating something new; originality, expressiveness, and difference.

Critical success factors. Those factors that may determine whether or not the effort is successful.

Cultural foundation. The underlying sense of group identity of the overall organization.

Culture. The group's sense of self; group identity. See chapter 10.

Culture Change. The shift of group identity within a team or organization. See chapter 10.

Customer. Any individual or organization that receives and evaluates the services of the producing team.

Customer value. The success dimension that provides value-added to customers.

Data collection/gathering. The process of gathering data together for the purpose of analysis; may or may not include data reduction.

Deliberation analysis (decision-making analysis). The study of organizational decision-making. As a key marker for organizational culture, this analysis and its resulting interventions become critical to successful HPT development.

Deliverable. A tangible, discrete output or outcome as a direct result of some activity.

Directive Change Management (DCM). A change strategy that works to align the behaviors of an organization. See chapter 8.

Employee value. The success dimension that provides value-added to employees.

Empowerment. The level of self-authority and self-power; may or may not be recognized by key stakeholders.

Entitlement. Having or believing that a right to benefits or privileges exists, exclusive of any contract or quid pro quo.

Facilitator. The preliminary level of intervention in HPT efforts; principally focused on the transition work activity. See chapter 25.

Gantt chart. A graphical description of project milestones projected onto a calendar; used to rapidly evaluate the progress of the project.

Go/No-Go. A milestone or event where the decision is made to either (1) go with the project and continue or (2) not go with the project and stop.

Goals. The overall targets of the effort. HPT goals are often superordinate goals that are overarching across the effort.

Ground rules. The sets of rules and constraints that the team agrees to abide by.

Guiding principles. A qualitative description of group-normalizing values and beliefs.

Hawthorne effect. A series of worker observations made in the 1930s at Western Electric's Hawthorne plan. Commonly refers to the effect of productivity increase being directly related to managerial supervision and attention—and then decreased in the absence of that attention.

High Involvement Team (HIT). A team that works to increase employee involvement significantly higher than the organizational norm. Typically, HITs primarily focus on employee value at the expense of other success dimensions.

High Performance Team. Any team that achieves a quantum leap in business results in less than a year—in all key success dimensions.

High Performance Team effort. Any team that attempts to become a High Performance Team; may or may not be successful.

High Performance Work System (HPWS). An integrated system of HPTs. For the purposes of this text, HPTs and HPWS are considered interchangeable.

HPT leader. The person initially designated as the leader of the effort; the key person accountable for the HPT goals and results. As a transition process, this role shifts from that of a conventional leader to a key team member throughout the HPT life cycle.

HPT member. A member of the HPT, this person initially has the responsibility to achieve the goals, transitioning to full accountability. Roles and responsibilities typically shift dramatically within the team.

HPT Non-Sponsoring Executive (NSE). Any organizational executive not directly responsible for the change effort, yet a key stakeholder in the HPT process.

HPT sponsor. The organizational executive responsible for the change strategy of the organization, within which the HPT effort is chartered.

HPT stakeholder. Any person or organization having an interest or a key stake in the outcome of the HPT effort.

Identity. The distinct personality, makeup, and emotional processes of the individual; a sense of self.

Implementation. The execution of plans to result in the desired outcomes.

Implementation, Full. A full immersion implementation, where the full scope of the project is performed at once. See chapter 36.

Implementation, Phased. A partial implementation, where portions of the project are implemented at a time. See chapter 36.

Implementation plan. A comprehensive plan, providing all necessary resources, timing, and information required for a successful implementation.

Intangible. Conceived and perceived without discrete sensory perception.

Integration plan. A plan to interface with key stakeholder groups as well as teams that may precede or proceed the working team.

Intervention. Any action or strategy designed to preclude, divert, or accelerate an otherwise natural direction or outcome.

Learnings. A collection of meaningful experiences that have impacted the individual or team, resulting in changed behavior or reaction.

Lessons learned. A series of learnings, typically in a deliberate, structured manner, evaluating previous experiences.

Linear work. The tasks, processes, and resources required to create a predefined product or service. Typically focused on the primary output of the organization.

Line of Sight. Direct interface and interaction with the group or concept; for example, a line of sight to the customer indicates personal contact and interaction between the customer and the team.

Magical thinking. The belief that something will happen simply as a result of declaring it.

Manager (role). Someone responsible for the work to be done, typically at the project level.

Mentor (role). Someone providing thought leadership and advice to the team without having routine interaction.

Metrics. Regular measurements that can be analyzed.

Metrics/monitoring plan. An outline of the specific measurements that will be monitored and analyzed throughout the implementation phase. This typically links directly to the implementation goals; in the most effective plans, overall goal achievement can be extrapolated from the monitored metrics.

Mission. The purpose of the team; defines whether or not the team is successful.

Mission Critical. A make or break factor in the mission's success.

Nonlinear work. The tasks, processes, and resources required to produce an outcome that is not predefined. Typically focused on decision making, planning, and intangibles.

Non-Sponsoring Executive (NSE). A key stakeholder not directly involved with the HPT effort.

Non–value-added (NVA). Does not provide a benefit in a success dimension.

Operational value. The success dimension that provides form/fit/function benefits of the product or service.

Order of magnitude. A factor of 10.

Organization. A group of people associated for a particular purpose; generally, the overall enterprise (as with a team, this is ultimately defined by the overall sense of group identity).

Organizational Development (OD) or **Organizational Effectiveness (OE).** Study related to the social aspects of work, specifically focused on organizations.

Organizational readiness. The level of desire for change, as applied to a specific change effort or outcome.

Organizational resilience. The ability of the organization to accept multiple changes; its adaptability and repeated acceptance of change.

Organization chart. A diagram outlining the positions or roles within the organization; typically includes reporting relationships.

Outsourcing. The process of transferring work from internal resources (employees) to external resources (contractors).

Passive/aggressive. A pattern of passive resistance for the purpose of indirect conflict.

Perception. The interpretation of sensory and environmental input.

Perspective. A subjective evaluation of objects or events of relative significance.

Phase. A discrete stage of development.

Power (organizational). Having significant influence over others.

Principle. A basic truth, value, or assumption.

Process. A series of actions, transitions, or functions resulting in a specific outcome.

Process map. A graphical representation of a process, demonstrating the relationship between discrete work tasks.

Process map, child. A derivation of the process map, typically drilling down another level of detail for clarity and understanding. Multiple child processes are ideally able to be integrated into an overall process map.

Process map, idealized. A process map that has no error conditions; the process described has no variances and no work-arounds.

Product. A tangible, discrete output that provides value, typically defined by its form, fit and function for a predefined purpose.

Product cycle times. The calendar time of duration required to produce a given product.

Re-engineering. The study of evaluating business and enterprise processes in a straightforward and linear way. Synonymous with *Business Process Redesign*.

Return on Investment (ROI) and **Return on Assets (ROA).** Financial calculation indicating the payback of any given investment or capital good.

Role modeling. The deliberate display of appropriate behavior for the purpose of demonstration.

Role and responsibilities. A function performed by an individual and his or her corresponding duties.

Sandbox. A listing of constraints, typically on a level with the HPT goals.

Self-Directed Work Teams (SDWTs). Teams that have internalized the traditional role of supervisor or manager.

Self-Managed Work Teams (SMWTs). Synonymous to SDWTs, with focus on goal achievement rather than task achievement.

Service. The provision of unique actions or benefits that provide value in and of themselves.

Shareholder value. The success dimension that provides benefits to the owners or ultimate custodians of the organization.

Sigma (statistical). A symbol for the standard deviation from the ideal process.

Six sigma (statistical). A process having no more than 3.4 defect/problem per 1 million opportunities.

Skilling. Having specific skillsets; may refer to the training process of instilling skillsets.

Skillsets. A set of skills or abilities that combine to perform specific tasks or meet the needs of certain types of work.

Slice team. A cross-functional or cross-organizational team.

Sociotechnical. Having a combined focus on both the social and technical aspects of work. Typically, this type of organizational design views the worker as an integral part of the work process.

Stakeholder. Any person or group having a stake in the outcome.

Status quo. The present or existing state (literally, state in which).

Steward (role). Person protecting a given resource, commonly associated with status quo maintenance.

Strategy. An integrated deliberate set of actions designed to achieve a specific goal or outcome.

Subject Matter Expert (SME). One who provides particular expertise on a given subject.

Success Dimension. Key business success dimensions include customer value, employee value, operational value, shareholder value, and cultural foundation.

Supervisor (role). Someone responsible for the work to be done, typically at the task level.

Supplier. An individual or group providing a service or component product to the producing team.

Task. A specific unit of work, typically minimal, with a defined beginning and end.

Tangible. Having a discrete boundary, typically discernible by physical senses.

Team. A group of people sharing a common identity and purpose.

Template. A pattern used as a guide for producing a product or service.

Thought leadership. Providing unique ideas and conceptual guidance for a given process or effort.

To-Be. The future state.

Touch time. The actual direct labor time required for the product or service.

Training plan. A strategy to provide necessary skilling for all key stakeholders required to achieve success.

Transition. The process of changing from one state or phase to another.

Transition plan. A deliberate plan to transition from As-Is to To-Be; typically comprehensive and detailed.

Value-added. Providing a positive benefit in a success dimension.

Variance. Any deviation from the expected performance of a process or the natural flow of work.

Work. The overall effort directed toward the creation of a service or product.

Work plan. A detailed projection of the specific work to be performed.

Work Re/Design. The process of defining the work of the team/organization. For HPTs, this includes a whole-system review by all members of the HPT and all key stakeholders of the effort. This is a coined term, combining Work Design (covering new work design) and Work Redesign (covering the redesign of existing work).

Index

About the Author

MARC HANLAN is Senior Partner of High Performance Work Team Consulting, LLC (HPWTC). He has a strong history of supporting large-scale change in a wide range of organizations, resulting in reduced costs, increased effectiveness, high employee commitment and high performance. As a pioneer in High Performance work teams since the early 1980s, he has helped organizations achieve breakthrough results in profitability, market share, safety, productivity, quality and employee involvement.

Building on more than 25 years of experience working with hundreds of High Performance Teams and thousands of employees, Mr. Hanlan has guided High Performance Teams from a range of positions, including line management at General Electric and support management at Exelon, as well as in consulting roles. Holding patents in process technologies, he is adjunct faculty for graduate programs in psychology, and currently advises, consults, and presents on the topic throughout North America and in Europe. He enjoys flying, astronomy, poetry, and most importantly, time with his family.

Mr. Hanlan enjoys networking with all groups reaching toward High Performance; he can be reached through the HPWTC website at *www.HighPerformanceWorkTeam.com.*

LEARNING MORE ABOUT HIGH PERFORMANCE

Learn about High Performance

1. *Read This Text.* Many readers find it helpful to read a section at a time, and others find it helpful to re-read the text as they progress through an HPT effort. The bibliography can be very helpful, as well.
2. *Use the Internet.* Additional case histories, additional resources, and HPT networking are available through HPWTC at www.HighPerformanceWorkTeam.com
3. *Partner with an Experienced Guide.* Whether the guide is from HPWTC, the HPT Network, or others with HPT experience, having a guide is important. As mentioned throughout this text, a Catalyst-level guide is a critical success factor.

Do High Performance

1. *Start an HPT,* even if a small pilot. As the text indicates, HPT is highly experiential. Start one. Today.
2. *Build on HPT.* Expand on success, and learn from missed opportunities.
3. *Network with other HPTs.* Join formal networks, and create informal ones. Provide feedback and offer learning to others. Renew the energy and creativity.
4. *Provide Feedback.* Let Marc Hanlan know of your efforts, successes, challenges, and learnings.

The most difficult step in High Performance is the first one . . . .